D1292830

Creating Value through International Strategy

Creating Value through International Strategy

Edited by

Africa Ariño

Pankaj Ghemawat

and

Joan E. Ricart

First published 2004 by
PALGRAVE MACMILLAN
Houndmills, Basingstoke, Hampshire RG21 6XS and
175 Fifth Avenue, New York, N.Y. 10010
Companies and representatives throughout the world

PALGRAVE MACMILLAN is the global academic imprint of the Palgrave
Macmillan division of St. Martin's Press, LLC and of Palgrave Macmillan Ltd.
Macmillan® is a registered trademark in the United States, United Kingdom
and other countries. Palgrave is a registered trademark in the European
Union and other countries.

ISBN 1–4039–3472–X

This book is printed on paper suitable for recycling and made from fully
managed and sustained forest sources.

A catalogue record for this book is available from the British Library.

Library of Congress Cataloging-in-Publication Data
Creating value through international strategy / edited by Africa Ariño,
    Pankaj Ghemawat, and Joan E. Ricart.
        p. cm.
    Includes bibliographical references and index.
    ISBN 1–4039–3472–X (cloth)
    1. International business enterprises—Management. 2. Strategic
    alliances (Business) 3. Competition. I. Ariño, Africa. II. Ghemawat,
    Pankaj. III. Ricart, Joan E.
    HD62.4.C74 2004
    658.1′8—dc22   2004047309

10   9   8   7   6   5   4   3   2   1
13 12 11 10 09 08 07 06 05 04

Printed and bound in Great Britain by
Antony Rowe Ltd, Chippenham and Eastbourne

Contents

List of Figures   viii

List of Tables   ix

Foreword by Jordi Canals   x

Acknowledgements   xiii

Notes on the Contributors   xiv

**1 Introduction: International Strategy and
    Location Specificity**   1
    Africa Ariño, Pankaj Ghemawat and Joan E. Ricart

Part I   Creating Value through International Expansion

2 Introduction to Part I   21
    Johanna Mair

**3 The Process of International Expansion in
    Knowledge-Intensive Settings: Research Questions,
    Theory and Summary of Findings**   26
    Walter Kuemmerle

**4 Multilatinas: Emerging Multinationals
    from Latin America**   43
    Jon I. Martínez, José Paulo Esperança and José de la Torre

**5 Corporate Governance and Globalization:
    Toward an Actor-Centred Institutional Analysis**   55
    Ruth V. Aguilera and George S. Yip

Part II   Sources of Value in Global Strategy

6 Introduction to Part II   71
    Carlos García-Pont

**7 Firm-Specific and Non-Firm-Specific Sources of
    Advantage in International Competition**   78
    Álvaro Cuervo-Cazurra and C. Annique Un

8   Chilean Foreign Direct Investment across Latin America:
    Alliances and Competitive Advantage   95
    Patricio del Sol

9   International Geography and History in Host Market
    Competitiveness of Foreign Multinational Enterprises:
    A Research Agenda   109
    Subramanian Rangan and Aldemir Drummond

Part III   Organizing MNCs for Value Creation

10 Introduction to Part III   125
    Bruno Cassiman and Giovanni Valentini

11 Dual Paths to Multinational Subsidiary Performance:
    Networking to Learning and Autonomy to Innovation   130
    Sunil Venaik, David F. Midgley and Timothy M. Devinney

12 Decentralization of R&D and Know-How Flows through
    MNEs: Some Stylized Facts and Insights from Theory   145
    Reinhilde Veugelers and Francesca Sanna-Randaccio

13 Multinational Investment and Organizational Risk:
    A Real Options Approach   165
    Jeffrey J. Reuer and Tony W. Tong

Part IV   Global Alliances and Networks

14 Introduction to Part IV   181
    Africa Ariño

15 Globalizing Professional Services: Are Networked
    Organizations an Answer?   185
    Peter Smith Ring

16 The Impact of Personal and Organizational Ties
    on Strategic Alliance Characteristics and Performance:
    A Study of Alliances in the USA, Israel and Taiwan   201
    Paul Olk, Shaul M. Gabbay and Tsungting Chung

Part V   Internationalization, Complexity and
         Organizational Transformation

17 Introduction to Part V   217
    Joan E. Ricart

18   **The Roles of the Corporate Level in the
     Internationalization Process of the Firm**   222
     Ádrian Atilio Caldart and Joan E. Ricart

19   **'Wireless Apostles' and 'Global Emperors':
     Strategies for Domination in a Global Arena**   238
     Mitchell P. Koza, Silviya Svejenova and Luis Vives

Index   255

List of Figures

3.1 Resource allocation for international
expansion – start-up firms versus established firms   39

4.1 An evolving process   47

4.2 An evolving process (modified integration–
responsiveness framework)   47

11.1 The theoretical model   133

15.1 The design space   192

16.1 Model of the proposed study   205

List of Tables

1.1	Strategy domains	3
1.2	Levels of international business strategy	12
1.3	The CAGE framework for country-level analysis	14
4.1	Outward FDI, 1989–99	45
4.2	Company and industry statistics	50
4.3	Summary of management processes	51
7.1	Types of advantage in international competition: source, location and conditions for achievement	82
8A.1	Chilean exports, imports and outbound and inbound foreign investment, 1975–2000	103
8A.2	Origin of Chilean imports and destination of Chilean exports, 2000	104
8A.3	Chilean foreign investments, by country of destination and economic sector, 1990–2000	104
11.1	Main constructs and their relationship in the model	137
11.2	Sample descriptors	138
11.3	Summary of empirical results	139
15.1	Forms of networked organizations in professions	192
16.1	Summary of results	209
19.1	Strategic behaviour profiles	243

Foreword

When IESE Business School was founded in 1958, the world was far from being global. Four decades later the world economy is a bit more integrated, but the claim that complete globalization is already achieved is farfetched. Yet, since its foundation, IESE has always shown a very strong international character that has helped shape its several educational ventures in Europe, Africa, Asia and America. In 2002, thanks to the generous contribution of Francisco and José Ma Rubiralta, IESE launched The Anselmo Rubiralta Center for Globalization and Corporate Strategy. Its mission is to promote inter-disciplinary research and generate useful ideas for the business community on the different dimensions of globalization.

This book provides not just a glimpse but also solid evidence on the work and challenges already undertaken by the Anselmo Rubiralta Center. It contains the papers submitted to an international conference held at IESE Business School in June 2003 on 'Value Creation Through International Strategies'.

Despite insistent media reports on this phenomenon and the unending debate about it, globalization is still a recent challenge for the business world. Other important challenges such as innovation, quality management or people development are essential to business development, whether local or international, and have been important topics for debate for many decades. This is not yet the case for globalization, a topic on which important research started to be developed only some thirty years ago and which has come of age in the last decade.

Yet, despite its short life, globalization is very important today for the business community and society at large for several reasons. The first is that we know some of the reasons that trigger firms' international expansion, and the different forms adopted, but we do not know whether the reasoning behind it is solid, why some firms adopt a certain strategy, or how the decision-making process that leads to a Crucial international scope actually works.

The second reason concerns how sustainable globalization itself is. The current level of market integration in the world economy is certainly higher than at any other point in time, but still far from complete. The potential for globalization in many industries seems to be important, but the fact of the matter is that local differences – even in those industries that seem to have all the qualities for becoming global – persist and sometimes pose formidable obstacles to further market integration. Can firms speed up this process? Can they do it in a way that the globalization process itself becomes more self-sustainable, stopping the clock of history from turning back?

Business leaders not only need to know more about the prospects of globalization, but also need to be familiar with what works and what does not work in global competition. In general, international expansion makes management more complex and, although some companies are very good at transferring knowledge and experiences from one country to another, in general, profitability of international operations is smaller than in the home market. In the same way that business strategy is an area where the rich conceptual progress made in the last two decades has been instrumental in helping firms polish up their managerial skills, research in international business strategy is important in helping business leaders manage the international expansion process better.

Although the proliferation of quality studies in this area over the past decades is tantalizing, there is still a need for integrative frameworks in international business. The papers presented in this book do not offer a closed, unified framework, but they do offer some useful coordinates to place solid research and real business experiences into a broader context on how to create value in international firms. The very same structure of the book around several areas – creating value through international expansion, sources of value in international competition, organizing MNCs for value, global alliances and networks, and corporate strategy and international expansion – will not only interest scholars and practitioners, but also help them conceptualize some of the knowledge already developed in this area in a useful way.

In the international arena, there is an entity, the subsidiary of a MNC, whose role has been in general played down in most of the literature on international business. If the current debate around the world sends some clear messages to multinational corporations, one stands out: globalization is not about homogeneity. Rather, it is about differences and how to make those differences compatible with the effort to standardize. In this process, MNCs' subsidiaries have a key and crucial role to play.

The same roaring cry on globalization heard today round the world also sends a clear message to scholars. We live and are likely to live for the little while in a world that falls short of perfect market integration.

As Pankaj Ghemawat[1] points out, we live in a state of incomplete cross-border integration that can be defined as semi-globalization. This looks like a messy situation, but this structural condition of partial integration leaves room for international business strategy to have a unique content, different from mainstream business strategy that focuses on a single country, or the global strategy scenario where the world is treated as one big country.

We are grateful to IESE Professors Africa Ariño and Joan Enric Ricart, and Harvard Professor Pankaj Ghemawat who did an outstanding job organizing the international conference and editing this book, and also to the authors who submitted excellent papers to the conference. I am also very grateful to Francisco and José Ma Rubiralta for their generous support to the study of globalization at IESE.

JORDI CANALS
Dean of IESE Business School

Note

[1] See P. Ghemawat (2003), 'Semiglobalization and International Business Strategy', *Journal of International Business Studies*, 34(2), 138–52.

Acknowledgements

This book would not have been possible without the help of many contributors. We are indebted to the authors for their work and their willingness to respond to our invitation to address the issue of value creation through international strategy. Their hard work has made this book possible. Those who supported this work also need to be recognized, all of the participants at the conference held at IESE Business School, University of Navarra in Barcelona, Spain, 15–17 June 2003, made a vital contribution to this book.

This conference provided the opportunity for the exchange of views among the more than forty participants gathered there. The conference was supported by the Anselmo Rubiralta Center for Globalization and Strategy at IESE. Many people supported both the conference and this book. Christine Ecker, David Pastoriza and Andrea Rocamora played an important part in the conference success. Gemma Golobardes, Noèlia Romero, and Luis Vives contributed greatly to the preparing of this book. Last but not least, we are especially grateful to Francisco and José Rubiralta whose generosity made this project possible, as well as other activities of the Anselmo Rubiralta Center.

AFRICA ARIÑO
PANKAJ GHEMAWAT
JOAN E. RICART

Notes on the Contributors

Ruth V. Aguilera is Assistant Professor at the College of Business and the Institute of Labor and Industrial Relations at the University of Illinois in Champaign-Urbana. She received her PhD and MA in Sociology from Harvard University. She has published in the *European Sociological Review, Academy of Management Review, Economic Sociology, International Journal of Human Resource Management, Journal of Industrial Relations, Organization Studies* and has several chapters in edited books on comparative corporate governance. She also co-edited a book with M. Federowicz entitled *Corporate Governance in a Changing Economic and Political Environment* (2003). Her current research interests are at the intersection of economic sociology and organization theory, with particular emphasis on corporate governance, mergers and acquisitions, institutional analysis and inter-corporate relations.

Africa Ariño is Associate Professor of General Management at IESE Business School, University of Navarra, Spain, where she serves as Associate Director for Faculty. She is also Academic Director of the Anselmo Rubiralta Center for Globalization and Strategy at IESE. She holds a PhD from the Anderson School at UCLA, an MBA degree from IESE, and a BA from the University of Barcelona. Her research interests include process issues in international strategic alliances, and understanding alliance contractual features. Among other outlets, her research has been published in the *Journal of International Business Studies, Journal of Management, Organization Science, and European Management Journal.*

Ádrian Caldart received his PhD in Management from IESE Business School in 2003. He is currently working as a Researcher at IESE and as a Visiting Professor at AESE Escola de Direcção e Negócios in Lisbon, Portugal. His research interests are corporate strategy, corporate entrepreneurship and governance.

Bruno Cassiman is Associate Professor of General Management at IESE Business School. He holds a PhD in Managerial Economics from the Kellogg School of Management. His research on innovation and strategy has been published in *The American Economic Review, The European*

Economic Review, The International Journal of Industrial Organization, Managerial and Decision Economics, and *Research Policy.*

Tsungting Chung is Associate Professor at the Department of Business Administration, National Yunlin University of Science and Technology, Yunlin, Taiwan, where he teaches international negotiation theory and practice, international management, and cross Taiwan strait commercial relations. Most of his research and publications are in the field of negotiation and strategic alliance. He received his PhD from the Graduate School of International Studies, University of Denver, USA.

Álvaro Cuervo-Cazurra holds a PhD in management from the Massachusetts Institute of Technology and PhD in Business Economics from the University of Salamanca and is an Assistant Professor at the University of Minnesota's Carlson School of Management. His current research lies at the intersection of strategic and international management, studying how firms develop resources to become competitive and how they then become international. Another line of research deals with corporate governance issues, studying the role and behavior of the board of directors.

Timothy M. Devinney is a Professor at the Australian Graduate School of Management (AGSM), and Director of the Centre for Corporate Change. He has published six books (the most recent being *Managing the Global Corporation* (with J. de la Torré and Y. Doz, 2000) and the forthcoming *Knowledge Creation and Innovation Management* (with D. Midgley and C. Soo)) and more than fifty articles in leading journals including *Management Science,* the *Journal of Business, the Academy of Management Review, Organization Science, California Management Review, Management International Review, Journal of Marketing* and the *Strategic Management Journal.*

Aldemir Drummond is Professor of Strategy and Organizations at Fundação Dom Cabral. His areas of research interest are strategy implementation, general management and international strategy. He holds a BSc in Economics and a MSc in Management, both from the Federal University of Minas Gerais, Brazil, and a PhD in Management Studies, from Cambridge University, UK. He was the Director of the Executive MBA Program at Fundação Dom Cabral, the leading executive education institution in Brazil, and later the Associate Dean for Human Resources at the same institution.

José Paulo Esperança is Professor of International Financial Management at ISCTE in Lisbon, Portugal, where he directs the management PhD programme. He has written and consulted on service industries, the internationalization of small firms, governance issues, and questions of international financing and venture capital. His publications have appeared in the *Journal of Multinational Financial Management, Journal of Applied Financial Economics*, and *Portuguese Review of Financial Markets*.

Shaul M. Gabbay is the Director of the Institute for the Study of Israel in the Middle East – ISIME at the Graduate School of International Studies, University of Denver. His research topics focus on social networks in the context of Israel and the Middle East. He has published numerous papers and books on strategic social networks and social capital.

Carlos García-Pont is Assistant Professor of Marketing at IESE Business School, University of Navarra. He holds a PhD from MIT, and a MBA. degree from IESE, and a degree in Industrial Engineering from the Polytechnic University of Catalunya. His work places special emphasis on the importance of alliances in understanding competitive strategy, organizational needs of market-oriented organizations in industrial markets and subsidiary strategy in global corporations. He has also done work in strategic management and marketing strategy. He has had extensive experience with both local and multinational organizations in his consulting activities, where he has worked mainly on those issues of interest.

Pankaj Ghemawat is the Jaime and Josefina Chua Tiampo Professor of Business Administration at Harvard University's Graduate School of Business Administration and Head of the Strategy Unit. He received his PhD in Business Economics from Harvard University, he worked as a consultant with McKinsey & Company in London during 1982 and 1983, and has taught at the Harvard Business School since then. In 1991, he was appointed the youngest full professor in the Business School's history. One strand of his research and teaching focuses on the dynamics of globalization and generic strategies for international firms, another is concerned with foundational issues in business strategy, particularly work on the topics of competitive dynamics, business scope, and complexity. Professor Ghemawat's publications include *Commitment* (Free Press, 1991), *Games Businesses Play* (MIT Press, 1997), and *Strategy and the Business Landscape* (Addison Wesley Longman, 1999), as well as several dozen articles and case studies. He serves on the editorial boards of *Management Science, Journal of International Business Studies,* the *Journal of Economics and Management Strategy, Long Range Planning,* the *Strategic Management Journal,* and *Strategic Organization.*

Mitchell P. Koza is Director General and Professor of International Strategy at the European Center for Executive Development (CEDEP) in Fontainebleau, France. A sociologist by training, he is primarily interested in issues of international competitiveness. He has published many papers in the major academic and practitioner outlets on strategic alliances, acquisitions and corporate transformation.

Walter Kuemmerle is Associate Professor of Business Administration at the Harvard Business School. His research interests fall within the domain of knowledge and capital management in a global economy. Presently, he studies entrepreneurship in different countries. He also studies the factors that induce firms to carry out foreign direct investment in R&D.

Johanna Mair is Assistant Professor of General Management at IESE Business School, University of Navarra (Spain). Her teaching and research focuses on strategy and social entrepreneurship. Before earning a PhD in Management from INSEAD (France) she was working in international banking and for the European Commission.

Jon I. Martínez is Professor of International Strategy and Management at ESE Graduate Business School, University of Los Andes, in Santiago, Chile. He has been visiting professor at UCLA, INSEAD and several other business schools around the world. Professor Martínez has centered his research on the internationalization process of small-to-medium size firms, multinational strategies and coordination mechanisms, and the strategy of subsidiaries of multinational companies. He is co-author of a book on international strategy, and has published several articles on these topics in such journals as *Strategic Management Journal, Journal of International Business Studies,* and *Sloan Management Review.*

David F. Midgley is Professor of Marketing and Coordinator of the Marketing Area at INSEAD. His research areas include the diffusion of innovations, global organization and e-business. He is the author of over 80 publications and a graduate of the Universities of Salford and Bradford in the United Kingdom.

Paul Olk (PhD, University of Pennsylvania) is Associate Professor of Management at the Daniels College of Business of the University of Denver. His primary research interest is the formation, management and performance of strategic alliances, with additional interests in international management, friendship networks, and knowledge development.

Subramanian Rangan (PhD Harvard University) currently works on the topic of global competition among and crossborder cooperation within multinational firms. Winner of the Haynes Prize (1988) for international business research, he has co-authored two books and published in *Academy of Management Review, Journal of International Business Studies*, and *Strategic Management Journal*.

Joan E. Ricart is Associate Dean for Research and the Doctoral Programme, and Chairman of the General Management Department at IESE Business School, University of Navarra in Spain. He holds Doctoral Degrees in Industrial Engineering (Universidad Politécnica de Catalunya, 1982), Managerial Economics (Northwestern University, 1984) and Economics (Universidad Autónoma de Barcelona, 1985). He is President of the European Academy of Management and Associate Editor in Chief for the *Journal of International Business Studies*. He has been a professor in the Universidad Politécnica de Catalunya and in the Universidad Autónoma de Barcelona, as well as visiting professor in many schools around the world. He has published several books and articles in international and national journals. His areas of interest are strategic management, economics of organizations, corporate governance, and organizational design. He was Chairman of the 17th International Conference of the Strategic Management Society, held in Barcelona in October 1997 and of the founding conference of the European Academy of Management, held in Barcelona in April 2001.

Jeffrey J. Reuer is Associate Professor at the Kenan-Flagler Business School at the University of North Carolina. His research focuses on corporate strategy and he uses information economics and real options to examine the structuring and implications of corporate investments such as alliances, acquisitions, and foreign direct investment.

Francesca Sanna-Randaccio is Professor of Economics at the Department of Systems and Computer Sciences of the University of Rome 'La Sapienza' and Visiting Professor of International Economics at the Free University of Bozen. She studied at the University of Rome, Johns

Hopkins University (MA in International Relations) and Oxford University (MLitt in Economics). She is a member of the Executive Board of the European International Business Academy (EIBA) and a member of the Executive Committee of the European Association for Research in Industrial Economics (EARIE). She has published a book and several articles in the fields of international economics, industrial organization and the economics of innovation. In recent years her research has focused on the interaction between firms' multinational expansion and innovative strategy, R&D internationalization, the impact of FDI on host and home countries and the effect of national and multilateral FDI policies.

Peter Smith Ring (PhD, UC Irvine) is Professor of Strategic Management, College of Business Administration, Loyola Marymount University. His research focuses on networks and alliances, processes for managing strategic alliances, the role of trust in alliance management, strategies for managing interactions between competitive and political environments, and public sector–private sector collaborations.

Patricio del Sol (PhD Stanford University) is Professor in the Department of Industrial Engineering and Systems at the Catholic University of Chile. He has published many articles and two books on competitive strategy and project evaluation. He has been consultant and director for numerous Chilean public and private institutions.

Silviya Svejenova is Lecturer at Cranfield School of Management (UK) teaching Strategy across its MBA programs and Organisation Theory to PhD and DBA students. Her research focuses on relationship management, from social networks to international alliances. She is engaged in in-company training in related areas in Spain, Germany and the UK.

Tony W. Tong is a PhD candidate in strategic management at The Ohio State University. His current research applies real options theory to corporate strategic investments. He has papers published or forthcoming in the *Academy of Management Annual Conference Best Paper Proceedings*, *Journal of Management Studies* and *Journal of World Business*.

José R. de la Torre is Dean of the Alvah H. Chapman Graduate School of Business and holds the Byron Harless Eminent Scholar at Florida International University. He was previously Professor of International

Business at the Anderson School at UCLA, and INSEAD. He is co-author of Managing the Global Corporation (McGraw-Hill, 2000) and serves as a director of several international companies. His recent research deals with the impact of e-commerce on global business, multinational corporate reaction to regional market liberalization, and the management of international collaborative agreements, which has appeared in the *Journal of International Business Studies, Management Science, Organization Science*, and the *California Management Review*.

C. Annique Un is Assistant Professor of Management at Cornell University's Johnson Graduate School of Management. She received her PhD from the Massachusetts Institute of Technology's Sloan School of Management. Her research is on the management of technology and innovation in multinationals. She teaches International Competitive Strategy and Strategic Knowledge Management to MBA and PhD students.

Giovanni Valentini is a doctoral student at IESE Business School. His work investigates the organizational design of innovation processes as a determinant of firms' technological and economic performance.

Sunil Venaik is a Senior Lecturer in the Enterprise and International Business cluster at the UQ Business School, The University of Queensland, Australia. Sunil has published in top-level international academic journals including *Organization Science* and *Management International Review*, presented papers at distinguished international academic conferences such as the Academy of International Business and the European International Business Academy, and consulted with leading national and multinational firms. Sunil's research focuses on the environment, strategy and management of small and large multinational firms and the implications of public policy on the performance of global firms and businesses.

Reinhilde Veugelers has been with KULeuven, Belgium, since 1985, where she obtained her PhD in Economics in 1990 with a thesis on 'Scope decisions of Multinational Enterprises'. She is currently a full professor in the Department of Applied Economics, where she teaches managerial economics and international business economics and a CEPR Fellow (London). She was a visiting scholar at Northwestern University's Kellogg Graduate School of Management and at Sloan School of Management, MIT, and visiting professor at UCL, Belgium, ECARES/ULBrussels, Paris I, France, UPF & UAB, Barcelona, Umaastricht. Her research is concentrated in the fields of industrial organization, international economics and strategy and innovation, and she has authored numerous publications on multinationals, R&D cooperation and alliances, and market integration in leading international journals. She obtained research grants for projects on cooperation in R&D (DWTC), the Europeanization of Industry (EC), inter-firm networks and international competition (EC), R&D strategies by Flemish Companies (IWT). She is currently co-promotor for the Flemish Government 'Steunpunt' on R&D statistics.

Luis Vives is a PhD candidate at IESE Business School. He has degrees in Business Administration and Music. He worked in a civil construction company. In 1999 he joined IESE, where he is completing his PhD in the Strategy – General Management Department. Since 2000, Luis Vives has been lecturer at the International Trade School (ESCI) in Barcelona and in 2003 he was visiting scholar at Rotterdam School of Management – Erasmus University. His current research is related to the coevolution in the telecommunications industry, and how deregulation and globalization are affecting these markets. Besides teaching, Luis Vives has been involved in independent consulting projects.

George S. Yip is Professor of Strategic and International Management at London Business School and Lead Fellow of the UK's Advanced Institute of Management Research. He conducts research on global strategy, global marketing, global governance, and strategic transformation. He is the author of *Total Global Strategy* (in ten languages).

1

Introduction: International Strategy and Location Specificity

Africa Ariño, Pankaj Ghemawat and Joan E. Ricart

Background

This book focuses on value creation through international strategy. This is a complex topic that requires us to delve into the interaction between places and firms, in order to try to understand the differences across locations and the logic whereby some firms are able to overcome or exploit such differences in order to create value (Ricart *et al.* 2004). In this introductory chapter, we will elaborate on some of the conceptual underpinnings of this book, particularly the notion of location specificity.

This volume results from a conference held in Barcelona at IESE Business School, University of Navarra, in June 2003, and sponsored by the Anselmo Rubiralta Center on Globalization and Strategy. The purpose of the conference was to overcome some of the constraints of distance (an important theme, it turned out, at the conference) and assemble a group of distinguished scholars to discuss papers and themes related to international strategy in a format that offered more room for extended, focused discussion than is often the case at conferences. The call for papers was deliberately broad. While our primary purpose in organizing the conference was to provide a forum for discussing research on how to create value through international strategy, we were also interested in work relating considerations of organizational structure and process to considerations of value creation. We sent invitations to submit papers to a group of scholars known for work spanning a wide range of disciplinary areas as well as methodologies, and were gratified by the response.

In order to encourage a lively discussion around the conference themes, we decided to move away from the traditional format of paper presentation followed by discussion. Instead, the individual presentations were wrapped into a panel-like format. One person served as a provocateur for each panel, setting the stage for it so as to provide a common ground to which the presenters could relate, and provoking discussion about broader themes and issues that cut across the papers in the panel. Eighteen papers were presented at the conference; the thirteen that survived a process of self-selection and revision (overseen by the provacateurs) are the chapters that are included in this volume, along with overviews of each panel or part of the conference by the provocateurs. Aiming to reach a broader audience than specialized journals, we asked the authors to remove technical detail that would be appropriate in other outlets and – within space limits – to be more extensive in terms of reviewing the research question and theory development.

The purpose of this introductory chapter is not to summarize individual papers or even the provocateurs' introductions to the five parts of this volume into which the papers are grouped, but to offer a particular perspective on the issues that they help resolve or highlight as unresolved. From our perspective, while there are some common threads that run through most of the chapters, it is useful to begin by dividing them into two groups: those primarily concerned with *strategy* in the traditional sense (Parts I and II) and those more focused on *organizational issues*, broadly defined (Parts III–V). This is, of course, an oversimplification: most of the papers in this volume have both strategic and organizational elements. Still, there *are* some systematic differences – across the two groups – in terms of the relative weight placed on traditional strategic concerns about *what* international expansion involves and yields versus organizational concerns centring on *how* international firms are managed.

On the strategy side, the chapters in Part I focus on the process of international expansion, and those in Part II on the value to be derived (or not) from internationalization. On the organizational side, the chapters in Part III provide fresh perspectives on long-standing organizational issues in international business, those in Part IV look at quasi-organizational rather than organizational forms – specifically, organizational alliances and personal networks – and those in Part V are concerned, among other things, with the complexities wrought by internationalization or required for its pursuit to be successful. The individual chapters are described in more detail in the provocateurs' introductions to each part of this volume. What we want to accomplish here is examine the emergent conference theme of location specificity, elaborate how it intertwines with the contributions in this volume and explore the implications for future research. These, in brief, are the tasks undertaken in the next three sections of this introduction.

The theme of location specificity

The fact that *location specificity* can be used to tie together the contributions in this volume should not be entirely surprising. To see why, it is useful to parse the field of strategy into the domains depicted in Table 1.1 (also discussed in more detail in Ghemawat 2003a). Note the somewhat paradoxical character of domain A, mainstream business strategy: by assuming total specificity (or, less frequently, total fungibility), it allots the least attention to actually coming to grips with either business/ usage specificity or location specificity. As a result, we have to look to domain B, that of mainstream corporate strategy, for interesting analyses of variations in the extent to which key firm activities, resources or knowledge are business-specific as opposed to generic, in the sense of being fungible across businesses. And we must also look to domain C, that of international business strategy, for analyses of variations in the extent to which activities, resources and knowledge are location-specific as opposed to generic in the sense of being fungible across locations. Domain D, featuring international corporate strategy, combines considerations of business/usage specificity and location specificity. The point of Table 1.1, however, is not to celebrate the synthesis in domain D but, instead, to make it clear that location specificity is essential if the international strategy is to have a distinctive content.

Table 1.1 Strategy domains

Focus		Increasing attention to business-specificity/non-specificity $\rightarrow$	
		Single business	Multiple businesses
Increasing attention to location specificity/ non-specificity $\uparrow$	Multiple countries/ locations	C International business strategy	D International corporate strategy
	Single country/ location	A (Mainstream) business strategy	B (Mainstream) corporate strategy

Source: Based on Ghemawat (2003a).

Surely a theme this critical could not have passed unnoticed in the international business literature! It hasn't. Economists who pioneered the study of the multinational enterprise (MNE) were the first to flag the significance of location specificity in this context. Hymer (1960) characterized location specificity as a source of disadvantages for MNEs that they had to compensate for with firm-specific advantages. Caves (1971) corrected Hymer on this point by reasoning that the assets underpinning horizontal direct investment by MNEs across national borders – that is, the sources of their firm-specific advantages over local competitors – had to be at least somewhat fungible across locations and matching that prediction to evidence that the assets most prominently associated with horizontal expansion were intangible – that is, relatively likely to exhibit some locational fungibility. Subsequently, Williamson (1979, 1985) shifted attention from the locational specificity of assets to general asset specificity – also supposed to subsume physical specificity and human specificity and, in later renditions, several additional categories as well – as the 'principal factor' in transaction cost economics. International business studies, animated by a similar interest in internalization – the captive deployment of specific assets as opposed to reliance on market mechanisms – proceeded in a parallel direction over a similar time frame, prompting Dunning (1998, p. 46) to note that:

> The contribution of the internalization school has done more to explain the existence and growth of the multi-activity firm than that of the MNE *per se*. This is because, with relatively few exceptions, the transaction and coordination costs identified with arm's-length intermediate product markets have not, in general, been specific to cross-border markets, or, indeed, to traversing space.

As a result, work within international business on location specificity remained limited and confined to a few applications such as Vernon's (1971) 'obsolescing bargain' theory of MNEs being held by host governments after making large location-specific commitments.

There is general agreement that this situation started to change in the late 1980s–early 1990s, with a renewal of interest in economic geography, particularly the economics of co-location (for example, Dunning 1998 or, for a broader perspective, Sorenson and Baum 2003). Recent work in this vein will briefly be discussed in the last section of this Introduction. The intent of this section is simply to summarize the analytics of location specificity and set out some analytical propositions as a basis for discussing both the research contributions in this volume and the opportunities for future work.

Location specificity is generally considered to be the attribute of an *asset* or *resource* (see Williamson 1985, p. 89) and refers to the extent to which the redeployment of an asset (or the output that it provides) to other locations impairs productive (supply-side) value. Location specificity, thus defined, is clearly a matter of degree. In addition, the Heckscher–Ohlin–Samuelson factor price equalization theorem reminds us that, at least under the benchmark assumption of price-taking behaviour, frictions in the trade of output of products or services from the asset as well as frictions in asset mobility itself are both necessary for there to be any room for location specificity. In the absence of either kind of friction, asset prices around the world would equalize, as would the profitability of serving one location as opposed to another with a particular asset.

The possible frictions in trade in the products or services provided by an asset include:

- Transportation costs/hazards/time requirements.
- Additional (generally positive) costs of transacting at a greater distance (including language and other cultural differences).
- Preferences for proximity/home bias.
- Legal/administrative/contractual restrictions on transacting at a distance.

Most of these barriers to mobility, but particularly the last one, can apply to the underlying assets as well as to the output they provide. In addition, on the supply side, one can also cite frictions associated with:

- Physical asset/input immobility.
- Complementarities with other immobile assets.
- Specific knowledge in the Hayekian sense of knowledge that is costly to move around (effectively a subcase of the previous point).
- Specialization to local conditions, with adaptation to new ones compromised by adaptation costs and/or complexity.

Most of these frictions can be studied on several different scales, ranging from the local through to the international. However, the international scale, in addition to being of particular interest to international business, has some broader attractions as well because it maximizes locational variation along various dimensions – cultural/social, administrative, geographic and economic – in a way that casts location specificity into particularly sharp relief.

The preceding list of dimensions of variation should also suggest that there are a broad array of differences across countries. Efforts to analyse known dimensions of difference and to add new ones occupy a good chunk of the current international business research agenda, which makes some sense. But some attention should also be given to the issue of how to move beyond essentially piecemeal consideration of a large number of individual dimensions of difference – that is, beyond models of low dimensionality towards *integrative frameworks*.

In addition, attention must also be paid to the inadequacies of *indexicality*. Many of the integrative frameworks that have been proposed for purposes of understanding the differences across countries (or locations) presume that countries can be assessed one-by-one or unilaterally against a common yardstick – possibly calibrated on the basis of the actual population distribution – to yield *meaningful rankings or contrasts*. Note that 'indexicality' in this sense encompasses not only cardinal indexes such as the World Economic Forum's Global Competitiveness Indexes (formerly one, now two) or Transparency International's Corrruption Perceptions Index but also ordinal ranking schemes such as Porter's (1990) 'national diamond' framework for calibrating the (relative) international competitiveness of different countries as home bases in specific industries. But the simplicity of indexicality is purchased at a price: there is inevitably a loss of information in reducing an entire structure to a simple index number or contrast[1]. For example, the physical distance between country pairs cannot be represented in terms of country-by-country index numbers. More broadly, indexicality is inattentive to the *bilateral* or *multilateral* character of many of the dimensions of difference among countries, which suggests that countries be envisioned as existing in (and even occupying) space in relation to each other instead of as an array along a common yardstick. Another way of putting this is that countries should be represented as *nodes in a network* rather than as a heap of structurally equivalent objects.

The tendency to neglect this point about bilateral (or more broadly, relational) measures is problematic for empirical as well as conceptual reasons. Consider what is probably the most systematic and successful attempt, so far, to integrate the implications of multiple dimensions of difference for cross-border economic activity: implementations of the 'gravity model' (primarily in international economics). The gravity model in economics bears a rough resemblance to Newton's law of universal gravitation, down to having originally been proposed in the economic context by an astronomer, James Stewart. The model posits that economic interactions between two locations are directly related to the *product of their economic mass* and inversely related to the *geographic distance between them* – as well as to measures of distance along other dimensions. Fitted relationships of this sort manage to explain half or even two-thirds of the variation in aggregate bilateral trade between each country pair, as a result of which gravity-based modelling has been described as supplying 'some of the clearest and most robust empirical findings in economics' (Leamer and Levinsohn, 1995, p. 1384). What is of particular relevance here is that bilateral measures of distance, broadly defined, 'often turn out in such models to exert effects comparable to if not much larger than unilateral measures'. To see what the bilateral–relational measures can bring in, think of a somewhat analogous problem: trying to assess the flow of ideas in an organization. Simply focusing on unilateral measures might involve focusing on things such as whether people sit in open cubicles or offices with floor-to-ceiling walls, the presence or absence of common areas (for instance, around the coffee machine) and so on. But while these are useful considerations, adding in information about how the various offices are situated in relation to each other should help us develop a much better, albeit still incomplete, understanding of who talks to whom.

Having emphasized the distinction between unilateral and bilateral–relational measures, it is useful to add that unilateral influences – that is, influences specific to individual countries rather than to country pairs – are by no means incompatible with careful consideration of the relational influences to which gravity models, almost by definition, draw our attention. A formal link is supplied by a unilateral measure of isolation (or integration), which captures unilateral country-specific attributes that generally decrease (or increase) a country's involvement in cross-border economic activities and which can be treated as a common component of that country's distances from other countries, or of barriers at its borders. For example, really isolated countries (characterized by unique, ingrown cultures, closed administrative policies, physical remoteness and so on) can be thought of as being relatively distant from everywhere else.

This broad way of looking at things has some strong implications for the study of location specificity. First, a simple focus on *spatial differentiation* – that is, differences across locations – will not suffice: attention must also be paid, in an integrated way, to *spatial interactions*. Second, for purposes of studying spatial interactions, it is useful to think of countries as being embedded in multidimensional space – that is, varying in their distances from each other – instead of simply lumping them into home versus an (undifferentiated) abroad. Third, and relatedly, work that focuses on interactions at very short distances – that is, interactions at what is effectively a common location (for instance, the rapidly growing body of literature on agglomeration economies) – is certainly of interest, but it is hard to know what to make of it without also having some insight into interactions across longer distances. Put differently, to focus the study of spatial interactions at the local level would, in the present context, be àkin to setting off to study networks but never getting past the individual nodes within them. Further implications of the not-so-implicit recommendation – that we need more work on interactions *across* locations – are investigated in the concluding section of this Introduction. But, first, it is time to relate the chapters in this volume to the conceptual framework for thinking about location specificity that has been developed in this section.

The contents of this volume

As mentioned in the first section of this Introduction, the theme of location specificity became clearer to us in the course of the conference and our subsequent attempts to tie together the papers presented at it, particularly those that evolved through the selection and revision process into the chapters in this volume. As a result, any attempt to map the chapters in this volume into the framework for thinking about location specificity developed in the previous section will necessarily be imperfect. Accordingly, this section (and, more broadly, this Introduction) should be thought of as offering one possible way of tying together the various contributions in this volume into a whole that is greater than the sum of its parts.

The chapters in Part I remind us that location specificity begins at home: that (most) multinational companies have *well-established home bases* that leave a strong imprint on their process of international expansion:

- Kuemmerle (Chapter 3) looks at how firms' position in their home market influences the process of international expansion. He compares international expansion decisions by established and entrepreneurial firms in terms of the *home-base-augmenting* or *home-base-exploiting* nature of those decisions.
- Martínez, Esperança and de la Torre (Chapter 4) compare management practices of MNEs competing in Latin America to those of *Multilatinas*

(local companies that have expanded operations within the region). When the expansion target is proximate to the home country companies may target lower levels of integration, coordination and control than those needed to expand to more distant targets.

- Aguilera and Yip (Chapter 5) argue that home market institutional structure is a source of variation in firm-level strategy. They examine how different corporate governance arrangements related to employees, shareholders, board of directors, top management teams and governments influence a firm's internationalization.

The chapters in Part II bring host as well as home countries into the picture, and suggest that it is useful to think of countries as existing in space, at varying distances from each other, instead of as simply varying between identical and absolutely separate (that is, instead of assuming location specificity to be either zero or total):

- Cuervo-Cazurra and Un (Chapter 7) present a framework built on the *resource-based* view of the firm that distinguishes between firm-specific and non-firm-specific advantages, and emphasize that different sources of advantage will prove more valuable depending on whether firms are competing at home or abroad and the type of competitors – domestic or international – that they face.
- Del Sol (Chapter 8) focuses on *group membership* as a source of advantage that extends to similar (low-distance) countries. He also analyses how a firm can bridge the distance to a host country by using joint ventures (JVs) with firms from other developing countries.
- Rangan and Drummond (Chapter 9) highlight the importance of *geographic and historical links* between countries in reducing the 'liability of foreignness' or distance by decreasing the costs of entering the market and increasing the cost effectiveness of their internal control mechanisms, thereby making it easier to manage international operations.

The chapters in Part III focus on some of the distinctive organizational challenges and opportunities engendered by location specificity and can be thought of as highlighting situations in which the home and host countries are relatively distant rather than close to each other along various dimensions:

- Venaik, Midgley and Devinney (Chapter 11) present a comprehensive model that examines the impact of five types of environmental pressures and two organizational conduct variables (autonomy and networking) on learning, innovation, and overall performance. Their findings suggest that there is not a unique *structure–conduct–performance* (SCP) path; instead, MNEs may be able to enhance performance by choosing different paths in different markets.

- Veugelers and Sanna-Randaccio (Chapter 12) focus on the challenges of moving knowledge around in the presence of *locational stickiness–specificity*. In particular, they study centralization–decentralization decisions related to research and development (R&D) centres in multinational companies and show that the location specificity of knowledge has a drastic effect on such organizational decisions.
- Reuer and Tong (Chapter 13) examine one of the potential advantages unlocked by location specificity: given variation across locations, *multimarket operation* has the potential to reduce risk. Realization of this potential is contingent, however, on firms ensuring that the appropriate organizational arrangements are in place since the costs of coordinating across distant locations depend on factors such as strategy, structure, and systems.

The chapters in Part IV focus on *interorganizational alliances and networks* and, by virtue of the quasi-organizational frame that they adopt, suggest that there are sometimes advantages to aligning organizational boundaries with the boundaries between locations, with both interorganizational and interpersonal networks serving as bridges across them:

- Ring (Chapter 15) highlights the importance of networks to successful internationalization in a knowledge-intensive sector, that of professional services. Professional service firms faced with the challenge of serving customers that are becoming more international may find it easier to bridge across organizations by forming *international networks* than by seeking to overcome the distance between locations on their own.
- Olk, Gabbay and Chung (Chapter 16) draw attention to the importance of *interpersonal relationships* as a complement to interorganizational relationships. They uncover better performance in high-technology alliances that are supported by personal ties than in those that are not.

The chapters in Part V delve even deeper into the organizational complexities of internationalization. Note that strategy making can be complex even in the single-country case in the sense of demanding choices along a number of policy dimensions that are distinct but inter-related and therefore must be made with some attention to *internal consistency*. International strategy has, in addition, to confront the complexities of operating across borders and the challenges, thereby exacerbated, of achieving the requisite degree of external consistency with presumably more varied environments:

- Caldart and Ricart (Chapter 18) study how internationalization fundamentally changed and complicated the sets of strategic issues facing their focal firm. Relying on evolutionary and complexity theories, they develop a framework for thinking about the complexities of international corporate strategy, and suggest ways in which the *corporate level of the organization* contributes to the firm's internationalization process
- Koza, Svejenova and Vives (Chapter 19) analyse international competition in wireless telecommunication services and illustrate firms' use of generic competitive strategies as heuristics to cope with such complexity. While each of the generic strategies that they examine supports a distinctive competitive position, each also places some limits on the *organizational capacity* to adapt to changes in the industry environment.

Beyond this volume

This volume, let alone this Introduction, cannot aspire to cover the full spectrum of issues raised by location specificity. Still, instead of simply ending with a non-specific call for additional work on this vast domain, it seems useful to identify some areas for future work that appear particularly fruitful. To organize strategy, it is useful to refer again to the discussion in Part B, which started with Table 1.1, and effectively developed into Table 1.2, with level 1 of international business strategy focusing on spatial/locational differentiation and levels 2 and 3 on spatial interactions over very short distances (one location) and variable distances (across locations), respectively. We shall now consider each level of analysis in more detail.

Regarding level 1, international business strategy obviously ought to take differences across countries seriously, but not to the point of focusing on local variation to the exclusion of all else. In other words, it would be useful to develop research that has implications for firms crossing borders that go beyond 'Never underestimate the importance of local knowledge' – even if one believes that many firms could still benefit

Table 1.2   Levels of international business strategy

Focus		Increasing attention to business-specificity/non-specificity →	
		Single business	Multiple businesses
Increasing attention to location specificity/ Non-specificity ↑	Multiple countries/locations	C International business strategy *Level 3: Interactions across locations* *Level 2: Localized interactions* *Level 1: Differences across locations*	D International corporate strategy
	Single country/ location	A (Mainstream) business strategy	B (Mainstream) corporate strategy

from taking local variation or knowledge more seriously. Or to use the terminology originally introduced by Pike (1954), we need 'etic' knowledge – the cross-country perspective of a detached observer – as well as 'emic' knowledge – the deep but narrow single-country perspective of a native participant. Purely 'emic' knowledge is actually more helpful for analysis at the national (or intranational) level than at the international level.

Level 2 research is somewhat complementary to level 1 research: for example, the two share an interest in industrial clusters–districts as, respectively, webs of particularly dense local interactions and as key markers of differences across locations. Indeed the fascination with clustering (or, more generally, geographic concentration) has led to a large amount of research revolving around one or more causal mechanisms: location-specific knowledge and human capital spillovers, demand externalities, time economies, reduction of holdup fears and the investment biases they can induce and purely pecuniary economies as well as traditional specialization based on comparative advantage. Interest has recently been concentrated on spillovers in particular and increasing-returns-to-scale mechanisms in general. Less attention has been paid to the interplay between such forces and the numerous *countervailing forces* that might encourage geographic dispersion, which is somewhat surprising for at least two reasons. First, at the industry level, there is scant evidence that geographic concentration is increasing broadly, or even just within the high-tech sector. Second, at the firm level, internationalization typically involves more rather than less geographic dispersion of the activities that a firm performs. Given the centrifugal forces that it must contend with, such a firm seems unlikely to find an unalloyed emphasis on the centripetal forces that lead to agglomeration economies very helpful.

Partly for this last reason, level 3 is where we think it most essential to encourage additional work. Several specific lines of work that are either directly related to this level of analysis or underpin it stand out as appearing to be particularly promising or essential:

- Further unbundling and exploration of the effects of distance on *cross-border economic activity*. While the gravity-based modelling in international economics that is cited in Part II has made substantial progress, it is overly focused on trade and insufficiently disaggregated (it doesn't get down to the industry level) to be ideal from the perspective of international business. Given these needs, the opportunities for international business researchers are obvious. In addition, we also seem to need general frameworks for thinking about why countries differ in ways relevant to cross-border economic interactions as a supplement to specialized models of individual dimensions of difference among countries. Table 1.3 presents one proposal in this regard, by one of us (Ghemawat 2001): the CAGE framework, with the acronym meant to evoke the Cultural, Administrative/political/ institutional, Geographic and Economic dimensions of differences across countries. Others might further unbundle some of the CAGE categories or modify or even recast them. But it is not necessary to agree on the best possible framework for thinking about this issue to accept the utility of some such framework(s) for organizing our thinking.
- Integration of network-analytic relational perspectives into traditional country analysis with its typical emphasis on *indexicality*. Despite the inadequacies of indexicality, there are strong impulses towards it for reasons of tradition, convenience, etc. Countering these impulses is likely to require not only additional research underlining and unbundling the importance of incorporating relational effects into country analysis but also deliberate attempts to seize researchers' and educators' interest, the development of appropriate 'middleware' (for instance, Table 1.3) and other teaching materials,

Table 1.3 The CAGE framework for country-level analysis

	Cultural differences	Administrative differences	Geographic differences	Economic differences
Bilateral measures	• Different languages • Different ethnicities/lack of connective ethnic or social networks • Different religions • Differences in national work systems • Different values, norms and dispositions	• Lack of colonial ties • Lack of shared regional trading bloc • Lack of common currency • Different legal system • Political hostility	• Physical distance • Lack of land border • Differences in climates (and disease environments)	• Differences in consumer incomes • Differences in availability of: – Natural resources – Financial resources – Human resources – Intermediate inputs – Infrastructure – Information or knowledge
Unilateral measures	• Traditionalism • Insularity • Spiritualism • Inscrutability	• Non-market/closed economy (home bias versus foreign bias) • Non-membership in international organizations • Weak legal institutions/corruption • Lack of government checks and balances • Societal conflict • Political/expropriation risk	• Land-lockedness • Geographic size • Geographic remoteness	• Economic size • Low *per capita* income • Low level of monetization • Limited infrastructure, other specialized factors

Source: Ghemawat (2001).

etc. Absent such proactivity, the cumulated weight of entrenched past practice will be hard to overcome.

- Recognition of *arbitrage strategies* that capitalize on the (substantial) remaining differences across countries or locations as well as strategies that simply try to cope with such differences while seeking to convert similarities into economies of scale or scope (see Ghemawat 2003b for an additional discussion). In an era in which the value chains for many manufactured products have been sliced up across many countries so as to perform each (footloose) activity in a relatively efficient location, and offshoring appears to be transforming services, at least some of the scope for arbitrage should be obvious. But its scope actually extends well beyond the familiar stereotype of low-cost labour for low-tech products and services to high-tech products and services (for example, Brazil's Embraer in regional jets or Indian companies in software services) and even further, to the other components – cultural, administrative/political/institutional and geographic – of the CAGE framework for thinking about the differences between countries that were presented in Table 1.3. Taking arbitrage seriously matters greatly for the conceptual structure of international business because it requires reframing the traditional strategic dilemma, balancing local responsiveness and global scale economies into a strategic trilemma involving local responsiveness, scale economies and absolute advantages of the sort that underlie arbitrage. Further conceptual as well as empirical work along these lines is obviously needed.

- Finally and most speculatively, the analysis of location specificity could probably be integrated better with the theory of *competitive advantage*. In particular, international business research that *has* been sensitive to issues of location specificity has tended to distinguish between location-specific advantages or disadvantages and firm-specific (competitive) advantages or disadvantages. Case studies, however, at least raise the possibility that the covariance between the location-specific and firm-specific effects may be what is of most interest, as opposed to simply a statistical inconvenience. Specifically, differential (firm-specific) capabilities at exploiting location-specific advantages, mitigating location-specific disadvantages or even altering the effective degree of location specificity seem as if they have a major impact on the outcomes of cross-border competition in many cases. In that spirit, thinking about how firms can exploit/counteract locational factors more effectively than direct and indirect competitors seems to offer a more interesting basis, both conceptually and practically, for thinking through international business strategy than a single-minded focus on separating out location-specific and firm-specific components of performance would. Put differently, there are advantages to thinking of success in international competition as being determined by the intersection of the differential opportunities offered by different locations and firms' differential abilities to seize on them rather than in terms of clearly separate locational and competitive factors.

Clearly, the challenges posed by these and other interesting areas for future work are considerable. But so are the opportunities. Our hope is that this volume will make some modest contribution to the broader research programme that has been identified in this introductory chapter.

Note

1. For a somewhat more extended discussion of indexicality in a broader social science context, see Abbott (2001), especially pp. 11–12 and Chapter 6.

References

Abbott, A. D. (2001) *Chaos of Disciplines* (Chicago: University of Chicago Press).

Caves, R. E. (1971) 'International Corporations: The Industrial Economics of Foreign Investment', *Economica*, 38 (149), 1–27.

Dunning, J. H. (1998) 'Location and the Multinational Enterprise: A Neglected Factor?', *Journal of International Business Studies*, 29 (1), 45–66.

Ghemawat, P. (2001) 'Distance Still Matters: The Hard Reality of Global Expansion', *Harvard Business Review* 79 (8), 137–47.

———'Semiglobalization and International Business Strategy', *Journal of International Business Studies*, 34 (2), 138–52.

———'The Forgotten Strategy', *Harvard Business Review*, 81 (11), 76–84.

Hymer, S. (1976/1960) *The International Operations of National Firms: A Study of Direct Foreign Investment* (Cambridge, MA.: MIT Press).

Leamer, E. E. and J. Levinsohn (1995) 'International Trade Theory: The Evidence', in Grossman and K. Rogoff (eds), *Handbook of International Economics* G. M. (Amsterdam: Elsevier Science), 1339–94.

Pike, K. L. (1954) *Language in Relation to a Unified Theory of Structure of Human Behavior* (Glendale, CA.: Summer Institute of Linguistics).

Portes, M.E. (1990), *The Competitive Advantage of Nations* (New York: Free Press).

Ricart, J. E., M. J. Enright, P. Ghemawat, S. L. Hart and T. Khanna (2004) 'New Frontiers in International Strategy', *Journal of International Business Studies*, 35(3), 175–200.

Sorenson, O. and J. A. C. Baum (2003) 'Geography and Strategy: The Strategic Management of Space and Place' in J. A. C. Baum and O. Sorenson (eds), *Geography and Strategy* (Amsterdam, Boston: JAI Press), 1–19.

Vernon, R. (1971) *Sovereignty at Bay: The Multinational Spread of US Enterprises* (New York: Basic Books).

Williamson, O. E. (1979) 'Transaction-Cost Economics: The Governance of Contractural Relations', *Journal of Law & Economics*, 22 (2), 233–61.

———— (1985) *The Economic Institutions of Capitalism: Firms, Markets, Relational Contracting* (New York, London: Free Press, Collier Macmillan).

Part I

Creating Value through International Expansion

2
Introduction to Part I

Johanna Mair*

Research on international expansion has a long tradition within the field of global strategy and international management (for example, Aharoni 1966; Johanson and Wiedersheim-Paul 1975; Buckley and Casson 1976; Johanson and Vahlne 1977). A large number of empirical and conceptual papers have contributed to our understanding of 'why' firms expand abroad by examining in detail the motives of firms to expand internationally (for instance, Ajami and Ricks 1981; Chung 2001). What is less understood is 'how' firms expand abroad, and how this process differs among regions and industries (Vermeulen and Barkema 2002; Werner 2002). In other words, we still do not have a comprehensive picture on the multiple facets of the process of international expansion. The chapters in Part I set out to contribute to the existing body of knowledge of the internationalization process by focusing on specific regions and adopting distinct perspectives.

All three chapters share the same underlying research question: 'how do firms expand internationally?' Furthermore they adopt an *internal perspective* to shed light on the internationalization process, while taking into consideration the importance of geography and firms' location. These developments are in line with the increasing interest in disentangling firms' development and economic growth in line with the advantages that location may offer (Sorenson and Baum 2003; Ricart et al 2004). As a result all three chapters look inside the firm to detect the particularities of the process, applying different perspectives and focusing on different aspects of expansion while at

---

* The help of Luis Vives, doctoral candidate at the IESE Business School, is highly appreciated in the preparation of this introduction to Part I of the book.

the same time acknowledging the importance of location specificity if necessary.

The individual chapters complement each other and contribute to our knowledge of the internationalization process as they vary in theoretical perspective, empirical focus (industry, geographic location) and methods. Kuemmerle (Chapter 3) uses cross-boarder decisions of thirty-two multinational firms and twenty-seven start-up firms to describe and compare the resource allocation process of start-ups and established firms in the context of internationalization. In terms of methods, Kuemmerle adopts a more narrow view and looks at resource allocation processes. He finds that characteristics of international process are determined by intrafirm context and motives of international expansion. Martinez, Esperança and de la Torre (Chapter 4) remain broad, and emphasize management and organizational processes as critical factors in the internationalization process, focusing on one particular geographical area (Latin America). In this setting, they compare organizational and management processes used by emerging multinationals 'Multilatina' companies (ML) with those employed by established multinational corporations (MNCs). The chapter explicitly aims at contributing to a theory of the evolution of MNCs. Finally, Aguilera and Yip (Chapter 5) assume that the institutional environment plays an important role in explaining different degrees of globalization between countries. They apply a corporate governance perspective to examine differences in the globalization patterns between countries. Aguilera and Yip introduce an actor-centred institutional model and elaborate how the most important corporate governance actors might influence globalization. To enhance parsimony, they delimit their conceptual analysis to Europe.

While the chapters do not focus directly on the effect of the home country context on the internationalization process, they offer interesting insights on how various factors associated with the home country influence international expansion. Martinez, Esperança and de la Torre, for example, stress organizational characteristics of the internationalizing company, such as size and R&D and new product development as important factors; Kuemmerle suggests that international expansion is driven partly by the knowledge available at the company's home base; and Aguilera and Yip emphasize the importance of the national governance systems in the decision to expand abroad.

Together, the chapters provide a holistic picture of the internationalization process. Their individual contributions can be summarized as follows.

1. *Martinez, Esperança and de la Torre* empirically investigate the process of evolution of a firm from a domestic company to a multinational corporation by comparing the strategy and structure of foreign MNCs competing in Latin America with companies that have gone abroad and expanded operations in the region (MLs). Building on different theories in the literature of international business they portray this process of evolution as starting with an internationalization process and ending with the consolidation–globalization process. Depending on the particular stage, a company needs distinct *organizational and management processes*. The authors test various hypotheses on differences in organizational and management processes with survey data on fifty-eight MNCs, operating in Latin America, and forty MLs, based in Argentina, Brazil, Chile, Mexico and Peru. The empirical findings support their claim that these two groups of firms use management processes differently, depending on the stage of development. While MNCs have a high need for efficiency and competitiveness and therefore require advanced processes to integrate, control and coordinate their operations across the region, MLs are more concerned with expansion and their needs to control, coordinate and integrate are significantly lower.

2. *Kuemmerle* investigates the process of international expansion by looking into the differences and similarities in the resource allocation decisions of large established firms in the electronics and pharmaceutical industry and fast-growing entrepreneurial start-up firms. Based on earlier work that showed that firms carry out foreign direct investment (FDI) in order to create new capabilities (the home-base-augmenting motive) or to exploit firm-specific capabilities (the home-base-exploiting motive), Kuemmerle advances and empirically tests the hypothesis that established firms are engaging first in home-base-exploiting expansion, while in start-up firms geographic expansion decisions of home-base-augmenting nature will occur before geographic expansion decisions of a home-base-exploring nature. For an established firm, home-base-augmenting investments entail higher levels of uncertainty than home-base-exploiting investments. For a start-up firm home-base-exploiting investments entail higher levels of uncertainty than home-base-augmenting ones. Furthermore the author suggests that start-ups pursue risky international expansion more aggressively.

   The analysis of survey and interview data on 156 expansion decisions corroborates Kuemmerle's initial hypotheses. An additional case study of four firms furthermore illustrates that the nature of the internal structural context is a critical determinant for the outcomes of the international expansion decision process. A common aspect of successful investment processes by both types of companies is the *permeability of organizational structures* for ideas and feedback.

3. *Aguilera and Yip* address the discrepancy in the degree of globalization between European companies. They introduce an original approach to study how national corporate governance systems affect globalization patterns by addressing the issue through the lens of corporate stakeholders. Aguilera and Yip's stylized actor-centred institutional model argues that each firm (actor) is embedded in a specific corporate governance context that is 'socially constructed' and shaped by the social and political processes induced by the interplay of *five key corporate governance actors or stakeholders* (employees, shareholders, board of directors, top management teams and governments). This specific governance context generates conflicts and coalitions, which in turn influence the firm's decisions regarding global strategy and global organization. As a result, Aguilera and Yip suggest that to understand international expansion strategies and to make expansion decisions it is important to analyse the dynamics of the different actors related to the firms.

In sum, the studies selected for Part I enrich the literature on global strategy in general and on the process of international expansion in particular. They go beyond investigating the motives of international expansion and address 'how' firms actually do expand abroad. The overall contribution can be summarized as following. First, the studies shed light on specific aspects of this process, such as the way firms allocate resources, use management processes and manage their stakeholders. Second, they broaden our knowledge by examining international expansion processes in less-studied regions such as Latin America or Europe, and less-studied industry backgrounds such as start-up firms. Finally, the studies are stimulating future empirical research by introducing novel and original perspectives.

References

Aharoni, Y. (1966) *The Foreign Investment Decision Process* (Boston, MA: Harvard University Press).

Ajami, R. A. and D. A. Ricks, D. A. (1981) 'Motives of Non-American Firms Investing in the United States', *Journal of International Business Studies*, 12(3), 25–34.

Buckley, P. J. and M. Casson (1976) *The Future of the Multinational Enterprise* (New York, Holmes & Meier).

Chung, W. (1991) 'Identifying Technology Transfer in Foreign Direct Investment: Influence of Industry Conditions and Investing Firm Motives', *Journal of International Business Studies*, 32(2), 211–29.

Johanson J. and J. Vahlne (1977) 'The Internationalization Process of the Firm: A Model of Knowledge Development and Increasing Foreign Market Commitment', *Journal of International Business Studies*, 8, 23–32.

Johanson, J. and P. Wiedersheim-Paul (1975) 'The Internationalization of the Firm: Four Swedish Cases', *Journal of Management Studies* (October), 305–22.

Ricart, J. E., M. J. Enright, P. Ghemawat, S.L. Hart and T. Khanna (2004) 'New Frontiers in International Strategy', *Journal of International Business Studies* 35(3), 175–200.

Sorenson, O. and J. A. C. Baum (2003) 'Geography and Strategy: The Strategic Management of Space and Place', in C. Baum and O. Sorenson (eds), *Geography and Strategy* A. (Amsterdam, and Boston: JAI Press), 1–19.

Vermeulen F. and H. Barkema (2002) 'Pace, Rhythm, and Scope: Process Dependence in Building a Profitable Multinational Corporation', *Strategic Management Journal*, 23, 637–53.

Werner, S. (2002) 'Recent Developments in International Management Research: A Review of 20 Top Management Journals', *Journal of Management*, 28(3), 277–305.

3
The Process of International Expansion in Knowledge-Intensive Settings: Research Questions, Theory and Summary of Findings

Walter Kuemmerle*

Introduction

The study of processes of international expansion of firms has a long tradition within the process literature. Yet, this stream of research is somewhat thin when compared to the overall body of work on resource allocation processes as well when compared to research on motives for international expansion of firms. There are several possible explanations for this. First, process research typically includes a substantial component of fieldwork. This type of research is hard enough when it is performed within one country, and considerably more challenging when it involves extended visits to multiple countries. Process research also typically examines rather complex phenomena and researchers may deliberately limit themselves to one country in order to control for variance.

Research on international expansion processes might thus be challenging, but it is also quite insightful – and increasingly important as more and more firms establish significant operations outside of their home country (OECD 1996). The purpose of this chapter is to investigate how firms, large and small, make resource allocation decisions for inter-

* The longer version of this chapter, containing the empirical analysis, appears in Kuemmerle (2004) I am grateful for comments by Teresa Amabile, Josh Lerner and Bill Sahlman and seminar participants at Harvard Business School and IESE. I am indebted to William J. Coughlin, Chad Ellis and Sylvia Lee for research assistance

national expansion. The chapter seeks to address a gap in the process literature, not just on the international dimension, regarding differences and similarities between large established firms and fast-growing entrepreneurial firms.

The chapter is made up of two sections. I will first review the relevant literature on international expansion and argue that large established firms have traditionally followed a product life-cycle model even though both opportunities and needs have changed since the early 1990s. Entrepreneurial start-up firms, on the other hand, have only recently started to expand abroad early in their lives. I will also review the literature on resource allocation and argue that established firms have generally followed a resource allocation process dominated by firm-specific structures. But the entrepreneur, or a few key individuals around her, often drove resource allocation decisions in entrepreneurial firms. The second section summarizes findings from a detailed empirical study reported elsewhere (Kuemmerle 2004).

International expansion and resource allocation processes

The rationale for international expansion

Why do firms expand abroad? Essentially, there are two reasons. Either firms seek to sell products and services in foreign markets or they seek to source certain inputs abroad which are simply unavailable or much more expensive at home. Firms might also carry out both activities – and, in fact, many firms do so over time. The next question then becomes: why are all firms not present everywhere around the world? The basic answer is that *national borders* continue to represent distinct barriers to factor mobility. These barriers include language, customs, norms, different time zones, geographic distance and many other factors not existing within countries, or at least not to the same degree as across borders. Many of these barriers are firm-specific. For example, an older firm might have a broader stock of managerial knowledge about its products and processes that enables it to expand into an additional country at lower cost than a start-up firm. In addition, many of these barriers are unilateral at the country level. For example, it is still more difficult to sell an American-manufactured car in Japan than it is to sell a Japanese-manufactured car in the USA. Barriers to factor mobility across country borders and heterogeneity in firm-specific capabilities thus continue to exist and lead to observed heterogeneity in cross-border expansion of firms.

Despite the implementation of powerful trade blocs such as the EU and NAFTA in the late twentieth century, international trade is still very costly (Ghemawat 2001). Even in such well-integrated goods market pairs as the USA and Canada, there is considerable price volatility. According to one estimate, a distance of only 2,500 miles within the USA caused price volatility similar to that observed by US–Canadian cross-border trade and a geographic distance of a few miles (Engel and Rogers 1996). And international trade is still the simplest form of international expansion. Establishing and maintaining a cross-border network of manufacturing and R&D sites is less simple. It is much more complex and costly than international trade because the firm needs to create a dense mesh of *intra-firm connections* among different units to make such a network fruitful (Bartlett and Ghoshal 1989; Doz and Prahalad 1991).

Yet, many costs of doing business on an international scale have decreased substantially over recent years. A three-minute telephone call from New York City to London, for example, cost $717.7 in 1927 and $0.84 in 1999 (in 1999 US dollars).[1] Shipping a 150 1b parcel by air from New York City to Hong Kong cost $2188.0 in 1960 and had decreased to $389.0 by 1999 (in 1999 US dollars). Even more dramatic, transporting a container via ship from Los Angeles to Hong Kong cost $10,268.0 in 1970 and a mere $1900.0 in 1999 (in 1999 US dollars) (Air Traffic Conference of America 2000; US Dept of Commerce 2000; US Census Bureau 2001). These developments have enabled all types of firms to expand their activities across borders at an unprecedented rate.

In earlier work I developed and tested a distinction among motives for FDI based on knowledge flows. I found that firms carried out FDI either to create new capabilities or to exploit existing firm-specific capabilities. I labelled the former motive 'home-base-augmenting' and the latter motive 'home-base-exploiting' (Kuemmerle 1999a). *Home-base-augmenting* investment occurs when firms seek to capture spillovers in a foreign environment with the intention of enhancing the firm's capabilities. An example of home-base-augmenting investment would be a firm establishing a research site in proximity to the home base of a major foreign competitor or in proximity to a major university. A firm will typically choose a home-base-augmenting investment over acquiring a technology licence if the firm expects to create new and valuable knowledge at that site that could not be licensed from anywhere or only at a higher cost. *Home-base-exploiting* investment occurs when a firm seeks to exploit its capabilities through a local presence rather than through exporting or granting technology licences. An example of home-base-exploiting investment would be a manufacturing plant in a foreign country that is established to benefit from lower labour cost or to shorten response times to local market demand.

I showed that between 1955 and 1996 the frequency of home-base-augmenting investments relative to home-base-exploiting investments had increased dramatically for a group of thirty-two multinational enterprises (MNEs). Between 1955 and 1965 only 7 per cent of new investments in R&D sites abroad by these firms were home-base-augmenting, but between 1986 and 1995 that number had increased to 40 per cent (Kuemmerle 1999b). Note that while that investigation pertained only to new R&D sites, the general finding is applicable to manufacturing sites and sales subsidiaries as well. Many manufacturing sites abroad might be established primarily to exploit firm-specific capabilities in a country where labor costs and other costs are lower. We can categorize these investments as 'home-base-exploiting'. This is the case with many pharmaceutical manufacturing facilities in Puerto Rico and with BMW's manufacturing plant in Thailand. Other manufacturing facilities might have a strong home-base-augmenting intention where the firm actively seeks to learn from the local environment. Northpole, the world's largest maker of camping tents, operates a large facility in China. This is not just to benefit from low labor costs, but also to monitor potential spillovers from a large number of suppliers of raw materials such as fibres, fabrics and dyestuffs that are available in the region.

The literature on international expansion of firms reflects the shift towards home-base-augmenting investments. In the 1960s and 1970s, scholars described and analysed a cycle where firms would first manufacture at home for domestic consumption, then export, then move to establish factories abroad for local consumption and finally, once these factories had reached a sufficient quality level, service even the home market with goods manufactured abroad (Hymer 1976; Vernon 1979). More recent studies have focused on alternative motives for international expansion, namely on investments that are home-base-augmenting in nature (Wesson 1993; Cantwell 1991; Kuemmerle 1999b; Chung and Alcacer 2001).

Home-base-augmenting investments became more prevalent for three reasons. First, and as documented above, *the cost of doing business across borders* declined dramatically because of technological progress and because of the elimination of a wide range of tariffs, at least between major industrialized and emerging market countries. Second, a *supply-side shift of knowledge* occurred. The quantity and quality of spillovers that firms could capture from universities and from other firms increased.

Universities around the world started to actively develop, offer and price intellectual property for use by firms and firms sought such spillovers (Jaffe 1989; Hakanson and Nobel 1993, Henderson and Cockburn 1996). Third, a perceived *demand-side shift for knowledge* occurred. In many instances firms, realized that their technological knowledge stock at the home base, while superior in quality, would not enable them to survive in the long run. Knowledge in entirely separate fields of technology was becoming increasingly relevant for new products in the long run: Fumio Kodama has labelled this phenomenon 'technology fusion' (Kodama 1992; Coombs, Narandren and Richards 1996).

It should come as no surprise that for an established firm home-base-augmenting international expansion typically entails higher levels of uncertainty than home-base-exploiting investments. In the latter case, the firm typically has a good understanding of the technology and of the requirements for making such an investment successful. By contrast, in the case of home-base-augmenting investments, firms seek to capture spillovers that are generally only vaguely defined *ex ante* and often do not even exist by the time the firm makes an expansion decision. In addition to this uncertainty, there is uncertainty as to how well the firm's home base will be able to absorb and process the newly created knowledge. The 'not-invented-here' syndrome has been described as a powerful inhibitor of knowledge absorption and exploitation within the firm (Katz and Allen 1982). As I will discuss below, this has important implications for the resource allocation process.

For start-up firms, the opposite applies: home-base-augmenting investments typically involve less uncertainty than home-base exploiting ones. Start-up firms typically do not have a large number of entrenched organizational routines that would make intrafirm knowledge absorption difficult. The start-up firm does not have a lot firm-specific capabilities as yet, and is in a learning mode (Bhide 1999). Second, home-base-exploiting investments at start-up firms typically involve considerable fixed costs, not just for capital equipment but also for the creation of a minimum set of administrative routines between the foreign site and the young firm's home base. These costs can put the entire firm's survival at risk if free cash flows are still volatile – or, even worse, if free cash flows are negative and remaining funds may not be sufficient to reach break-even.

The resource allocation process and international expansion

The expansion of firms across country borders is associated with considerable uncertainty about the *benefits* and *costs* of such a decision. In practice, the basic economic aspects of an international expansion decision are generally more hampered by a lack of hard data than comparable domestic expansion decisions. This lack of reliable data affects both established firms and start-ups, but there are important differences between the two types of firms. This section will first discuss the international expansion of established firms and then focus on the international expansion of start-up firms.

In established MNEs several, if not many, individuals are involved in the decision making process for a new subsidiary. Additional uncertainty arises from conflicting views among the managers involved (Cyert and March 1963). Essentially, all the classic challenges described by studies of resource allocation processes apply here. These include: (1) a lack of transparency regarding the long-term outcome of managerial decisions and (2) a lack of alignment between managerial incentives (at different levels within the firm) and the overall strategy of the firm (Bower 1970; Burgelman 1983). Since organizations are 'fundamentally political entities' (Pfeffer 1992), senior managers should strive to design resource allocation processes that make constructive use of multiple managerial perspectives at different levels in the organization and that encourage an *open dialogue* about (sometimes radically) different choices, while rewarding each manager involved for her relative contribution to the decision. This is, of course, much easier said than done. Several researchers have documented that investments that enhance an established firm's current competences are undertaken more rapidly than investments that would jeopardize existing firm competences for the benefit of establishing new ones (Tushman and Anderson 1986; Christensen and Bower 1996).

In the international context, these typical challenges are compounded by all the issues that make international business more complex than domestic business: national culture, business practices, consumer preferences, different local factor conditions and differences in the rule of law.

What do we know specifically about resource allocation processes in an international context? Quite little, as it turns out. An early study documented the haphazard nature of foreign expansion (Aharoni 1966), while other authors argued that international expansion was a gradual process where discrete expansion decisions were not necessarily well-planned or rational. Furthermore, in only very few instances did managers involved in an expansion decision really consider overall firm strategy and synergies with the rest of the firm's existing international network. This lack of rationality in expansion decisions seemed to be more pronounced in larger firms and if a larger number of individuals were involved in the decision making (Malnight 1995; Johanson and Vahlne 1990).

At the same time, managers seem to learn from international expansion, even though their initial investment decisions might be unsuccessful. In my own research I found that managers often systematically under-estimated the cost of geographic expansion (Kuemmerle and Ellis 1999). In line with this finding, a study of established multinational firms showed that these firms had a reduced risk of failure as they sought to *further* expand their presence, while firms taking their first expansion steps often failed (Mitchell, Shaver and Yeung 1992). These findings suggest a punctuated equilibrium of either a sizeable international presence or no presence abroad at all. Cross-border JVs also seem to be a somewhat inferior alternative to fully owned subsidiaries, at least as far as the management of intrafirm knowledge is concerned. A recent study has argued quite convincingly that fully owned subsidiaries are better facilitators of knowledge flows across country borders than cross-border JVs (Almeida 2002).

In general, process rather than structure seems to be the important driver of success in multinational firms. Bartlett and Ghoshal have argued that the transnational corporation is successful because it prepares managers for natural conflicts that arise in an ever-changing matrix structure (Bartlett and Ghoshal 1990). A study of cross-border JVs has also argued that process variables such as resource allocation and knowledge internalization have a stronger impact on the success of a cross-border JV than structural variables such as duration or ownership (Hamel 1991).

With this in mind, how do resource allocation processes for inter-national expansion in large multinational firms and in fast-growing entrepreneurial firms compare? The literature on this topic is very small, presumably because the phenomenon of young firms expanding abroad is relatively new. However, the number of so-called 'global start-ups' has risen strongly since 1995s. Global start-ups can be defined as firms that establish dedicated sites abroad during the first year of their existence (Kuemmerle 2002). Dramatically lower costs of doing business across borders have created the opportunity for entrepreneurs to expand abroad early and to preempt competitors from copying the basics of a business idea.

Global start-ups are different from established multinational firms in at least three important ways. First, they typically are strongly influenced by the *personalities of their founders* and during the early days of the firm the founders' capabilities dominate relative to the capabilities of the firm as a whole. Resource allocation decisions to expand abroad are thus driven primarily by the founders and their vision or by early employees of the firm who often have risk profiles similar to the founders'. Several studies have found that prior international exposure of the founders has a strong positive influence on a young firm's propensity to expand abroad (McDougall and Oviatt 1996). Organizational routines and the internal structural context, as defined by Bower, play a less important role in start-ups than in established firms (Bower 1970).[2] This might give the start-up firm some advantages, as decision making processes are faster and less encumbered by structural context factors than in established firms. However, it can also put start-up firms at a disadvantage because, presumably, not all structural context is bad. The inability of many start-up firms to eventually become a successful multinational firm often has a lot to do with the lack of attention that the founders paid to the nurturing of a conducive structural context inside the firm.

Second, start-up firms are quite *resource constrained*, and carry little overhead because of their small size. This makes resource allocation decisions more transparent than in large firms. Budgeting systems in large firms typically use an *internal benchmark* that is set by the Chief Financial officer's (CFO's) office, such as a rate of return or a payback period, to evaluate projects. Not surprisingly, most expansion projects that reach the relevant decision making body show that they have passed these previously set hurdles. Often, this is not a reflection of the true nature of the project, but a result of working the system – forecasts get tweaked so that the project passes the hurdle. This happens particularly when the firm does not have a reliable system of *ex post evaluation* for past expansion decisions. In start-up firms things are different. There are hardly any set return hurdles; the most important constraint is typically available cash; and because the firm is in survival mode it monitors its cash carefully. Because of the small size of the firm, the entrepreneurs are almost always directly involved in important expansion decisions, especially regarding geographic expansion (Kuemmerle 2002), and their continued involvement in the firm ensures a post-investment review of the critical assumptions. In summary, in start-up firms there are few, if any, initial set hurdles. Start-up firms are also sufficiently small that those who make a geographic expansion decision will be directly confronted with its outcome.

Third, most entrepreneurs and senior managers in start-up firms readily acknowledge that they are in a *learning mode*. This has a rather fundamental impact on their approach toward resource allocation processes.

Most decisions will be seen as trials and therefore monitored more carefully than is the case in many large firms (Bhide 1992; Sahlman, Stevenson and Roberts 1999). In learning mode, start-up firms generally have an easier time reversing an international expansion decision. The online auction firm eBay in 2002 shut down its operations in Japan, a country where Yahoo! had developed a leading market share because of eBay's late entry and because Yahoo!'s auctions were free of charge. It is doubtful that the average established multinational firm would have taken such a drastic exit decision so quickly.

Venture capital funding, which many start-ups receive, is further conducive to a learning mode. Venture capital financiers prefer to release financing to entrepreneurial firms in stages. This encourages spending discipline and a thorough periodic review of the business. Start-up firms in fact probably benefit from this initial spending discipline even beyond the time when venture capitalists are involved in the firm.

All this is not to say that established firms always fall short in their resource allocation processes when it comes to competing against entrepreneurial start-ups. Some established firms succeed in maintaining the entrepreneurial culture of their resource allocation process throughout their international expansion. One detailed case study documented that at 3M a combination of several factors led to a uniquely entrepreneurial resource allocation process. It included a transparent information system and simple but ambitious performance goals, as well as an understanding among senior managers that their most important role was to coach junior managers as they learned how to allocate resources and a culture that cherished well-intended failure (Bartlett and Mohammed 1994).

Another study examined the corporate venturing process in an established firm and found that an internal structural context that allowed for entrepreneurial activity at the operational level and enabled middle managers to conceptually understand the link between such activity and outcomes was conducive to successful corporate venturing (Burgelman 1983). Finally, a study of foreign subsidiaries of diversified multinational firms found that the performance of these subsidiaries was positively correlated with the presence of a local entrepreneurial culture within the subsidiary (Birkinshaw, Hood and Jonsson 1998).

Overall, it seems crucial for established firms to keep their resource allocation processes flexible and transparent over time, particularly when it comes to investment projects in untried areas that require improvisation (Scott 1987). A key problem in such projects is that ideas get intercepted and do not 'bubble up' from the front line of management to the top of the firm.

Comparing international expansion decisions

I have argued that in established firms home-base-augmenting invest-ments are typically associated with a higher level of uncertainty than home-base exploiting investments because the outcome of a learning effort (and that is what home-base-augmenting investments are about) is generally less predictable than the application of an existing capability to a market opportunity and because the 'not-invented-here' syndrome might limit the absorption of new knowledge into the firm. The internal structural context probably also drives managers to suggest predictable projects (that is home-base-exploiting ones) rather than uncertain projects.

I have also argued that in start-up firms the opposite is true, and that home-base-exploiting investments are associated with higher degrees of uncertainty than home-base-augmenting ones. Start-ups are generally very resource constrained and most home-base-exploiting investments involve considerably higher fixed costs than home-base-augmenting ones Furthermore, start-up firms typically have fewer specific capabilities that they can exploit internationally, and there is more uncertainty associated with the long-term value of these existing capabilities than in large established firms. In eBay's early days, for example, it was not at all clear that running online auctions was a capability that would be difficult to replicate for others and hence valuable. It was even less clear whether this capability would have a similar value outside of the USA. Would consumers in the UK and Japan accept eBay's business model as enthusiastically as they did in the USA? eBay's decision to expand abroad was thus more risky than the decision of an established auction house like Sotheby's to set up shop in a new country would have been.

Finally, most start-up firms that decide to expand beyond their borders will probably first invest abroad with a home-base-augmenting objective, because their business at home is still very much in an experimental mode and there is much to be learned by further refining the business model. Using the framework of Cohen and Levinthal, one can argue that start-up firm's 'absorptive capacity' is high (Cohen and Levinthal 1994) and that this reduces the uncertainty of home-base-augmenting investments.

If one maps the two types of investments on a matrix where one axis measures the degree of stability of the internal structural context for resource allocation processes and where the other axis measures the degree of uncertainty associated with the investment, Figure 3A.1 emerges. Figure 3A.1 is a behavioural model derived from the careful examin-ation of a number of case studies and from the existing literature, and suggests that for established firms, the relative uncertainty of home-base-augmenting investments versus home-base-exploiting investments is larger than for start-up firms. Figure 3A.1 also suggests that for start-up firms home-base-augmenting investments are less uncertain than home-base-exploiting investments.

One way to verify the information in Figure 3A.1 would be to study a number of expansion cases in detail and to measure the degree of uncertainty associated with each decision. Since there are considerable measurement problems associated with this approach, I suggest a simple alternative measure: relative timing of home-base-augmenting versus home-base-exploiting investments. One would imagine that established firms and start-ups alike would carry out the *less uncertain* type of investment *first*, even though the motives for this behaviour might differ.

In established firms, the tendency towards carrying out less uncertain expansion investments first might be driven by operating managers' seeking to maximize their private benefits. If intrafirm information systems are imperfect and if the internal structural context is more focused on punishing failure (well-intended or not) than rewarding success, operating managers will prefer to propose and champion low-uncertainty expansion investments. In start-up firms, on the other hand, the tendency towards carrying out less uncertain geographic expansion investments will most likely be driven more by the firm's desire to survive during its critical early stages than by a manager's desire to maximize private rather than firm benefits. The reason is that maximizing of private benefits by managers is detected more easily in start-up firms, and very often the principals themselves rather than the agents make key resource allocation decisions. And the principals (that is, the founders) are strongly focused on firm survival.

The assumption that more uncertain investments will be undertaken later than less uncertain investments hinges on the premises that the state of the world at more distant points in time is more difficult to predict than at closer points in time and that managers and entrepreneurs have a strong interest in the survival of their firms. There is little doubt about the two premises in the mainstream literature on economics and sociology.

The question arises, however, why either type of firm would carry out the more uncertain type of investment at all. In established firms, the answer lies in the fact that in the long run top managers will advocate the more uncertain type of investment and that under their influence the internal structural context for this type of investment becomes more favourable. Often, such a change in internal structural context will be temporary because it is associated with the newness of a significant change, such as a new CEO taking charge (Khurana and Nohria 2002). In start-up firms, the answer lies in the fact that if the young firm survives its core business presumably stabilizes and generates free cash flows that can be used for geographic expansion decisions involving high fixed costs.

This reasoning leads to the following three hypotheses:

- **H1:** In established firms geographic expansion decisions of a home-base-exploiting nature will occur *before* geographic expansion decisions of a home-base-augmenting nature
- **H2:** In start-up firms geographic expansion decisions of a home-base-augmenting nature will occur *before* geographic expansion decisions of a home-base-exploiting nature
- **H3:** In start-up firms the time-lag between geographic expansion of low and high levels of uncertainty is *shorter* than in established firms

Summary of findings

I now summarize the findings from an empirical study reported elsewhere (Kuemmerle 2004). Data for the established firms were drawn from an analysis of all R&D sites that a sample of thirty-two multinational firms in the electronics and pharmaceutical industries established up to 1995 anywhere outside of their home countries. Altogether, 156 expansion decisions across borders were examined. Data for the start-up firms come from a sample of firms that I studied between 1996 and 2002. Altogether, this sample contained twenty-seven firms. The firms in the sample were active in twenty-six countries and the sample represented eighteen home-base countries. Results from statistical tests support the three hypotheses above. Established firms typically carried out home-base-exploiting investments four years before home-base-augmenting investments. Start-up firms, on the other hand, carried out home-base-augmenting activities about 1.5 years before home-base-exploiting activities. All results were significant at least at the 1 per cent confidence level.

I then examined four case studies in great detail. All four of them pertained to expansion decisions involving high uncertainty. For the established firms, I studied a successful and an unsuccessful home-base-augmenting investment. For the start-up firms, I studied a successful and an unsuccessful home-base-exploiting investment. The four cases suggest that the nature of the *internal structural context* is a critical determinant for the outcomes of the international expansion decision process, especially when a decision entails significant resource commitments and high levels of uncertainty for the firm. Three aspects of this context are particularly relevant:

- *First,* ideas and investment proposals need to 'bubble up' from operating managers to top management without distortion. The entire resource allocation process needs to be framed as an opportunity for operating managers and corporate staff. This entails a deep understanding among corporate staff not only about the resource allocation process itself but also about substantive matters in an investment proposal and about the sources of uncertainty in it. In the ideal case, corporate staff will amplify the pieces of information in the proposal that need particular attention by top management.
- *Second,* top management needs to follow a decision making process that addresses the uncertainty of an investment proposal by involving all parties within the firm who can contribute to the decision in a practical way and who will most likely be involved in its implementation. In other words, the resource allocation process needs to be framed as a process that copes with uncertainty partially by creating *early ownership* of the project among a *variety of constituencies* within the firm.
- *Third,* top management and operating managers should be keenly aware that highly uncertain investments such as R&D sites abroad need intensive *monitoring and nurturing* immediately after the investment decision. If the investment decision is negative, a consensus should evolve that the quality of the decision making process was high. This happens primarily through clear and open intrafirm communication and prepares the way for future successful decisions. If the investment decision is positive, the decision needs to be framed such that voluntary ownership for the project evolves almost immediately after the decision at various levels in the firm.

Established firms face challenges regarding all three aspects. Owing to their larger size, established firms have more layers of *hierarchy* and more *formal communication channels* than small firms; it is thus more likely that investment ideas get distorted or never reach decision makers. In large firms, it is also more complex to include all parties that might be involved in the implementation in the decision making process, simply because their number is large. Finally, the implementation and nurturing of the international site during its early phases is challenging because of limited management attention in a large firm.

Entrepreneurial firms face different challenges, especially concerning the second aspect – that is, the involvement of all constituencies that can contribute to a practical investment outcome. While investment proposals generally 'bubble up' fairly quickly to the entrepreneur and often even originate from her, the young firm typically lacks the capabilities necessary to assess the international expansion decision. This is particularly true for home-base-exploiting decisions that require a deep understanding of cost structures and actual pace of ramp-up of a local site. Even though all relevant constituents within the firm (operating managers and entrepreneur) may be involved in the resource allocation process, the entrepreneur often dominates this process so much that a balanced assessment is difficult. Thus, the very strengths of the entrepreneurial firm – its smaller size and less formal routines – can represent a disadvantage because they do not give enough voice to those managers who might be able to counterbalance a lopsided view of the entrepreneur.

Figure 3.1 Resource allocation for international expansion – start-up firms versus established firms

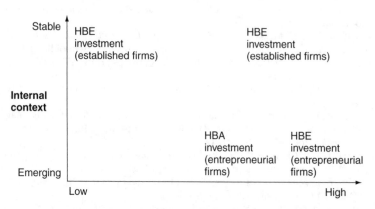

Notes: HBA = Home base augmenting investments intended to increase the firms' set of capabilities.
HBE = Home base exploiting investments intended to increase the firms' set of capabilities.

Notes

1. The cost for a three-minute telephone call from New York City to San Francisco also declined, from $136.8 (in 1999 dollar) in 1920 to $0.90 in 1999. The cost of a call from New York City to London thus declined by a factor of 854, while the cost for a call from New York City to San Francisco declined by a factor of 152 over a roughly comparable period of time.
2. Bower, in his process model of resource allocation (1970), defines three factors–phases: definition, impetus and structural context. 'Definition' is the process of determining the basic technical and economic characteristics of a project. 'Impetus' refers to the rate at which general managers within the firm publicly commit to the project and 'structural context' is defined as a set of organizational forces that influence the process of definition and impetus. In Bower's model it is particularly the structural context and its elements that top management can shape.

References

Aharoni, Y. (1966) *The Foreign Investment Decision Process* (Boston, MA: Harvard Business School Press).

Air Traffic Conference of America (2000) *Air Cargo*.

Almeida (2002), Paul 'Are Firms Superior to Alliances and Markets? An Empirical Test of Cross-Border Knowledge Building', *Organization Science* 13(2), 147–61.

Bartlett, C. and S. Ghoshal (1989) *Managing across Borders: The Transnational Solution* (Boston, MA: Harvard Business School Press).

————(1990) 'Managing Innovation in the Transnational Corporation', in C. A. Bartlett, Y. Doz and G. Hedlund (eds), *Managing the Global Firm* (London: Routledge).

Bartlett, C. and A. Mohammed (1994) *3M Optical Systems: Managing Corporate Entrepreneurship*, 9-395-017 (Boston, MA: Harvard Business School Press).

Bhide, A. (1992) 'Bootstrap Finance: The Art of Start-Ups', *Harvard Business Review* (November–December), 110–17.

————(1999) *The Origin and Evolution of New Business* (Oxford: Oxford University Press).

Birkinshaw, J., N. Hood and S. Jonsson (1998). 'Building Firm-Specific Advantages in Multinational Corporations: The Role of Subsidiary Initiative', *Strategic Management Journal*, 19(3), 221–41.

Bower, J. L. (1970) *Managing the Resource Allocation Process: A Study of Corporate Planning and Investment* (Boston, MA: Harvard Business School Press).

Burgelman, R. A. (1983) 'A Process Model of Internal Corporate Venturing in the Diversified Major Firm', *Administrative Science Quarterly*, 28, 223–44.

Cantwell, J. (1991) 'The International Agglomeration of R&D', in M. Casson (ed.) *Global Research Strategy and International Competitiveness* (Oxford: Basil Blackwell).

Christensen, C. M. and J. L. Bower (1996) 'Customer Power, Strategic Investment and the Failure of Leading Firms', *Strategic Management Journal*, 17, 197–218.

Chung, W. and J. Alcacer (2001) *Knowledge Seeking and Location Choice of Foreign Direct Investment in the United States*, Working Paper. (New York City: New York University).

Cohen, W. M. and D. A. Levinthal (1994) 'Fortune Favors the Prepared Firm', *Management Science*, 40(2), 227–52.

Coombs, R., P. Narandren and A. Richards (1996) 'A Literature-Based Innovation Output Indicator', *Research Policy* 25, 403–13.

Cyert, R. M. and J. G. March (1963) *A Behavioral Theory of the Firm* (Englewood Cliffs, NJ: Prentice-Hall).

Doz, Y. L. and C. K. Prahalad (1991) 'Managing DMNCs: A Search for a New Paradigm', *Strategic Management Journal*, 12, 145–64.

Engel, C. and J. Rogers (1996) 'How Wide is the Border?', *American Economic Review*, 86 (5), 1112–1125.

Ghemawat, P. (2001) 'Distance Still Matters: The Hard Reality of Global Expansion', *Harvard Business Review* (September), 137–47.

Hakanson, L. and R. Nobel (1993) 'Determinants of Foreign R&D in Swedish Multinationals', *Research Policy* 22, 396–411.

Hamel, G. (1991) 'Competition for Competence and Inter-Partner Learning Within International Strategic Alliances', *Strategic Management Journal*, 12, 83–103.

Henderson, R. and I. Cockburn (1996) 'Scale, Scope, and Spillovers: The Determinants of Research Productivity in Drug Discovery', *The Rand Journal of Economics*, 27, 32–59.

Hymer, S. H. (1976) *The International Operations of Multinational Firms: A Study of Foreign Direct Investment* (Boston, MA: MIT Press).

Jaffe, A. B. (1989) 'Real Effects of Academic Research', *American Economic Review*, 79(5), 957–70.

Johanson, J. and J.-E. Vahlne (1990) 'The Mechanism of Internationalisation', *International Marketing Review*, 7(4), 11–24.

Katz, R. and T. J. Allen (1982) 'Investigating the Not Invented Here (NIH) Syndrome: A Look at the Performance, Tenure, and Communication Patterns of 50 R&D Project Groups', *R&D Management*, 12(1), 7–19.

Khurana, R. and N. Nohria (2000) *The Performance Consequences of CEO Turnover*, Working Paper. (Boston, MA: Harvard Business School Press).

Kodama, F. (1992) 'Technology Fusion and the New R&D', *Harvard Business Review* (July–August).

Kuemmerle, W. (1999a) 'The Drivers of Foreign Direct Investment into Research and Development', *Journal of International Business Studies*, 30 (1), 1–24.

————(1999b) 'Foreign Direct Investment in Industrial Research in the Pharmaceutical and Electronics Industries – Results from a Survey of Multinational Firms', *Research Policy*, 28(2–3), 179–93.

————(2002) 'Home Base and Knowledge Management in International Ventures', *Journal of Business Venturing*, 17, 99–122.

————(2004) 'The Process of International Expansion: Comparing Resource Allocation in Established Firms and Entrepreneurial Start-ups', in J. L. Bower and C. Gilbert (eds), *Strategy as Resource Allocation* (Oxford: Oxford University Press).

Kuemmerle, W. and C. Ellis (1999) *Internet Securities, Inc.: Financing Growth*, 9-899-149 (Boston, MA: Harvard Business School Press).

Malnight, T. W. (1995) 'Globalization of an Ethnocentric Firm: An Evolutionary Perspective', *Strategic Management Journal* 16, 119–41.

McDougall, P. P. and B. M. Oviatt (1996) 'New Venture Internationalization, Strategic Change and Performance: A Follow-Up Study', *Journal of Business Venturing*, 11, 23–40.

Mitchell, W., J. M. Shaver and B. Yeung (1992) 'Getting There in a Global Industry: Impacts on Performance of Changing International Presence', *Strategic Management Journal*, 13, 419–32.

OECD (1996) *Globalization of Industry – Overview and Sector Reports*. (Paris: OECD).

Pfeffer, J. (1992) 'Understanding Power in Organizations', *California Management Review*, 34, 29–50.

Sahlman, W. A., H. H. Stevenson and M. Roberts (eds) (1999) *The Entrepreneurial Venture*, 2nd edn (Boston, MA: Harvard Business School Press).

Scott, R. W. (1987) *Organizations: Rational, Natural and Open Systems* (Englewood Cliffs, NJ: Prentice-Hall).

Tushman, M. L. and P. Anderson (1986) 'Technological Discontintuities and Organizational Environments', *Administrative Science Quarterly*, 31(3), 439–66.

US Census Bureau (2001) *US Statistical Abstract*, 121st edn. (Washington, DC).

US Department of Commerce (2000) *Containerized Cargo Statistics* (Washington, DC: US Department of Commerce, Maritime Administration, Office of Trade Studies and Statistics).

Vernon, R. (1979) 'The Product Cycle Hypothesis in a New International Environment', *Oxford Bulletin of Economics and Statistics*, 41(4), 255–67.

Wesson, T. (1993) *An Alternative Motivation for Foreign Direct Investment*, Unpublished Dissertation. (Cambridge, MA: Harvard University).

4
Multilatinas: Emerging Multinationals from Latin America

Jon I. Martínez, José Paulo Esperança and José de la Torre *

Introduction

Different theories in the field of international business have attempted to explain from various perspectives the evolution of firms from local to global. The *stages theory* (Johanson and Vahlne 1977) and the *entry strategies* framework (Root 1987) focus on the first steps of the whole process and explain how a company goes abroad and penetrates foreign markets. The *internalization* (Buckley and Casson 1976; Rugman 1981) and the *eclectic* (Dunning 1980) theories take an economist's perspective, to explain why a company becomes a MNC, internalizing transactions instead of using market mechanisms, but neglect the processes and stages involved in this transformation. The *structural theories* (Stopford and Wells 1972; Egelhoff 1982) do consider evolution, but their perspective may be too 'architectural' (according to Bartlett 1983). Finally, the *integration–responsiveness* (I–R) framework (Bartlett 1986; Prahalad and Doz 1987) assumes that the company is already a MNC that operates subsidiaries in several countries, so they too tend to ignore the expansion process.

──────────

* The statistical assistance of Ivo Nuno Pereira at ISCTE, and Paulo Albuquerque and Charlotte Ren, both PhD candidates at the Anderson School at UCLA, is gratefully acknowledged. Nancy Hsieh, Odir Pereira, Jenna Radomile and Mirthala Rangel provided extraordinary assistance in generating questionnaire returns. The financial support of UCLA's Center for International Business Education and Research is also gratefully acknowledged.

The need for a new framework is paramount to explain a new type of company increasingly active in the international arena – the *emerging MNC*, relatively smaller than its international rivals and usually emerging from middle-income nations. Latin America in the 1990s provides an exceptional setting for the understanding and predicting of a type of organization which is arising in many parts of the globe and may play a crucial role in the organization of cross-border economic activity, as well as spreading the globalization process.

The relevance of the new generation of MNCs has not been ignored in the literature. Liesch and Knight (1999) underline the lack of a robust theory to explain the internationalization process, especially for small and medium enterprises (SMEs). They complain, in particular, that we still do not have an appropriate explanation of how and why internationalization arises, suggesting that this gap can be addressed by 'outlining a linkage between foreign expansion and the role of information and knowledge' (1999, p. 391). Although suggesting a number of interesting research hypotheses, this study lacks empirical evidence. Some attempts at analysing real new MNCs have, however been made. Mascarenhas (1997) concentrated on 'international specialists', firms with limited resources who outsource multiple functions, particularly manufacturing and marketing activities. Leung and Yip (2003) also analyse a set of new multinationals, all based in the Asia-Pacific region who became important suppliers to more traditional MNCs and active acquirers across borders, these twenty-four firms are termed 'global original equipment manufacturers' (OEMs) and confirm that the required knowledge for internationalization can be obtained through 'softer' modes such as learning from clients rather than the 'harder' modes of setting up strong research and development (RvD) departments. Both the theoretical and empirical approaches converge on their concern with the need for a comparison between the emerging type of MNC and the more established, larger, rich countries-based MNC.

This chapter concentrates on the organizational and management processes that MNCs require for implementing their strategies in the regions and countries where they compete, comparing the emerging MNCs with their more experienced rivals.

The emerging MNC and Latin America

The 1990s were a period of growth for worldwide flows of foreign direct investment (FDI), reflecting a period of economic optimism and rising globalization. However, the traditional home countries, namely the USA and several European nations (such as the UK and the Netherlands), with a vast experience in foreign expansion, were joined by a group of medium-income countries whose local firms became active in the international arena. Indeed, outward FDI based in many of these countries expanded significantly faster than FDI based in the richer nations. The Latin American region as a whole, and several specific nations within the region, provide a dynamic example of this new trend, as shown in Table 4.1.

The estimation of the average geometric growth rate between the average for 1989–93 and 1999 shows that outward FDI grew faster in the region than in the world as a whole, with countries such as Argentina, Mexico and particularly Chile exhibiting a significant growth. Although a few of the firms that pioneered the foreign expansion from middle-income countries are large, such as the Mexican CEMEX or the Brazilian Companhia Vale do Rio Doce, most are relatively small, suggesting a decreasing minimum size for internationalizing firms. In a study based on US small firms, Manolova *et al.* (2002) observe that they are less likely to internationalize than Asian and European small firms.

It is not surprising that an increasing interest on small firm internationalization is getting a rising attention on the literature. One of the most focused perspectives comes from the field of international entrepreneurship (McDougall, Shane and Oviatt 1994; Westhead, Wright and Ucbasaran 2001). Most of these studies concentrate on demographic characteristics of the international entrepreneurs, such as age and size. The resource constraints of firms operating in a foreign context, formerly observed within the Hymer–Kindleberger paradigm,

Table 4.1   Outward FDI, 1989–99 (FDI Outflows, $US billion)

	1989–93 annual average	1994	1995	1996	1997	1998	1999	Yearly growth rate (%)
World	221.4	282.9	357.5	390.8	471.9	687.1	799.9	23.9
Latin America and the Caribbean	6.93	6.09	7.31	5.82	15.05	9.41	27.33	25.7
Mexico	0.18	1.06	−0.26	0.04	1.11	1.36	0.8	28.2
Argentina	0.31	1.01	1.5	1.6	3.66	2.17	1.2	25.3
Brazil	0.52	0.62	1.16	0.52	1.66	2.61	1.4	17.9
Chile	0.17	0.91	0.75	1.19	1.87	2.8	4.86	74.9

Source: United Nations, *World Investment Report* (2000).

are also exploited in the context of small multinationals. While some studies have analysed the role of human capital to overcome such disadvantages (Manolova *et al.* 2002), others have focused on the high-technology sector, apparently fertile to the emergence of small MNCs (McDougall, Shane and Oviatt 1994; Bloodgood, Sapienza and Alameida 1996).

The limited resources of small MNEs are also looked at from the main-stream perspective, in international business, of international cooperation. Oviatt and McDougall (1994, 1995) concentrate on international new ventures and global start-ups. Knight and Cavusgil (1997) address the 'born global' firm as a typical case of early internationalization.

The evolutionary theory stemming from the Scandinavian school has also influenced several students of small firm internationalization (Coviello and McAuley 1999). Smaller firms are even more prone to valuing geographic and psychic proximity when they venture abroad.

The problem associated with most of the research on emerging MNCs is that it is still mostly exploratory and almost exclusively based in case studies. Machado da Silva, Casali and Fernandes (2001) on Brazilian firms and the October 2000 special issue of the *Journal of Business Research* are examples of such studies in the context of emerging Latin American firms. The evolution of the organizational structure and the coordination and control mechanisms within the new smaller firms, by contrast with the more experienced, larger and more mature rivals, is still basically to be understood. This chapter attempts to shed light on this issue, in one the most fertile home regions for this new type of organization, Latin America (Chudnovsky, Kosacoff and López 1999; see Robles, Simon and Haar 2003). Learning on the experience and special characteristics of the new type of MNC, given the contemporary environment, is also much needed to help in defining the set of policies necessary for risk avoidance and value creation.

An evolving MNC

The evolution of a firm from a domestic company to a multinational organization involves several processes, as depicted in Figure 4.1. As many authors have reported in the literature, companies need to be prepared to compete in the international league. This process of becoming a professional firm means that the company has to acquire management skills and practices, and hire the right people to compete in an efficient way in the local marketplace. Once the firm has developed enough competence, it is ready to initiate the internationalization process.

Local environment	International environment	Global environment
Domestic company	Emerging MNC	Consolidated MNC
'Professionalization' process	Internationalization process	Consolidation/Rationalization process

Figure 4.1 An evolving process

Through this process, the company starts selling and producing in a few countries and thus becomes an *emerging multinational company*. Finally, once the company is competing and expanding into several markets as if it were a local competitor, often duplicating activities in different countries within a region, it starts realizing that the rationalization and consolidation of such activities would bring cost efficiencies and learning of key ideas that can be transferred to other affiliates in order to cope with an ever-more global environment (Douglas and Craig 1989).

An emerging MNC is therefore a firm that is still developing its internationalization process and so is expanding in a number of countries and enhancing local market penetration. Considering the framework of Figure 4.2, which was inspired by the integration–responsiveness framework (Prahalad and Doz 1987), these embryonic multinationals are entering the box on the left lower cornes, and differ from experienced or consolidated MNCs in that they usually have a much lower level of integration and localization of value-chain

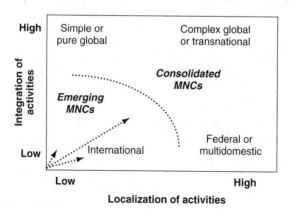

Figure 4.2 An evolving process (modified integration–responsiveness framework)
Note: Integration is defined as the degree of coordination and standardization of product offerings and attributes, value-chain activities and functional tasks across subsidiaries and HQs. Localization is the degree of dispersion of value-chain activities across markets together with their level of responsiveness to local conditions.

activities. Consolidated multinationals, that can take various forms – such as *federal* or *multidomestic, simple* or *pure global*, or *complex global* or *transnationals*, depending on the author – are still growing in a number of countries, but marginally when compared to emerging MNCs.

In terms of management and organizational processes, which are the core of this chapter, emerging MNCs are less developed in the quantity and quality of such processes than consolidated MNCs. As these companies are facing the consolidation and rationalization of their global operations in order to be more efficient and competitive, they need more sophisticated processes and mechanisms to integrate, coordinate and control their worldwide activities. Several authors have reported the value of these processes and devices to integrate, coordinate and control the dispersed operations of multinational companies (Galbraith 1973; Doz and Prahalad 1981; Martínez and Jarillo 1989). This theory of the evolving MNC suggests that as emerging MNCs evolve into consolidated ones, they need more management and organization processes such as centralization of decision making, formalization of policies and procedures, planning and budgeting, reporting and control, socialization and acculturation and coordination devices to integrate their operations.

Given that the emerging MNCs that we are considering in this chapter come from Latin America, we will call these companies *multilatinas* (MLs). From this point on, we will identify consolidated MNCs simply as MNCs.

Empirical research

Based upon the previous framework we have defined two sets of research propositions regarding the special characteristics of MLs, and the theory based on differences of coordination mechanisms and other management processes as compared with MNCs:

- *Special characteristics*: MLs are at an earlier stage of development compared to MNCs, which means they are smaller in size, less geographically diversified in sales and have lower levels of R&D investment and rate of introduction of new products.
- *Management processes*: MLs present a lower degree of formalization of policies and procedures than MNCs; MLs exhibit less complex and sophisticated planning systems than MNCs; MLs employ less frequent reporting and control devices then MNCs; MLs show lower use and frequency of coordination mechanisms than MNCs; MLs reveal a less cohesive and unified culture across units as compared to MNCs.

As a result of globalization and pressures for integration, MLs have increased their level of regional coordination less than MNCs.

Empirical analysis and data collection

In order to test these research propositions, we conducted a mail survey by using a detailed structured questionnaire which was applied to companies competing in Latin America. The survey was taken between December 2000 and July 2001. The sample was separated in two groups:

- *Foreign MNCs competing in the region, based in North America and Europe.* We took 449 MNCs in Europe (172) and North America (277). A total of Eighty firms were disqualified for various reasons and an additional Eighty-six firms refused to participate, mainly owing to corporate policy. After multiple sampling we obtained fifty-eight usable responses.
- *Local companies from Argentina, Brazil, Chile, Mexico and Peru* that had expanded to other countries within the *'Multilatinas'* region. We sent the questionnaire to 154 companies in eight countries. The final number of usable responses was forty.

We have therefore a combined sample of ninety-eight companies operating in several Latin American countries. Both groups compete in a wide range of industries, from consumer 'low-tech' products to industrial 'high-tech' goods, including services.

Findings

Results show that MNCs are considerably bigger in terms of number of employees and sales than MLs. They are also more international than MLs, given that, on average, 42 per cent of their sales come from abroad (out of their home region – that is, North America, Europe) as compared to 24 per cent in the case of MLs. Table 4.2 presents interesting information regarding company 'demographics', as well as some selected strategy indicators and industry variables.

Regarding strategy and competitive variables, MNCs invest significantly more money in R&D (close to 4 per cent of their global sales) than MLs (about 2 per cent of their sales). Their rate of new product introduction is higher as well, which means that between 10 and 20 per cent of their sales come from products or services introduced in Latin

Table 4.2   Company and industry statistics

Variables	Scale	Mean		T-test
		MLs	MNCs	significance
Number of employees worldwide	*N*	11,290	55,114	***
Total global sales	million US$	1,238	13,956	***
Sales in home region	%	76	58	***
R&D intensity	low (1) – high (7)	2.10	3.63	***
Rate of introduction of new products	low (1) – high (7)	3.20	3.81	*
Homogeneity of demand	dissimilar(1) – homogeneous(7)	4.55	5.07	*
Domestic competition	local firms(1) – sub sidiaries MNCs (7)	3.57	4.52	**

Note: $* p < 0.1; ** p < 0.05; *** p < 0.01$.

American markets since 1998. The same figure for MLs is 5–10 per cent. These results suggest that MNCs, on average, would be better prepared than MLs to compete in global markets where technology and innovation are crucial factors.

With respect to industries where they compete, MNCs enjoy more homogeneous markets than MLs, and face more 'multinational' competition. On average, MLs compete in industries where local firms control about 55 per cent of market share, while MNCs operate in sectors where the domestic competition counts for less than 40 per cent of the market. All these results confirm the special characteristics of MLs, showing that most of them are smaller, less internationalized and less innovative than their more experienced rivals.

Table 4.3 presents the main results of this study, showing a summary of the management processes. As we can see, several variables present significant statistical differences between means of MLs and MNCs when applying the *T*-test. Some variables are aggregates, such as the locus of decision making, which is composed of fifteen dimensions, and corporate control and reporting that includes nine.

Results are not clear for variables that tried to measure the autonomy versus centralization of decision making. However, concerning formalization of corporate relationships, MNCs are more formal than MLs, as predicted earlier. The same is true for strategic planning and budgeting, where MLs demonstrate a less sophisticated or simpler level than MNCs. By contrast, no significant difference was found for socialization

Table 4.3 Summary of management processes

Variables	Scale	Mean		T-test
		MLs	MNCs	significance
Locus of decision making *a*	autonomy (1) – centralization (7)	3.72	3.99	–
Formalization of corporate relations	very low (1) – very high (7)	4.18	4.79	*
Strategic planning and budgeting	annual budget (1) – complex (7)	4.13	4.68	*
Corporate control and reporting *b*	non-existent or annual (1)– frequent (7)	2.31	3.41	***
Coordination mechanisms *c*	rare (1) – frequent (5)	3.12	3.18	–
Socialization or acculturation	diverse culture (1) – common culture (7)	5.18	4.96	–
Regional coordination *d*	increased (1) – decreased (7)	2.27	2.04	**

Notes: * $p < 0.1$; ** $p < 0.05$; *** $p < 0.01$.
a Average of fifteen variables.
b Average of nine variables.
c Average of seven variables.
d Average of fifteen variables.

or acculturation or use of coordination mechanisms such as organizing task forces or management transfers.

It is clear that MNCs ask for more frequent reports than MLs, as a means of output control – this is the most significant difference found between MLs and MNCs. The change in regional coordination is also stronger within MNCs than MLs, suggesting a larger response to changing environmental conditions.

Conclusions and implications

This study has focused on the concept of 'evolution of MNCs' from emerging companies that are penetrating and installing production facilities in foreign and usually hear by countries, to more experienced and consolidated ones whose main concerns are not which new markets to enter, but how to be more efficient and competitive in the large number of countries where they are already competing. The evolving MNC thus goes through stages with different needs and competitive situations on the path from 'emerging' to 'consolidated' status.

We have observed that management processes are used differently by these two groups of firms in the Latin American market. As MNCs are more internationalized and operate in more differenciated environments, their needs for efficiency and competitiveness are higher, requiring more advanced and sophisticated processes and mechanisms to integrate, coordinate and control their operations across the region, and they need to use them more frequently. MLs, the emerging MNCs from Latin America, seem to be more concerned with expansion than efficiency, exhibiting lower levels of integration, coordination and control. Although a low level of coordination does not necessarily prevent a successful expansion into geographically and psychically close host countries (mainly other Latin American nations), it may bring significant risks as these firms carry a larger share of their business away from the home region.

In general, the results of this research tend to confirm our pattern of the evolving MNC. This is specially the case of processes such as formalization of corporate policies, strategic planning and budgeting and reporting and control. Others, such as centralization of decision making and socialization or acculturation respectively obtained mixed and poor results. Finally, we found good evidence that MNCs have increased their coordination levels within the region to a greater extent than MLs.

Our general conclusion with managerial implications is that emerging MNCs, and 'Multilatinas' in the specific context of Latin America, have much to learn from experienced and consolidated MNCs. This learning of management processes and coordination devices will be decisive in the struggle for foreign market entry, especially in more distant regions, as well as for being profitable and raising overall company value. This is the challenge they have to face as they follow the process of evolution we have postulated in this chapter.

References

Bartlett, C. A. (1983) 'MNCs, Get Off the Reorganization Merry Go Round', *Harvard Business Review*, March–April.
————— (1986) 'Building and Managing the Transnational: The New *Organizational* Challenge' in M. E. Porter (ed.), *Competition in Global Industries*. (*Boston, MA: Harvard Business School Press*), 367–401.
Bloodgood, J. M., H. J. Sapienza and J. G. Almeida (1996) 'The Internationalization of New High Potential US Ventures: Antecedents and Outcomes', *Entrepreneurship Theory and Practice*, 20(4) 61–76.
Buckley, P. J. and M. Casson (1976) *The Future of Multinational Enterprise* (London: Holmes & Meier).
Chudnovsky, D. B. Kosacoff and A. López (1999) *Las multinacionales latinomericanas: sus estrategias en un mundo globalizado* (Buenos Aires: Fondo de Cultura Económica de Argentina).

Coviello, N. E. and A. McAuley (1999) 'Internationalization and the Smaller Firm: A Review of Contemporary Empirical Research', *Management International Review*, 39(3), 223–56.

Douglas, S. P. and C. S. Craig (1989) 'Evolution of Global Marketing Strategy: Scale, Scope and Synergy', *Columbia Journal of World Business*, 24(3), 47–59.

Doz, Y. and C. K. Prahalad (1981) 'Headquarters Influence and Strategic Control in MNCs', *Sloan Management Review*, 23(1), 15–29.

Dunning, J. (1981) 'Toward an Eclectic Theory of International Production: Some Empirical Tests', *Journal of International Business Studies*, 11(1), 9–31.

Egelhoff, W. G. (1982) 'Strategy and Structure in Multinational Corporations: An Information Processing Approach', *Administrative Science Quarterly*, 27(3), 435–58.

Galbraith, J. (1973) *Designing Complex Organizations* (Reading, MA: Addison-Wesley).

Johanson, J. and J. E. Vahlne (1977) 'The Internationalization Process of the Firm – A Model of Knowledge and Increasing Market Commitments', *Journal of International Business Studies*, 8, 23–32.

Knight, G. A. and S. T Cavusgil (1997) 'Early Internationalization and the Born-Global Firm: Emergent Paradigm for International Marketing', Working Paper, Michigan State University, CIBER.

Leung, A. and G. S. Yip (2003) 'The Global OEM: The Transformation of Asian Supplier Companies', Chapter 7 in J. Birkinshaw, S. Ghoshal, C. Markides, J. Stopford and G. Yip (eds), *The Future of the Multinational Company* (London: John Wiley).

Liesch, P. W. and G. A. Knight (1999) 'Information Internalization and Hurdle Rates in Small and Medium Enterprise Internationalization', *Journal of International Business Studies*, 30(1), 383–94.

Machado da Silva, C. L., A. M. Casali and B. R. Fernandes (2001) 'Internationalization and Organizational Change: A Multi Case Study of Brazilian Organizations', *Latin American Business Review*, 2(3–4), 61–96.

Manolova, T. S., C. G. Brush, L. F. Edelman and P. G. Greene (2002) 'Internationalization of Small Firms: Personal Factors Revisited', *International Small Business Journal*, 20(1), 9–31.

Martínez, J. I. and J. C. Jarillo (1989) 'The Evolution of Research on Coordination Mechanisms in Multinational Corporations', *Journal of International Business Studies*, 20(3), 489–514.

———(1991) 'Coordination demands of international strategies', *Journal of International Business Studies*, 22(3), 429–44.

Mascarenhas, B. (1997) 'Small International Specialists', *Journal of International Management*, 3(3), 169–86.

McDougall, P., S. Shane and B. Oviatt (1994) 'Explaining the Formation of International New Ventures: The Limits of Theories from International Business Research', *Journal of Business Venturing*, 9(6), 469–87.

Oviatt, B. M. and P. P. McDougall (1994) 'Towards a Theory of International New Ventures', *Journal of International Business Studies*, 25(1), 45–64.

———(1995) 'Global Start-Ups: Entrepreneurs on a Worldwide Stage' *Academy of Management Executive*, 9(2), 30–43.

Prahalad, C. K. and Y. Doz (1987) *The Multinational Mission: Balancing Local Demands and Global Vision* (New York: Free Press).

Robles, F. Simon and J. Haar (2003) *Winning Strategies for the New Latin Markets*, (NJ: Financial Times/Prentice-Hall).

Root, F. R. (1987) *Entry Strategies for International Markets* (Lexington, MA: Lexington Books).

Rugman, A. M. (ed.) (1981) *Inside the Multinationals: The Economics of Internal Markets* (London: Croom Helm).

Stopford, J. M. and L. T. Wells, Jr. (1972) *Managing the Multinational Enterprise* (New York: Basic Books).

Westhead, P., M. Wright and D. Ucbasaran (2001) 'The Internationalization of New and Small Firms: A Resource-Based View', *Journal of Business Venturing*, 16(4), 333–58.

5

Corporate Governance and Globalization: Toward an Actor-Centred Institutional Analysis

Ruth V. Aguilera and George S. Yip *

Introduction

Despite globalization, multinational companies (MNCs) continue to be heavily influenced by the *institutional context* of the country in which their corporate headquarters are located (Ferner and Quintanilla 1998). For example, European MNCs accounted for 32 per cent of the world's 500 largest firms in 2001 (*Fortune Global 500*, 2002). But there is a large discrepancy between each European country's share of the top 500 MNCs and its share of population or gross domestic product (GDP). So the UK accounts for 22 per cent of all Western European companies in the *Fortune Global 500* in 2002, but only 15 per cent of population (in Western Europe) and 17 per cent of GDP; while Italy accounts for similar proportions of population and GDP but only 5 per cent of European *Fortune Global 500* MNCs. In this chapter, we argue that the discrepancy in the degree of globalization is partially explained by the country's institutional environment. In particular, we draw on actor-centred institutionalism to identify how corporate governance actors might influence globalization.

Previous studies examining variations in globalization have not addressed the role of national corporate governance systems from the corporate stakeholders' point of view. In this chapter, we develop a

* We gratefully acknowledge the support of the UK Economic and Social Research Council.

theoretical framework that shows how differences among European corporate governance systems can significantly explain variation in the globalization of MNCs.

Various explanations exist for MNCs' globalization discrepancies, such as the history of industrialization (Gerschenkron 1962; Chandler, Amatori and Hikino 1997) and the relative advantages of companies from different national bases (Porter 1990). 'Globalization' constitutes both geographic spread and global integration of strategy and organization (Yip 1992, 2003, p. 1). Our interest lies in explaining these two aspects of globalization, particularly the latter, rather than the more traditional focus on explaining a firm's percentage of international revenues.

An actor-centred institutional analysis

Our main assumption is that the institutional environment – and, in particular, corporate governance stakeholders – will shape firms' globalization patterns. Although there exist different schools of thought within institutional theory (see DiMaggio and Powell 1991; Whitley 1992, 1999; Hall and Soskice 2001; Scott 2001; Aguilera and Jackson 2003; Federowicz and Aguilera 2003), we view institutions as influencing the *range* but not determining *outcomes* within organizations. In addition, we do not deny the agency role of actors within organizations (Oliver 1991) and hence stress the interplay of institutions and firm-level actors (Sharpf 1997). Institutions shape the social and political processes of how actors' interests are defined ('socially constructed'), aggregated and represented with respect to the firm. However, institutions are themselves the result of strategic interactions in different domains generating shared beliefs that in turn impact those interactions in a self-sustaining manner (Aoki 2001; Aguilera and Jackson 2003). The task for our actor-centred institutional model is, therefore, to specify how the role of each governance actor is shaped by different national institutional domains and thereby generates different types of conflicts and coalitions within the firm, in turn influencing the firm globalization patterns through different elements of global strategy and global organization.

We consider the most important governance actors who might affect globalization: employees, shareholders, the board of directors, top management teams and governments. Obvious omissions are customers and competitors, but being external to the firm they have less interaction with corporate governance. In sum, we examine in detail the mechanisms by which the corporate governance context in which each actor is embedded influences the actor's decisions on key aspects of globalization.

This theoretical exercise fills two important gaps in the international business literature. First, to our knowledge there is only one study looking at the corporate governance dimensions of the multinational firm and internationalization patterns. Fukao's (1995) analysis of the corporate governance of the multinational *vis-à-vis* its subsidiaries is the closest in the field of global strategy. Second, an edited volume by Morgan, Kristensen and Whitley (2001), on the organization of the MNC across institutional and national divides, demonstrates the 'relatively limited institutionalization of worldwide governance regimes' (p. 32). Their argument is the starting point for examining how differences in governance affects globalization.

Corporate governance as a source of variance in globalization

We conceptualize 'corporate governance' broadly as the *set of interests and practices undertaken by shareholders and stakeholders of the firm*. We focus on how five main governance actors (employees, shareholders, the board of directors, top management teams, and government) behave towards the firm. We have identified these five governance actors because they are representative of the different interests shaping firm strategy. These interests are not always aligned. Since our level of analysis is the country, we necessarily stylize our conceptualization of each governance actor within a given country, making them almost 'ideal-types'. Moreover, we limit our discussion to the Corporate governance systems of the headquarters or home country, as that is the regime that has the most influence. While, the Corporate governance rules of countries in which the MNC has important subsidiaries will also have some influence, this tends to be much less than that of the home country.

Existing frameworks for globalization usually have three constructs: industry globalization drivers, global strategy elements and global organization factors (for example, Yip 1992). Government drivers are frequently included under industry aspects, but focus on intercountry rules such as trade and foreign direct investment (FDI) regimes. But these government drivers of globalization ignore intracountry rules in terms of governance. These prior studies also neglect the moderating effects of institutions. Admittedly, studies of the globalization of *countries* placed heavy emphasis on institutions (for example Porter 1990; Rugman 2000). However, studies of the globalization of *companies* have not. Institutional theory would say that historical legacies and national institutional complementarities explain the behaviour of country MNCs. The essence of global strategy theory is the balance among industry drivers and strategy (Porter 1986; Yip 1989; Morrison 1990) and organization and strategy (Prahalad and Doz 1987; Bartlett and Ghoshal 1989; Martínez and Jarillo, 1989; Birkinshaw and Morrison 1995; Westney and Zaheer 2001). Similarly, institutions create a balance and constraint on possible strategies and organizational forms.

Corporate governance is likely to affect all aspects of global integration. Using Yip's (1992) categories, these aspects are the five elements of *global strategy* – global market participation, global products and services, global activity location, global marketing and global competitive moves; and the four elements of *global organization* – global organization structure, global management processes, global human resources and global culture. In this chapter, we provide a systematic analysis of how Corporate governance might affect global strategy and global organization, which in turn will shape the patterns of globalization. The rest of this chapter discusses how particular aspects of Corporate governance, especially as related to actors in Corporate governance within an institutional context, affect globalization outcomes.

Roles of corporate governance actors in globalization

In this section, we conduct a stylized theoretical analysis to explain the logic that could predict how each corporate governance actor will behave towards global strategy and global organization that in turn will lead to a particular pattern of globalization mode. It is worth noting that this discussion refers to ideal-types for case of categorization.

Employees

The role of home country employees in corporate governance varies by country, as determined by the existing institutional arrangements. As discussed earlier, we focus on home–HQ countries, as any role of employees in corporate governance is overwhelmingly shaped at the corporate rather than the subsidiary level. Admittedly, there can be local roles, such as in the closing of facilities and local work rules, but these operate at a lower level of strategy.

Employees can have different mechanisms for influencing firm governance, depending on the corporate governance regime in which they operate. Examples of employee voice are board representation, work councils, equity ownership, unions, consultation rights and rules on working conditions and job security. The capacity of employees' to *influence the firm* will have important effects for the firm's ability to undertake global strategy and organization. We operationalize employees' involvement in terms of their ability to influence the firm's decision making.

Regarding the strategy dimensions of global integration, a strong corporate governance role for employees should be favourable to *global market participation*, as this latter applies to the global expansion of sales and therefore should favour home employment rather than threaten it. Similarly, the strong involvement of labour in firm governance shapes the characteristics of global products and services. A successful *global product strategy* requires not just the right design but also the ability to manufacture to world-class standards. Companies based in countries that for whatever reason cannot produce to world-class standards will, therefore, find it hard to adopt a global product strategy. On the other hand, too much employee involvement can have deleterious effects on product or service quality.

Conversely, employees having a strong voice within the firm's corporate governance should: (1) make it harder for an MNC to relocate activities globally outside the home country, (2) have a small negative effect on the use of global marketing, at the margin, strong home country employees may prefer marketing that retains national identity; and (3) make it harder for an MNC to make global competitive moves, as these often require sacrifice of home country position, resources, revenues or profits, and hence domestic jobs or working conditions.

Regarding the effects on global organization, we would expect that employees having a strong corporate governance role will not favour any global strategy lever because they would contribute to either fewer home country jobs or to decrease the quality of home country jobs. For instance, the implementation of global human resource (HR) policies is likely to transplant jobs across different subsidiaries and to introduce efficiency policies that are likely to impoverish home country employment practices such as work organization or performance incentives.

Shareholders

Shareholders of large public MNCs (which are our focus) play differing roles in different countries. At one extreme, the USA and the UK have mostly arm's length, neutral shareholders, who are focused on maximization of shareholder value. Although many American and British shareholders are large institutions, these have to date played mainly passive roles. Japan also has many institutional shareholders, but these tend not to be neutral and often act as part of a network ('*keiretsu*') that supports the role of the company within the network and, hence, incumbent management. Germany has many companies where different stakeholders, particularly banks and institutional shareholders, play a leading role in influencing corporate policy.

We distinguish between *neutral shareholders* and those with *vested interests (partial)*. By 'neutral' we mean that the overriding concern of the shareholders is to maximize profits and shareholder value. Interested shareholders also care about other objectives, sometimes ahead of shareholder value. Employee shareholders nearly always have the partial interest of some bias against maximizing shareholder value in favour of employment levels, pay or conditions. We consider shareholders such as banks or institutional investors as partial interest shareholders, as they will have several interests at stake in addition to shareholder value maximization. In Japan, institutional shareholders hold maintenance of the overall *keiretsu* as a major objective. In Germany, institutional shareholders typically have close ties and loyalty to management. In all countries, state shareholders pursue additional objectives such as maintaining employment, national security, competitiveness and prestige. Family shareholders also tend to be concerned with the family's legacy, loyalty to employees and tradition, and can also be risk averse. This latter point generally applies to second or later generations than to that of the founders.

In summary, neutrality or partiality is a function of several shareholder attributes: the typical roles in a country of institutional shareholders and of governmental shareholders, the prevalence of first versus second or later generation family shareholders, the extent of shareholdings by managers and lastly the degree of concentration that will allow the exercise of shareholder influence. Hence we prefer to use neutrality versus partiality of shareholder interests as the key defining characteristic of shareholder behaviour that affects globalization, although partial shareholders will need some degree of concentrated ownership in order to exercise influence.

We expect that shareholders will manifest different positions regarding the five global strategy levers. First, most shareholders, whether neutral or partial, should be in favour of *global market participation*, as that usually helps rather than hurts domestic interests such as higher firm revenues. Second, we argue that whether shareholders are neutral or partial probably has little effect on the ability of MNCs to produce *globally competitive products and services*. For example, Japan and Germany produce on average the highest quality global products (as confirmed in various surveys) and have similar types of shareholder interests (large institutions that favour incumbent management and the status quo).

France and Italy have relatively large shareholdings by partial government shareholders but are not as successful in producing global products except in some niche areas (especially in the case of Italy). The USA and UK have similar corporate governance in terms of having mostly neutral shareholders. But the USA has many more companies with successful global products while Britain has almost no global products left, but a significant number of globally competitive services (especially in finance, airlines and creative industries).

Third, neutral shareholders should favour *global relocation of activities* if that is in the best interests of the company and ultimately shareholder value. Some types of partial shareholders may oppose global relocation; in particular, significant equity ownership by home country employees makes it difficult for companies to move jobs overseas. Many government shareholders also seek to protect domestic employment. Some family shareholders may also have sentimental or altruistic reasons for preserving domestic employment. Fourth, partial shareholders should have a small negative effect on the use of *global marketing*. At the margin, some home country shareholders, such as employees and governments, may prefer marketing that retains national identity. Second and later generation family shareholders may also seek to preserve a company heritage that has a national identity. Finally, partial shareholders with home country interests, such as employees and governments, should make it harder for an MNC to make *global competitive moves*, as these often require sacrifice of home country position, resources, revenues or profits, and hence domestic jobs or working conditions.

The existing literature provides little guidance on the relationship between shareholder interests and global organization. First, even partial shareholders with domestic interests should favour *global organization structures* so long as the home country is dominant. An exception is that state owners may favour country-based organization structures, or a domestic–international split in order to preserve home country jobs, investment, or influence. A change from national family ownership to foreign or neutral ownership can trigger reorganization toward a global structure. Second, partial shareholders should favour *global management processes* so long as the home country processes dominate. Third, some types of partial shareholders, especially employees, should make it harder for an MNC to have *global HR policies*, as they will favour the employment and advancement of home country nationals. Family shareholders may also find it hard to apply neutral global HR policies. Finally, firms controlled by family shareholders and domestic employee shareholders may find it hard to create a *global culture*.

Board of directors

Boards of directors vary importantly in terms of their structure, composition and activeness (Daily and Dalton 1994). German boards have a dual structure, with a supervisory board ('*Aufsichsrat*') above a management board ('*Vorstand*'). The supervisory board has various statutory duties, particularly the appointment of the members of the management board and supervision of their actions. German companies with very restricted shareholdings can take the form of a GmbH and operate with only one board. In the UK, most boards adhere to the Cadbury Report's recommendation of having a non-executive chairman; in the other countries, the roles of chief executive (CEO) and chairman are often combined, especially in the USA. Another aspect of board structure is the role of committees, which varies depending on the strategic leadership of the board. In general, we do not believe that board structure *per se* makes a difference to globalization.

The composition of boards in major OECD countries varies by both custom and law. British boards have a high proportion, usually a majority, of corporate executives, with very few external directors. On the other hand, British chairmen are typically outsiders. In contrast, US boards mostly have a majority of outside directors, but the chairman is usually an insider, either a past or current CEO. French boards are becoming Anglicized owing to foreign institutional investor pressures. German supervisory boards are required by the Co-Determination Laws to have employee representatives, their number and proportion depending on the size of the company. In the other countries, labour representation and participation in firm decision making is rare, except where they are significant shareholders. State owned firms also tend to have higher labour representation. Japanese boards usually include representatives of other *keiretsu* members.

Countries also vary in the extent to which major shareholders have board representation. In the USA and UK, large institutional shareholders have only very recently sought representation on boards. In contrast, in Germany, and France, it is the norm to have major shareholders, such as banks or institutional investors, sitting on the board. Boards with a majority of directors who represent shareholders are more likely to globalize. They are less risk averse than boards dominated by non-shareholders, because they will be less constrained by non-shareholder interests such as the preservation of HQ country jobs and investment. Hence, such firms are more likely to favour globalization strategies, particularly global market participation and global activity location, even if they adversely affect stakeholders such as HQ country employees and suppliers. Similarly, such firms are more likely to use global management processes because they will seek value-maximizing behaviour more than preservation of traditional, country centred methods.

The insider–outsider split probably has mixed effects on globalization. On the one hand, outsiders (unless they represent special interests) should be able to make the most neutral tradeoffs about the risks involved in globalization. Boards dominated by neutral outsiders should be less risk averse than boards dominated by insiders, because they do not have their shares or job security at stake. Outsider directors are more likely to favour globalization strategies, particularly global market participation and global activity location, as they have few, if any, ties to HQ country employees. On the other hand, insiders typically have motives of empire building and incentive pay to offset any inherent preference for the status quo. Hence, performance evaluation and reward are also critical.

Globalization should be affected by boards having *partial* members: representatives of employees, network partners, suppliers, customers, governments or non-governmental organizations (NGOs). Partial boards will bias decisions away from pure profit and shareholder value maximization, and hence the optimal globalization strategy, in favour of their particular constituencies. We predict that employee, government and NGO board representatives pose might prevent fully-fledged globalization in order to promote their own interests. In contrast, representation of major shareholders, provided they have neutral interests, as discussed earlier, should favour globalization. Generally speaking, we will argue that, other things being equal, neutral boards will be more likely to favour the right globalization strategies.

We propose that globalization strategies will be most facilitated by having boards that have *neutral* interests favouring shareholder value. British and American boards rate highest on these measures, German boards lowest and French, Italian and Japanese boards in between. Having already discussed how employee and shareholder roles affect each of the nine elements of globalization, we need not repeat this analysis for boards. We propose that neutral boards will favour all nine elements of global strategy and organization.

Top management teams

Top management teams (TMTs) vary across countries in terms of their mobility and their background. In general, we expect that TMTs comprising mobile, professional managers are more likely to globalize. The more important distinction is whether the TMT acts in a *fiduciary* as opposed to an *autonomous* basis. Top managers with lifetime employment in the firm are more likely to act as fiduciaries for stakeholder interests and be more conservative about globalization. Similarly, those top managers who view themselves as professional managers rather than as specialists in a function are also more likely to make the balanced assessments needed for globalization. We expect that companies with mobile, professional TMTs will favor all nine elements of global strategy and organization, and adopt the most aggressive globalization strategies.

Governments

Governments can intervene in a business in two main ways. First, they set the general rules and regulatory regimes that apply to all companies in a country or all companies within a given category (for example, telecommunications companies). These rules and regimes also typically distinguish between domestic and foreign firms, and between domestic activities and foreign activities. For example, there may be general rules about the export of jobs and the import of foreign labour, or about the closing of operations. Second, governments may intervene in individual cases, such as whether to allow a particular company to be sold to a foreign buyer. Governments have many interests to motivate their behaviour. In the case of globalization, the two most important interests are probably the enhancement of national competitiveness and the preservation of employment. Both interests are likely to conflict with MNCs' free pursuit of globalization, especially in the short term. In general, MNCs seek to ignore HQ country considerations if at all possible in their globalization decisions, while national governments will inherently seek to intervene in favour of their country; and governments in the HQ country have the greatest influence in corporate governance. Countries differ in the degree to which their governments intervene in the affairs of MNCs, for ideological, political and legal reasons.

We first explore the relationship between interventionist governments and global strategy. Interventionist governments are more likely to encourage *global market participation* so long as jobs are not exported. They will also prefer exports as the mode of market participation rather than the setting up of overseas subsidiaries. They should in theory favour the development of globally successful *products and services*. In practice, protection often, but not always, produces less competitive products. In addition, they will make it harder for MNCs to *locate* activities globally outside the home country, usually to preserve employment.

Even liberal governments, such as that of the USA, can discourage some global relocations. Although they will probably be neutral as to whether domestic MNCs use global as opposed to national *marketing*, such governments may have a slight preference for preserving aspects of national identity. Interventionist governments should make it harder for an MNC to make *global competitive moves*, as these often require sacrifice of home country position, resources, revenues or profits, and hence domestic jobs or working conditions.

As for the relationship between interventionist government and global organization, protectionist governments should: (1) favour global *organization structures* so long as the home country is dominant; (2) favour *global management processes* so long as the home country processes dominate; (3) make it harder for an MNC to have *global HR policies*, as they will favour the employment and advancement of home country nationals; as well as (4) make it harder for an MNC to implement a global, rather than home country, *culture*.

Conclusion

The above analysis argues that strong roles for each corporate governance actor predict particular globalization models. Our proposed theoretical model fills a gap in the global strategy and organizational literature in that it accounts for the institutional factors that might shape organizational globalization. Drawing from actor-centred institutionalism, we select five key governance actors that will influence a firm's globalization strategy. Our model suggests that in order to understand corporate behaviour such as globalization strategies, it is necessary to comprehend the dynamics of the different actors related to the firm.

A critical contribution of our theoretical model stems from the systematic comparative perspective that permits comparisons across countries. Future research should operationalize the proposed conceptual variables and empirically test our propositions.

When firms need to grow, managers have different diversification choices. If they choose to tap into other markets through geographical diversification, then they should be aware of the actor-centred institutional factors that will determine their globalization decisions. Understanding the institutional environment within which firms operate at the national level will allow managers to align the different actors' interests and capabilities with their own firms' globalization modes.

To a large extent the MNC behaviour we have described as favouring globalization – risk taking, willingness to change, long-term maximization of profits and shareholder value and neutrality toward domestic national interests – is also the same as that favouring the long-term health and competitiveness of a nation's companies. Hence the national corporate governance systems that favour globalization also favour long-term corporate competitiveness.

References

Aguilera, R. and G. Jackson (2003). 'The Cross-National Diversity of Corporate Governance: Dimensions and Determinants', *Academy of Management Review*, 28(3), 447–465.

Aoki, M. (2001) *Towards a Comparative Institutional Analysis* (Cambridge, MA: MIT Press).

Bartlett, C. A. and S. Ghoshal (1989) *Managing Across Borders: The Transnational Solution* (Boston, MA: Harvard Business School Press).

Becht, M. and A. Roel (1999) 'Blockholding in Europe: An International Comparison', *European Economic Review*, 43, 10–49.

Birkinshaw, J. and A. Morrison (1995) 'Configurations of Strategy and Structure in the Multinational Subsidiary', *Journal of International Business Studies*, 26(4), 729–54.

Chandler, A., F. Amatori and T. Hikino (1997) *Big Business and the Wealth of Nations* (Cambridge: Cambridge University Press).

Daily, C. M. and D. Dalton (1994) 'Bankruptcy and Corporate Structure: The Impact of Board Composition and Structure' *Academy of Management Journal*, 37(6), 1603–17.

DiMaggio, P. J. and W. W. Powell (1991) 'Introduction' in P. J. DiMaggio and W. W. Powell (eds), *The New Institutionalism in Organizational Analysis* (Chicago, IL: Chicago University Press) 1–38.

Federowicz, M. and R. Aguilera (eds) (2003) *Corporate Governance in a Changing and Political Environment: Trajectories of Institutional Change on the Europe Continent* (London: Palgrave Macmillan).

Ferner, A. and J. Quintanilla (1998). 'Multinationals, National Business Systems and HRM: The Enduring Influence of National Diversity or a Process of "Anglo-Saxonization"', *International Journal of Human Resource Management*, 9(4), 710–31.

Fortune Global 500 (2000) http://www.fortune.com/fortune/global 500

Fukao, M. (1995) *Financial Integration, Corporate Governance, and the Performance of Multinational Companies* (Washington, DC: Brookings Institution).

Gerschenkron, A. (1962) *Economic Backwardness in Historical Perspective. A Book of Essays* (Cambridge, MA: The Belknap Press of Harvard University).

Hall, P. A. and D. Soskice (2001) *Varieties of Capitalism: The Institutional Foundations of Comparative Advantage* (Oxford: Oxford University Press).

Martinez, J. I. and J. C. Jarillo (1989) 'The Evolution of Research on Coordination Mechanisms in Multinational Corporations', *Journal of International Business Studies*, 20(3), 489–514.

Morgan, G., P. H. Kristensen and R. Whitley (2001) *The Multinational Firm. Organizing Across Institutional and National Divides* (Oxford: Oxford University Press).

Morrison, A. J. (1990) *Strategies in Global Industries: How US Businesses Compete* (Westport, CT: Quorum Books).

Oliver, C. (1991) 'Strategic Responses to Institutional Processes', *Academy of Management Review*, 16, 145–79.

Porter, M. E. (1986) 'Changing Patterns of International Competition', *California Management Review*, 28 (2), 9–40.

————(1990) *The Competitive Advantage of Nations* (New York and London: Free Press and Collier Macmillan).

Prahalad, C. K. and Y. L. Doz (1987) *The Multinational Mission: Balancing Local Demands and Global Vision* (New York: Free Press).

Rugman, A. M. (2000) *The End of Globalization* (London: Random House Business Books).

Scharpf, F. W. (1997) *Games Real Actors Play. Actor-Centered Institutionalism in Policy Research* (Boulder, CO: Westview Press).

Scott, W. R. (2001) *Institutions and Organizations* (Thousand Oaks, CA: Sage).

Westney, D. E. and S. Zaheer (2001) 'The Multinational Enterprise as an Organization', Chapter 13, in A. M. Rugman and T. L. Brewer (eds), *The Oxford Handbook of International Business* (Oxford: Oxford University Press), 349–79.

Whitley, R. (1999) *Divergent Capitalisms: The Social Structuring and Change of Business Systems* (Oxford: Oxford University Press).

————(ed.) (1992) *European Business Systems. Firms and Markets in Their National Contexts* (London: Sage).

Yip, G. S. (1989) 'Global Strategy . . . In a World of Nations?', *Sloan Management Review*, 31(1), 29–41.

————(1992) *Total Global Strategy* (Upper Saddle River, NJ: Prentice-Hall).

————(2003) *Total Global Strategy II: Updated for the Internet and Service Era* (Upper Saddle River, NJ: Prentice-Hall).

Part II

Sources of Value in Global Strategy

6

Introduction to Part II

Carlos García-Pont

One major issue brings the three chapters in Part II together: the search for the *sources of competitive advantage*. Chapters 7–9 deal with this issue. Cuervo-Cazurra and Un (Chapter 7) develop an exhaustive framework to identify the sources of competitive advantage of multinational companies (MNCs). In their framework they go down to local unit (subsidiary) level to identify sources of competitive advantage. The other two chapters, del Sol, (Chapter 8) and Rangan and Drummond (Chapter 9), are more detailed, in that their focus is the performance of specific subsidiaries from two different points of view. Del Sol looks at the performance of subsidiaries from a common home country. The perspective adopted is that of a developing country in its efforts to develop successful international firms. Rangan and Drummond look at performance of subsidiaries in a common host country, focusing on international competition rather than international expansion. However, in trying to identify the sources of advantage in the host country, they end up finding geographical and historical reasons that might as well have their origins in the international expansion processes of competing firms.

A significant stream of multinational enterprise (MNE) research has dealt with the strategy and performance of MNEs overall. Whether they had to pursue a local or global strategy was partly determined by the industry where they were developing their activities: firms in global industries had to pursue global strategies; firms in local industries had to pursue local strategies. Of course, MNEs evolve to acknowledge that the world was not divided into local and global industries, nor into global and local firms. Life is more complex. Firms do have to respond to pressures for national responsiveness. At the same time, they have to respond to pressures for global efficiency in order to achieve economic rationality. Models of firms evolve to be multifocal firms (Prahald and

Doz 1987), transnational corporations (Bartlett and Ghoshal 1989), heterarchies (Hedlund 1986) or metanational firms (Doz, Santos and Williamson 2001). Firms were responding to both pressures and incorporating the pressure for global learning or for operational efficiency through increasing coordination and configurational needs at the overall level of the firm and at the level of each one of its value chain activities (Porter 1986).

In fact, all these MNE firm models were positing that by adopting a certain kind of organizational paradigm the overall performance of the multinational would improve. They all focused on the MNE as a whole, taking into consideration the myriad environments where it was performing its activities. In fact, all of these perspectives highlighted the need to treat different units differently: 'MNEs must be conceptualized as a differentiated network' (Nohria and Ghoshal 1997, p. 4). Every subsidiary plays in a different field, which is determined by the *local environment*.

These alternative conceptions of the MNC view subsidiaries as contributors to a complex networked firm (Hedlund 1986; Ghoshal and Bartlett 1990; Nohria and Ghoshal 1997). These models propose that MNCs cannot be conceptualized as hierarchical structures, but rather as a puzzle whose pieces have to fit each other to create a bigger and better picture. Paramount to the source of advantage to the MNE is thus the source of advantage of its *individual operating units*, the subsidiaries. As a consequence, the term 'subsidiary strategy' started to be taken into consideration. Subsidiaries were encouraged to be proactive in developing value adding initiatives, not only to their local operations, but to the parent's overall business. Subsidiary development through initiative taking is a rich strand of the literature that emphasizes the shift to the strategic importance of these units (Birkinshaw 1998a, 1998b; Delany 2000).

However, the recent focus on the definition and development of subsidiary strategy has not been paralleled by study of subsidiary performance and the identification of subsidiaries' sources of advantage. Subsidiaries are organizational units that have to define their performance parameters. Each one will have a certain defined role within the overall network of the MNC. Certain subsidiaries will be considered *manufacturing platforms*, those are manufacturing bases that contribute to the complete value chain of the business. Other subsidiaries will have a *market orientation*, and will have to achieve a certain level of profitable market share, contributing to the overall gross margin of the MNC. Others will be a mix of these two, or will have special relevance within certain activities of the value chain of the complete business. Each one will have different ways to measure their performance. But the interesting issue that brings these chapters together is not the different roles that subsidiaries play in the multinational network, but the identification of the sources of subsidiary performance.

Let us start with Cuervo-Cazurra and Un's Chapter 7. They develop a comprehensive framework to incorporate the sources of advantage in international competition, divided into *firm-specific* and *non-firm-specific* advantages. The former is a characteristic of the analysed unit; the latter is a characteristic of the countries involved. Their perspective is that of the *resource-based view* (RBV) of the firm, which will not be the subject of discussion. RBV highlights sources of competitive advantage, but does not talk of the competitive interaction or industry structure, which themselves have an important impact on company performance.

What relates Chapters 7–9 is the analysis of the second dimension identified by Cuervo-Cazurra and Un. Three categories are identified under this second dimension: home country advantage, host country advantage and cross-country advantage. These three categories are a development of the more generic location advantage that has already been discussed in the literature. Market imperfections are at the heart of the development of the MNC (Buckley and Casson 1976). It has been argued that international business should play more attention to location-specific advantages, given that thus distinguishes international management from 'mainstream strategy of the business and corporate varieties' (Ghemawat 2003). The focus on home, host and cross-country advantages contribute to this discussion. While home and host country advantage, especially in their non-firm-specific form, have already been considered, the cross-country advantage is the most interesting. It focuses on the advantages provided by the fact of having operations in a certain pair or group of countries. Locational advantage is thus not only country-specific but *relational*, and it is worthwhile considering whether having operations in one country provides firms with a competitive advantage *vis-à-vis* competitors who don't. Considering the relational advantage of having operations in any two given countries brings up a more strategic issue, implying that the advantages provided by location do have a *combinatory potential*. It is known that resources and capabilities can enhance the competitive advantage that they provide through their combination. Furthermore, following the RBV of the firm that Cuerro-Cazzura and Un use in their framework, resources and capabilities that alone do not provide a competitive advantage can become advantages when combined (Amit and Shoemaker 1993). Firms do have a combinatory capability that can itself be a source of competitive advantage. One can thus conclude that as much as location itself can provide advantage to multi-national firms, the combination of locations can be a significant source of advantage that has failed so far to be studied. Chapters 8 and 9 contribute to the further identification of these location-based combinatory advantages.

The focus of del Sol's Chapter 8 is the *sources of advantage* for subsidiaries. His unit of analysis is the subsidiary of Chilean firms in other South American countries. Del Sol is thus controlling for home country advantage. The question underlying the argument is what sources of advantage subsidiaries have. Del Sol centres his arguments not on specific subsidiary resources, but on the characteristics of the parent firms: what are the characteristics of the parent firms that can improve subsidiary performance? Two concrete variables are considered – whether the Chilean parent belongs to a business group and whether the subsidiary is a joint venture (JV) with a partner from a developed third country.

The chapter considers first the characteristics of the Chilean parent firm. Pertaining or not to a business group can be considered a firm-specific advantage with a country bias. In developing countries, being a member of a business group provides a greater source of socio-economic legitimacy and business units belonging to business group have easier access to resources than individual business units. This argument has been shown not to hold in developed countries. Firm-specific advantages can also interact with specific home characteristics; the characteristics that provide advantage to firms from a certain country might not apply to firms from a different country. Del Sol thus provides arguments for the existence of firm-specific advantages that are *country-specific*. Not every firm in Chile belongs to a business group; however, every Chilean firm that belongs to a business group does have an advantage over other Chilean firms, an argument that might not hold for firms from Germany or the USA.

The chapter considers second whether the subsidiary is wholly owned or whether it was established with a partner. Del Sol is not arguing that subsidiaries that are JVs perform better than other subsidiaries, but that JVs with specific parent characteristics do better than others. He argues that partnering with a firm from a developed country increases the performance of the subsidiary: Interestinery Del Sol and Duran (2002) found that local partners did not increase profitability. It has traditionally been argued that local partners contribute local knowledge that might improve subsidiary performance by decreasing environmental uncertainty and might have some host country related advantage, that is, local knowledge. In the Latin American case, this reasoning might not apply. The liberalization process in Latin America had already been experienced by Chilean firms in their own country, thus Chilean firms were more knowledgeable about the uncertainties in the local business environment than their potential local partners. Del Sol and Duran identify a home country advantage that emerges from the *institutional setting* in which firms have developed their businesses compared with the setting where the FDI is done – that is, home country advantage is not an absolute source of advantage but relates to the differences between the countries.

The results on which Del Sol comments in Chapter 8 show that FDI with a partner from a developed country shows better results than FDI with parents form elsewhere. His line of argument is that local governments deal with more care with firms from developed countries. It is clear that this line of reasoning does not hold for countries that share the same level of economic and institutional development where there is a relational advantage between the two countries. It is not the host or home country advantage that determines the performance of FDI, it is the *difference in development* of the countries involved that influences performance.

Following del Sol, we can identify home country advantages that arise from the institutional setting where they grew up. We can also identify relational advantages that are specific to the pair of countries involved, suggesting one dimension – economic and institutional development – along which the countries can develop relational sources of advantage.

Rangan and Drummond provide a different perspective in Chapter 9. Instead of analysing what can be added to the home country advantage which is controlled for in del Sol's setting, they try to examine competition in the host country. They compare the performance of subsidiaries in the same country, and the discussion is framed under what Cuervo-Cazurra and Un call 'Foreignness' as a source of advantage. As the latter authors state 'the advantage of foreignness is the edge obtained by a firm in a given host country as a result of being from a particular country'. Rangan and Drummond argue that the less the liability of 'foreignness', the better the performance in a particular host country. The liability of 'foreignness' is understood as the familiarity with local information, laws and language. When analysing what lies behind liability of foreignness they propose geography and historical links, which both reduce the costs of entering the market and increase the cost effectiveness of their internal control mechanisms, making it easier to manage inter-national operations. What in fact they do is to establish the relational source of advantage along different lines from Del Sol's Chapter 8. Rangan and Drummond account for geographical and historical links among countries to establish a *relational advantage space*. Countries that are close in their geography and history are able to combine their cap-abilities in a better way.

Taken together, these three chapters suggest the need to redefine location-based advantage. It is not that home or host resources are not important, but this relational view might complement them. In order to evaluate locational advantage, one has to take into account the rela-tion between the home and the host country, so that a combination of location-based advantages can improve the competitive position of the firm. Del Sol is asking what are the best sources of advantage from a country perspective, suggesting that *development distance* is a source of competitive advantage in the host country. Rangan and Drummond argue that history and geography are sources of competitive advantage in the host country. Further research is needed to develop locational relational advantage if we are to further understand FDI performance.

References

Amit, R. and P. J. H. Shoemaker (1993) 'Strategic Assets and Organizational Rent', *Strategic Management Journal*, 14(1), 33–46.

Bartlett, C. A. and S. Ghoshal (1989) *Managing across Borders: The Transnational Solution*, (Boston, MA: Harvard Business School Press).

Birkinshaw, J. (1998a) 'Foreign-Owned Subsidiaries and Regional Development: The Case of Sweden', in J. Birkinshaw and N. Hood (eds), *Multinational Corpor-ate Evolution and Subsidiary Development* (London: Macmillan).

————(1998b) 'Introduction and Overview', in J. Birkinshaw and N. Hood (eds), *Multinational Corporate Evolution and Subsidiary Development* (London: Macmillan).

Buckley, P. J. and M. C. Casson (1976) *The Economic Theory of the Multinational Enterprise* (London: Holmes & Meier).

Del Sol, P. and P. Duran (2002) 'Responses to Globalization in Asia and Latin America: Chilean Investment Alliances across Latin America', Laeba Working Paper, 5.

Delany, E. (2000) 'Strategic Development of the Multinational Subsidiary through Subsidiary Initiative-Taking', *Long Range Planning*, 33, 220–44.

Doz, Y., J. Santos and P. Williamson (2001) *From Global to Metanational: How com-panies win out in the Knowledge Economy* (Boston, MA: Harvard Business School Press).

Ghemawat, P. (2003). 'The Forgotten Strategy', *Harvard Business Review*, 81(11), 76–89.

Ghoshal, S. and C. A. Bartlett (1990) 'The Multinational Corporation as a Differentiated Interorganizational Network', *Academy of Management Review*, 15, 603–25.

Hedlund, G. (1986) 'The Hypermodern MNC: A Heterarchy?', *Human Resource Management*, 25(1), 9–35.

Nohria, N. and S. Ghoshal (1997) *The Differentiated Network: Organizing Multinationals Corporations for Value Creation* (San Francisco, CA: Jossey Bass).

Porter, M. E. (1986) 'Competition in Global Industries: A Conceptual Framework', in M. E. Porter (ed.), *Competition in Global Industries* (Boston, MA: Harvard Business School Press).

Prahalad, C. K and Y. L. Doz, (1987) *The Multinational Mission: Balancing Local Demands and Global Vision* (New York: Free Press).

7

Firm-Specific and Non-Firm-Specific Sources of Advantage in International Competition

Álvaro Cuervo-Cazurra and C. Annique Un *

Introduction

In this chapter we provide a comprehensive analysis of the sources of the firm's advantage in international competition. The analysis of competitive advantage has been a primary concern of strategic management (Rumelt, Schendel and Teece 1994) and especially of resource-based theory (RBT) (Wernerfelt 1984). RBT argues that the firm achieves an advantage over competitors based on its advantageous or strategic resources (Barney 1991; Amit and Shoemaker 1993; Peteraf 1993). According to this theory, only resources exclusive to the firm can form the basis of its advantage – that is, the sources of advantage are *firm-specific*. This argument assumes that competitors are located in the same geographical area and have access to the same types of external resources. However, when we

* This chapter is a revised and summarized version of a paper presented at the First International Workshop on Creating and Appropriating Value from Global Strategy at IESE. The comments of Carlos García-Pont, Stephanie Lenway, Steve Tallman, Andy Van de Ven and participants at the Strategic Management Research Seminar at the University of Minnesota, the Strategic Management Society meeting in Paris and the First International Workshop on Creating and Appropriating Value from Global Strategy at IESE helped improve previous versions. The financial support of the International Programs Office at the University of Minnesota and IESE is gratefully acknowledged. This chapter was developed while the first author was visiting the Department of Applied Economics and Management, Cornell University. All errors remain our error.

extend the analysis of advantages to internationally competing firms in different locations, the picture changes. Access to different external resources in different locations, or the firm's 'foreignness', can assist the company in achieving an advantage relative to firms in other locations. Such advantages are available to a group of firms – that is, the sources of advantage can also be *non-firm-specific*.

We therefore consider six sources of advantage, three of which are firm-specific (parent, subsidiary and multinational) and three of which are non-firm-specific (home, host and 'foreignness'). We analyse not only how, but also where, each of these sources can support the firm's advantage. These arguments built on the application of RBT to the analysis of multinational enterprises (MNEs) (Tallman 1992; Tallman and Fladmoe-Lindquist 2002), studying the development and use of resources to achieve an advantage. They also build upon the extension of the Ownership, Location Internalization (OLI) paradigm of international production (Dunning 1977) to the study of advantages (Rugman and Verbeke 1992) that separates firm from location, and home from host resources. This framework assists managers in distinguishing among sources of advantage and using appropriate ones against different types of competitors, at both home and abroad.

Sources of advantage in international competition

Before explaining our classification of advantages, we provide some definitions of the concepts of firm and location resources, and distinguish between the transferability of *resources* and the transferability of the *advantage*. This aids our understanding of the sources of advantage and the conditions for success.

Firm and location resources and the competitive advantage of the firm

Firm resources are the tangible and intangible assets that are tied semi-permanently to a firm (Wernerfelt 1984; Teece, Pisano and Shuen 1997). We classify them into three types, based on their ability to provide a competitive advantage. First, *advantageous* or *strategic* resources (Amit and Schoemaker 1993) provide the firm with a competitive advantage because they are VRIS (valuable, rare, difficult to imitate and difficult to substitute) (Barney 1991). This is the case, for example, of an innovative technology that is protected by a set of patents. Second, *disadvantageous* resources provide the firm with a competitive disadvantage because they create problems for the firm's operations. This is the case, for example, when core capabilities become core rigidities, limiting the firm's ability to change and adapt to new market realities (Leonard-Barton 1992). Third, *neutral* resources are necessary for the firm's operations, but are not sufficient to provide an advantage (Montgomery 1995) – that is, they are complementary assets. However, they are still important because they create problems for the firm when they are missing. For example, access to bank finance is commonly used by firms and not likely to provide an advantage. However, the firm that lacks this access will suffer from financial constraints to investment that harm its operations (Fazzari, Hubbard and Petersen 1988).

The firm benefits not only from the firm resources it possesses, but also from access to *external or location resources*, which the firm uses in its activities, in combination with firm resources (Penrose 1959). Parallel to the definition of firm resources, we define 'location resources' as the tangible and intangible assets tied semi-permanently to a location. These include, for example, developed capital markets or skilled low cost labour. Location resources emerge not only as part of the country's endowment (Ricardo 1819), but also thanks to the actions of governments (North 1990; Murtha and Lenway 1994), as well as to industry, supply and demand interactions (Porter 1990) and to technological and organizing principles in the country (Kogut 1991). They can be also classified as advantageous, disadvantageous, or neutral according to the advantage they provide to firms in a given location that have access to them, in comparison to firms in other locations that do not have such access.

The cross-country transferability of resources and of competitive advantage

In analysing these advantages, we separate the challenge of transferring resources across countries, enabling the internationalization of the firm, from the challenge of transferring the advantage provided by those resources across countries, enabling the *successful* internationalization of the firm. First, the transferability of resources depends on their characteristics. Tangible resources, such as distribution systems, are difficult to transfer across countries because they are physically linked to a place (Rugman and Verbeke 1992). Intangible resources, such as knowledge, face few physical limitations to their transfer, but are still difficult to successfully transfer across locations because they are geographically specific (Hu 1995) or because they have tacit components that limit their use abroad (Kogut and Zander 1993). This transferral difficulty also applies to location resources (Kogut 1991). Nevertheless, the firm will need to transfer some resources abroad if it is to internationalize. It can do this directly, using foreign direct investment (FDI), by transferring resources developed in the home country to another country to perform value added activities there. It can also do so indirectly through trade, by using resources to create products that are exported and sold abroad.

Second, even when the firm can transfer resources across countries and internationalize, the advantage provided by those resources in one country may not transfer to another. The VRIS characteristics that give a resource its advantageous character in one location do not always exist in the new foreign location (Tallman 1992). For example, the resources of the firm do not create value for clients abroad because they have different needs, owing to differences in geography and climate, wealth, or culture and local taste (Bartlett and Ghoshal 1989). Resources that are rare in one country may be plentiful in another – such as, for example, the limited access to external finance that is prevalent in developing countries but not in developed countries (Booth *et al.* 2001). Local competitors may have developed their own resources that imitate or substitute for the resources of the foreign firm (Dawar and Frost 1999). Whereas in this chapter we will assume that the firm is able to transfer resources and internationalize, we will not assume that the transfer of advantage accompanies the transfer of resources abroad; we will discuss the conditions for achieving such an advantage in other countries.

Firm-specific and non-firm-specific sources of advantage

Table 7.1 summarizes the framework that we use in the following sections. It highlights the main differences among the various sources of advantage, and summarizes the conditions for their success in providing an advantage to the firm. We separate into three types the firm-specific advantages in international competition – that is, the advantages from which only the focal firm benefits. This classification is based on the location of the advantage:

(1) The *parent advantage* is the advantage the firm derives from a given firm resource developed in its home-country operation.
(2) The *subsidiary advantage* is the advantage the firm derives from a given firm resource developed in a foreign or host country operation.
(3) The *multinational advantage* is the advantage the firm derives from a given resource developed to manage operations across countries.

We also separate into three types the non-firm-specific advantages, those from which a group of firms in a particular location benefits:

Table 7.1 Types of advantage in international competition: source, location and conditions for achievement

	Location of advantage		
	Home country	**Host country**	**Cross-country**
	PARENT	**SUBSIDIARY**	**MULTINATIONAL**
	Source: Firm resources developed in the home country operation	*Source*: Firm resources developed in the host country operation	*Source*: Firm resources developed to manage across borders
	Location of advantage and conditions for its achievement:	Location of advantage and conditions for its achievement:	Location of advantage and conditions for its achievement:
Firm-specific	(1) Provides an advantage to the firm against competitors operating in its home country if the firm resources are VRIS there	(1) Provides an advantage to the firm against competitors operating in the host country if the resources are VRIS there	(1) Provides an advantage to the firm against domestic competitors operating in the home country if the arbitrage across operations and countries is strategically coordinated
	(2) Provides an advantage to the firm against competitors operating in a host country if the firm resources can be transferred (directly or indirectly via firm products) and are VRIS in the host country, even though they were not necessarily VRIS in the home country	(2) Provides an advantage to the firm against competitors operating in the home country if these firm resources can be transferred (directly or indirectly via firm products) and are VRIS in the home country, even though they were not necessarily VRIS in the host country	(2) Provides an advantage to the firm against domestic competitors operating in the host country if the arbitrage across operations and countries is strategically coordinated
		(3) Provides an advantage to the firm against competitors operating in a third country if these firm resources can be transferred (directly or indirectly via firm products) and are VRIS in the third country, even though they were not necessarily VRIS in the host country	(3) Provides an advantage to the firm against multinational competitors operating in the firm's home or host countries if the firm's management of resources is better

Specificity of advantage

HOME

Source: Access to location resources in the home country

Location of advantage and conditions for its achievement:

(1) Does not provide an advantage to the firm against competitors operating in its home country because other firms there have access to the location resources

(2) Provides an advantage to the firm against competitors operating in a host country if the location resources can be transferred only through the firm (directly or indirectly via firm products) and are VRIS in the host country

(3) Does not provide an advantage to the firm against competitors from its home country operating in a host country because they have access to the same location resources

HOST

Source: Access to location resources in the host country

Location of advantage and conditions for its achievement:

(1) Does not provide an advantage to the firm against competitors operating in the host country because other firms there have access to the location resources

(2) Provides an advantage to the firm against competitors operating in its home country if these location resources can be transferred only through the firm (directly or indirectly via firm products) and are VRIS in the home country

(3) Provides an advantage to the firm against competitors operating in a third country if these location resources can be transferred only through the firm (directly or indirectly via firm products) and are VRIS in the third country

(4) Does not provide an advantage to the firm against competitors from the host country operating in the home or third countries because they have access to the same location resources

'FOREIGNNESS'

Source: Foreign character or particular country of origin of the firm

Location of advantage and conditions for its achievement:

(1) Does not provide an advantage to the firm against domestic competitors operating in its home country because they have the same country of origin

(2) Provides an advantage to the firm against domestic competitors operating in a host country if its foreign character or particular country of origin is valued by people (individuals or government) in the host country

(3) Provides an advantage to the firm against other foreign competitors operating in a host country if its particular country of origin is preferred by people (individuals or government) in the host country

(4) Does not provide an advantage to the firm against competitors from its home country operating in a host country because they have the same country of origin

Non-firm-specific

Specificity of advantage

(1) The *home advantage* is the advantage generated from accessing a given external resource in the home country.
(2) The *host advantage* is the advantage experienced from accessing a given external resource in a host country.
(3) The *advantage of 'foreignness'* is the advantage derived from being foreign or from a particular country of origin that is favoured in a given host country.

In these definitions we specify *given* resources, rather than resources in general, because only some resources will support the advantage, and because this advantage will vary across locations. We now describe each in detail, indicating the conditions and location where the advantage is realized.

Firm-specific sources of advantage

The parent advantage

The parent advantage is the competitive edge provided by some firm resources developed to serve clients and face competitors in the firm's home country. We use the term 'parent' to denote the close link with the origin of the firm and because the operation in the home country is, in many cases, considered the parent organization. In this definition we do not consider resources developed to manage across countries, such as the capabilities of headquarters discussed in diversification studies (Markides 2002); these are included in our discussion of multinational advantage (p. 86).

The parent advantage enables the firm to achieve an edge in its country of origin when some of its resources are VRIS and are thus rendered advantageous in comparison to competitors' resources. Moreover, this advantage induces the firm to internationalize (Hymer 1976; Tallman 1992); managers assume that the advantage the firm enjoys in its original operation can be replicated abroad. The firm uses existing resources to expand into other locations and achieve an additional return over investments already made (Penrose 1959). Such internationalization is possible when the firm's resources have a degree of excess capacity (Chatterjee and Wernerfelt 1991) or are subject to non-rival consumption, and can be transferred abroad, as is the case for a resource such as knowledge (Kogut and Zander 1993).

The parent advantage is realized in a host country when these firm resources are advantageous in comparison to the resources of host country firms. The resources transferred from the parent operation must be rare in the new host environment, valuable in serving clients in the host country and must not have been imitated or substituted by competitors there. For example, the technology that enabled US firms to create innovative products after the Second World War helped them achieve an advantage abroad because clients desired the products, while competitors there were unable to match the innovative capabilities of the US firms (Vernon 1966). Alternately, even when the resources transferred are merely neutral in the home country, they may become advantageous in the host country. For example, a firm with technological expertise similar to that of its home country competitors, which is thus on an equal footing with other firms in its home country, may find that this same technology gives it an edge in another country where competitors are less technologically sophisticated. Although managers rarely focus on these neutral resources when evaluating the foreign expansion of the firm, these can nevertheless help the firm internationalize successfully, at least while no home country competitors enter the host country. By this point, the firm may have developed a subsidiary advantage that helps it fend off home country competitors.

The subsidiary advantage

The subsidiary advantage is the advantage possessed by a firm that has developed some resources in the host country operation to create value for clients in competition with local firms. This advantage is independent of, and in addition to, resources that have been transferred from the home country operation that are VRIS in the host country – that is, the parent advantage. It is based on resources developed by the subsidiary that are advantageous in the host country.

Not many subsidiaries benefit from their own subsidiary advantage. The creation of a subsidiary advantage entails conscious effort. It may not be developed, for example, because managers at headquarters have ethnocentric attitudes and dismiss ideas not developed in the home country (Perlmutter 1969), because the subsidiary is perceived as an implementer and is not allowed to develop its own resources (Bartlett and Ghoshal 1986) or because the MNE follows an international or global strategy and keeps tight control over subsidiaries (Bartlett and Ghoshal 1989). In these situations, the subsidiary achieves an advantage in the host country thanks to parent resources and merely acts as an outlet for the products of the parent.

Subsidiary managers might nevertheless develop the subsidiary's advantageous resources, either as part of their mandate or on their own (Birkinshaw, Hood and Jonsson, 1998; Rugman and Verbeke 2001). For example, subsidiary managers may perceive the opportunity or need to serve the clients better in the host country, and decide to develop some innovative capabilities to do so. Once this occurs, the subsidiary not only achieves a subsidiary advantage, but it can also become a contributor or strategic leader and support the advantage of other operations (Bartlett and Ghoshal 1986). The technological capability developed in the host country may enable the subsidiary to become a centre of excellence (Moore and Birkinshaw 1998), for example. For this to occur, the advantageous firm resources developed by the subsidiary must be transferable to the home country operation, and the advantage provided by them must also be transferable. Some of the neutral resources developed by the subsidiary may even become advantageous in the home country. The subsidiary may for instance, develop marketing capabilities that are on par with those of competitors in the host country, but that are superior to the capabilities of competitors in the home country, giving the firm a lead at home.

The subsidiary advantage can help the firm not only in its home country operation, but also in subsidiaries in third countries. Subsidiary resources can be transferred to existing operations in third countries to support the advantage there. Or the MNE can even use the advantageous subsidiary resources to enter into new countries without having to rely exclusively on the parent advantage (Barkema and Drogendijk 2001). In this case, the subsidiary acts as the new parent for the expansion into the third country.

The multinational advantage

The multinational advantage is the advantage enjoyed by the MNE that has developed resources to manage and strategically coordinate multiple operations across the globe. It differs from the ability to transfer resources across countries, which we consider to form part of the parent and subsidiary advantages. Here we refer to the role of headquarters and its contribution to each of the operations in the diverse countries, including those at home. The multinational advantage provides the firm with the flexibility to arbitrage across countries and, for example, intensify or reduce production as the competitive conditions across countries change (Kogut 1985). It also gives the firm the ability to retaliate in oligopolistic industries (Knickerbocker 1973), hedge across currency areas (Aliber 1970), diversify risks across countries (Agmon and Lessard 1977), or bargain with national governments (Stopford and Strange 1992). This advantage is a *result* of the firm's international operations rather than a source of them. Despite this, it needs to be actively developed.

The firm can alter its structure (Stopford and Wells 1972), the relationships among subsidiaries (Prahalad and Doz 1987; Bartlett and Ghoshal 1989), its human resource management practices (Hedlund 1986) and its control mechanisms (Rugman and Verbeke 2003) to facilitate the strategic coordination of resources, especially knowledge (Kogut and Zander 1993) in the network of operations (Ghoshal and Bartlett 1990).

Such multinational advantage helps the firm achieve the upper hand in relationship to firms that are not international, either at home or in a host country, by providing it with global efficiency, multinational responsiveness and worldwide learning (Bartlett and Ghoshal 1989). These abilities to arbitrage across countries and operations are difficult to imitate or substitute by firms that are not international. For example, when demand in the home country is strong, the MNE is able to increase production beyond the capacity of the plants in the country and cover the additional demand, whereas domestic competitors there are constrained in their ability to increase production beyond full capacity in the short run. However, the multinational advantage will enable the firm to achieve only parity against other MNEs, unless the firm is better in some aspects of *coordination of relationships* among the multiple operations within the network, since other MNEs also have the ability to arbitrage across operations and countries. For example, a firm present in more countries than other MNEs can use this to achieve higher flexibility in production or in its retaliation strategy.

Non-firm-specific sources of advantage

The home advantage

The home advantage is the advantage of the firm with access to location resources in the home country, particularly those that are in better conditions than in other countries. It is non-firm-specific because all firms operating in the home country have access to these resources; they can use them as inputs in their production processes (Penrose 1959). As such, location resources in the home country are neutral; they do not provide an advantage at home.

However, location resources in the home country can provide an advantage abroad. For example, the home country may have large pools of skilled but low-cost labour, which enable the firm to reduce its labour costs in production in comparison to firms located in a host country with high-cost labour. Such a home advantage will help the firm export competitively to that host country; it will not give the firm an edge in the host country against firms from the same home country, however, because these firms have access to the same location resources at home.

Location resources help the firm obtain an advantage abroad if, in addition to being VRIS relative to location resources in the host country, they are difficult to move across borders on their own. If this is the case, only firms located in the home country can benefit from access to them. Otherwise, the advantage will be temporal. While the firm can establish control over its firm resources in order to ensure that it benefits from the value they create, it cannot establish control over location resources and prevent their movement to other countries. For example, a firm that benefits from accessing investors with abundant capital at home cannot prevent investors from providing funds to firms located in a host country where capital is scarce. As such, although the access to investors is initially advantageous for firms in the home market, the mobility of this resource reduces the possibility of supporting a home advantage.

When the location resources can be transferred across countries, the firm has an incentive to establish controls over them to limit foreign competitors' access to them. The firm thus benefits from exclusive access to advantageous location resources. The firm can do this on its own, acquiring or establishing contractual controls over the supply of the desired resources and foreclosing competitors' access (Hart and Tirole 1990). This is the case, for example, for the South African diamond firm De Beers, which controls a large percentage of global diamond production. Alternatively, the government can grant the firm control over location resources, helping it to internationalize successfully (Aggarwal and Agmon 1990). For example, the Chilean government gave the copper firm Codelco control over the largest copper mine in the world, helping the firm become the leading exporter of copper.

Nevertheless, location resources at home can, on their own, be difficult to transfer across countries (Kogut 1991). They may be associated with home country neutral resources that limit their application in other countries. This occurs, for example, when contractual relationships are associated with specific institutions (North 1990); in this case, the firm accesses location resources and combines them with its own firm resources to facilitate their transfer across countries and realize the home advantage (Fladmoe-Lindquist and Tallman 1994).

The host advantage

The host advantage is the advantage of a firm that has access to external resources in the host country, specifically ones that are superior to those available in other countries. Access to these location resources in the host country will not be advantageous in that country, since all companies there have access to the source; location resources are neutral within the host country.

However, the host advantage can help the firm in its home country. The success of these location resources in providing an advantage to the firm at home depends on whether these location resources are VRIS relative to those at home. Moreover, these advantageous host resources need to be transferable to the home country only through the firm; otherwise, domestic competitors in the home country can obtain them through imports, which will result in no advantage to the firm. The transfer to the home country can be done directly; in this case, the firm becomes the channel for transferring location resources. This is the case, for example, for firms in developing countries that obtain access to American capital markets through American Depositary Receipts (ADRs), substantially reducing the cost of their finance relative to competitors that must rely on domestic sources of funds. Alternatively, the transfer can occur indirectly; in this case, the firm establishes production facilities in the host country in order to access advantageous location resources, combine them with its firm resources and create cheaper or better products, which it then sends home. This is the case, for example, for US firms that establish assembly plants in Northern Mexico, using skilled low-cost labour to assemble components that have been imported from the USA into finished products, which are then transported back to the USA. The host advantage can help the firm not only in its home country, but also when it is competing against firms in a third country: the firm can transfer location resources from the host country to achieve an edge in the third country.

The desire to access these advantageous location resources abroad may be what led to the firm's internationalization in the first place (Dunning 1993). The firm expands abroad in order to obtain access to natural resources, such as petroleum that are imperfectly distributed across countries. It may also internationalize in order to achieve efficiency by accessing location resources that allow it to reduce its production costs, such as low-cost skilled labour. Alternatively, it may move across borders in order to obtain access to strategic assets or capabilities that are available in the host country, such as clusters of technological expertise. These three motives reflect the desire to obtain access to location resources that are more easily available, and of better quality, than those in the home country.

The advantage of 'foreignness'

The advantage of 'foreignness' is the edge obtained by a firm in a given host country as a result of being from a particular country. When individuals in the host country perceive the firm's country of origin in a positive fashion, the firm enjoys an additional advantage, especially in the marketing of products (Bilkey and Nes 1982; Peterson and Jolibert 1995). The firm's products are not necessarily superior to local products, but individuals' preference for the firm's country of origin positively affects its products. A second dimension of the advantage of 'foreignness' exists when the host country governments give preferential treatment to foreign firms (Stopford and Strange 1992). For example, the host country government may offer tax incentives or subsidies that are available only to foreign investors. This advantage is non-firm-specific because one characteristic common to several firms, country of origin or 'foreignness', becomes advantageous. It appears only when the firm crosses its national borders.

The advantage of 'foreignness' does not provide the firm with an edge over local firms in its home country because other firms there have the same country of origin – that is, those competitors have imitated the potentially advantageous resource. For the same reason, it does not provide an advantage in a host country against firms coming from the same home country. However, it can provide an edge over competitors from other foreign countries whose country of origin is not perceived as positively in the host country. This is the case, for example, for Swiss watch makers, whose products command a premium abroad over those of firms that produce in countries not perceived as having a special skill in watch making, such as Hong Kong. The advantage of 'foreignness' can even provide a lead over local competitors in the host country, such as, for example, when foreign firms are viewed as more legitimate (Kostova and Zaheer 1999).

Although the advantage of 'foreignness' depends on consumers' perceptions of the firm's country of origin, and is not subject to firm influence, the firm can strengthen this perception. The firm can choose to highlight the country of origin of the products, especially when it enters the host country and advertises its products (Suzuki 1980). Moreover, this advantage of 'foreignness' is more beneficial for firms in areas perceived to be in line with the positive appeal of the country, such as Italian fashion design or Japanese miniaturization.

Conclusions

The extension and application of RBT to the analysis of the firm's advantage in international competition clarifies previous approaches and provides a unifying explanation. It highlights the benefits of both firm-specific and non-firm-specific sources of advantage. All of these advantages are based on the development of, access to, or use of resources. This framework assists managers of MNEs in understanding the sources of the advantages that accompany international competition, separating those that are firm-specific, and thus subject to direct managerial action, from those that are non-firm-specific and less subject to influence.

The framework presented has important implications for the use of diverse sources of advantage against different types of competitors. RBT highlights the heterogeneity that exists among firms. An MNE that enjoys all the advantages described will not always be able to use all of them against its competitors; the characteristics of the competitors determine which advantages the MNE can use against them. When the MNE competes against domestic competitors in its home market, it can benefit from its parent, subsidiary, multinational and host advantages. It will not benefit from home and 'foreignness' advantages because domestic home competitors have access to location home resources and have the same country of origin as the MNE. When the MNE competes against domestic competitors in a host country, it can benefit from parent, subsidiary, foreignness, home and multinational advantages. It will not benefit from the host advantage because domestic host competitors have access to the same location host resources. Finally, when the MNE competes against other MNEs with a similar international presence, it can benefit from its parent and subsidiary advantages. It may also benefit from the 'foreignness' and multinational advantages, as not all other MNEs will have the same country of origin and a similar ability to strategically coordinate resources across countries. It will not benefit from the home and host advantages because other MNEs with operations in the same countries have access to the location home and location host resources. As such, rather than conceptualizing the advantage of the firm in absolute terms, managers should ideally view it as coming from *multiple sources*, and existing only relative to different competitors. This will assist them in deploying the most appropriate sources of advantage against each of their competitors.

References

Aggarwal, R. and T. Agmon (1990) 'The International Success of Developing Country Firms: Role of Government-Directed Comparative Advantage', *Management International Review*, 30, 163–80.

Agmon, T. and D. R. Lessard (1977) 'Investor Recognition of Corporate International Diversification', *Journal of Finance*, 32, 1049–55.

Aliber, R. Z. (1970) 'A Theory of Direct Foreign Investment', in C. Kindleberger (ed.), *The International Corporation: A Symposium* (Cambridge, MA: MIT Press).

Amit, R. and P. J. H. Schoemaker (1993) 'Strategic Assets and Organizational Rent', *Strategic Management Journal*, 14, 33–46.

Barkema, H. G. and R. H. J. Drogendijk (2001). 'A New Internationalization Process Model: Theory and Evidence', Paper presented at the Academy of Management Annual Meeting (Washington, DC).

Barney, J. (1991) 'Firm Resources and Sustained Competitive Advantage', *Journal of Management*, 17, 99–100.

Bartlett, C. A. and S. Ghoshal (1986) 'Tap Your Subsidiaries for Global Reach', *Harvard Business Review*, 64(6), 87–94.

——— (1989) *Managing Across Borders: The Transnational Solution* (Boston, MA: Harvard Business School Press).

Bilkey, W. J. and E. Nes (1982) 'Country-of-Origin Effects on Product Evaluations', *Journal of International Business Studies*, 13, 89–99.

Birkinshaw, J., N. Hood and S. Jonsson (1998) 'Building Firm-Specific Advantages in Multinational Corporations: The Role of Subsidiary Initiative', *Strategic Management Journal*, 19, 221–41.

Booth, L., V. Aivazian, A. Demirguc-Kunt and V. Maksimovic (2001) 'Capital Structures in Developing Countries', *Journal of Finance*, 56, 87–130.

Chatterjee, S. and B. Wernerfelt (1991) 'The Link Between Resources and Type of Diversification: Theory and Evidence', *Strategic Management Journal*, 12, 33–48.

Dawar, N. and T. Frost (1999). 'Competing With Giants: Survival Strategies for Local Companies in Emerging Markets', *Harvard Business Review*, 77(2) 119–29.

Dunning, J. H. (1977) 'Trade, Location of Economic Activity and the MNE: A Search for an Eclectic Approach', in B. Ohlin, P. O. Hesselborn and P. M. Wijkman (eds), *The International Allocation of Economic Activity* (London: Macmillan).

———(1993) *Multinational Enterprises and the Global Economy* (New York: Addison-Wesley).

Fazzari, S. M., R. G. Hubbard and B. Petersen (1988) 'Financing Constraints and Corporate Investment', *Brookings Papers on Economic Activity*, 141–206.

Fladmoe-Lindquist, K. and S. Tallman (1994) 'Resource-Based Strategy and Competitive Advantage among Multinationals', in P. Shrivastava, A. S. Huff and J. E. Dutton (eds), *Advances in Strategic Management*, 10 (Greenwich, CT: JAI Press).

Ghoshal, S. and C. A. Bartlett (1998) 'The Multinational Corporation as an Inter-organizational Network', *Academy of Management Review*, 15, 603–25.

Hart, O. and J. Tirole (1990) 'Vertical Integration and Market Foreclosure', *Brookings Papers on Economic Activity*, 205–86.

Hedlund, G. (1986) 'The Hypermodern MNC: A Heterarchy?', *Human Resource Management*, 25, 9–45.

Hu, Y.-S. (1995) 'The International Transferability of the Firm's Advantages', *California Management Review*, 37, 73–88.

Hymer, S. H. (1976) *The International Operations of National Firms: A Study of Direct Foreign Investment.* (Cambridge, MA: MIT Press).

Knickerbocker, F. T. (1973) *Oligopolistic Reaction and the Multinational Enterprise* (Cambridge, MA: Harvard University Press).

Kogut, B. (1985) 'Designing Global Strategies: Profiting from Operational Flexibility', *Sloan Management Review*, 27, 27–38.

———— (1991) 'Country Capabilities and the Permeability of Borders', *Strategic Management Journal*, 12 (Special Issue on Global Strategy), 33–47.

Kogut, B. and U. Zander (1993) 'Knowledge of the Firm and the Evolutionary Theory of the Multinational Corporation', *Journal of International Business Studies*, 24, 625–45.

Kostova, T. and S. Zaheer (1999) 'Organizational Legitimacy under Conditions of Complexity: The Case of the Multinational Enterprise', *Academy of Management Review*, 24, 64–81.

Leonard-Barton, D. (1992) 'Core Capabilities and Core Rigidities: A Paradox in Managing New Product Development', *Strategic Management Journal*, 13, 111–26.

Markides, C. (2002) 'Corporate Strategy: The Role of the Centre', in A. Pettigrew, H. Thomas and R. Whittington (eds), *Handbook of Strategy and Management* (London: Sage), 98–138.

Montgomery, C. A. (1995) 'Of Diamonds and Rust: A New Look at Resources', in C. A. Montgomery (ed.), *Resource-Based and Evolutionary Theories of the Firm: Towards a Synthesis* (Boston, MA: Kluwer Academic).

Moore, K. and J. Birkinshaw, J. (1998) 'Managing Knowledge in Global Service Firms: Centers of Excellence', *Academy of Management Executive*, 12(4), 81–89.

Murtha, T. and S. Lenway (1994) 'Country Capabilities and the Strategic State: How National Political Institutions Affect Multinational Corporations' Strategies', *Strategic Management Journal*, 15, 113–29.

North, D. C. (1990) *Institutions, Institutional Change, and Economic Performance* (New York: Cambridge University Press).

Penrose, E. (1959) *The Theory of the Growth of the Firm* (Oxford: Oxford University Press).

Perlmutter, H. (1969) 'The Tortuous Evolution of the Multinational Corporation', *Columbia Journal of World Business*, 4, 9–19.

Peteraf, M. A. (1993) 'The Cornerstones of Competitive Advantage: A Resource-Based View', *Strategic Management Journal*, 14, 179–91.

Peterson, R. A. and A. J. P. Jolibert (1995) 'A Meta-Analysis of Country-of-Origin Effects', *Journal of International Business Studies*, 26, 883–900.

Porter, M. E. (1990) *The Competitive Advantage of Nations* (New York: Free Press).

Prahalad, C. K. and Y. L. Doz (1987) *The Multinational Mission* (New York: Free Press).

Ricardo, D. (1819) *On the Principles of Political Economy and Taxation*, 1st American edn (Georgetown, DC: J. Milligan).

Rugman, A. M. and A. Verbeke (1992) 'A Note on the Transnational Solution and the Transaction Cost Theory of Multinational Strategic Management', *Journal of International Business Studies*, 23, 761–71.

———— (2001) 'Subsidiary-Specific Advantages in Multinational Enterprises', *Strategic Management Journal*, 22, 237–50.

———— (2003) 'Extending the Theory of the Multinational Enterprise: Internalization and Strategic Management Perspectives', *Journal of International Business Studies*, 34, 125–37.

Rumelt, R. P., D. E. Schendel and D. J. Teece (eds) (1994) *Fundamental Issues in Strategy: A Research Agenda* (Boston, MA: Harvard Business School Press).

Suzuki, N. (1980) 'The Changing Pattern of Advertising Strategy by Japanese Business Firms in the US Market: Content Analysis', *Journal of International Business Studies*, 11, 63–72.

Stopford, J. and S. Strange (1992) *Rival States, Rival Firms: Competition for World Market Shares* (Cambridge: Cambridge University Press).

Stopford, J. and L. Wells (1972) *Managing the Multinational Enterprise: Organization of the Firm and Ownership of the Subsidiaries* (New York: Basic Books).

Tallman, S. B. (1992) 'A Strategic Management Perspective on Host Country Structure of Multinational Enterprises', *Journal of Management*, 18, 455–71.

Tallman, S. and K. Fladmoe-Lindquist (2002) 'Internationalization, Globalization, and Capability-Based Strategy', *California Management Review*, 45, 116–35.

Teece, D. J., G. Pisano and A. Shuen (1997) 'Dynamic Capabilities and Strategic Management', *Strategic Management Journal*, 18, 509–33.

Vernon, R. (1966) 'International Investment and International Trade in the Product Cycle', *Quarterly Journal of Economics*, 80, 190–207.

Wernerfelt, B. (1984) 'A Resource-Based View of the Firm', *Strategic Management Journal*, 5, 171–80.

8

Chilean Foreign Direct Investment across Latin America: Alliances and Competitive Advantage

Patricio del Sol*

Introduction

One of the most surprising responses of Chilean firms to the trend towards economic liberalization trend that began in Chile in 1975 and spread through Latin America from 1985 onwards was their outbound foreign direct investment (FDI) across the region. In their pursuit of this regional strategy, Chilean firms have often been supported by Chilean and foreign strategic alliances. This chapter focus on these alliances in order to arrive at a better understanding of what firms from emerging countries can do to improve the prospects of success in their investments abroad.

This chapter is rather unique in that it examines FDI from one emerging country to another, and alliances between firms from developed countries with firms from an emerging country (Chile) other than the one where the investment is located (the host country). Although there is a relatively large body of literature on FDI and alliances, most of it analyses FDI from developed countries,[1] and focuses on alliances between companies from developed countries with firms from the host country.[2]

---

* I would like thank my colleagues Joe Kogan and Carlos García-Pont for their insightful comments without which this chapter would have been very different. This chapter was originally presented at the 1st International Workshop Creating Value through Global Strategy (Barcelona, 15–17 June 2003), held by the IESE Anselmo Rubiralta Center on Globalization and Strategy. I am grateful to the Center for inviting me to participate in the Workshop, and for their financial support.

In this study we pose the one question and its mirror image:

- Do partners add value to Chileans firms when investing outside Chile?
- Do Chilean firms add value to their partners (some from developed countries) when the latter invest outside Chile?

Answering the first question is not trivial. Alliances, especially with foreign firms, may seem to be a solution for many firms who lack the resources and capabilities needed to compete internationally.[3] Indeed, some highly respected authors consider that alliances are essential. Yves Doz and Gary Hamel (1998, p. xiii), for example, assert that 'the strategic alliance has become a cornerstone of global competitiveness', while Kenichi Ohmae (1989) holds that 'globalization mandates alliances, makes them absolutely essential to strategy'. Other authors, however, take the view that alliances cannot add much value. A case in point is Michael Porter, one of the world's best-known strategists, who argues that 'alliances as a broad-based strategy will only ensure a company's mediocrity, not its international leadership' (Porter 1990a; see also Porter 1998, pp. 194, 339–40).

The answer to the second question is even more interesting. It is puzzling that much Chilean outbound FDI was joint ventures (JVs) between Chilean firms and firms from developed countries. Why would an American firm contemplating an investment in Argentina invite a Chilean firm to participate as a partner? Traditional theories of FDI cannot explain such a phenomenon.

For several years now, economists have been addressing a number of important questions related to the competitive liberalization processes that have taken place around the world.[4] However, business strategists are only just starting to examine the issue of how companies operating in countries that have undergone such reforms should respond to the changes. Khanna and Rivkin (2001) is an example of a recent stream of research that focuses on strategy and competition in developing countries that have adopted liberalization policies.[5] This chapter has been written in the context of this new research, and focuses on the competitive advantage of firms from emerging countries. We begin with a brief overview of Chilean firms' responses to the globalization pressures originated by the economic liberalization in the region, including their investments across Latin America. This is followed by an analysis of whether Chilean and foreign partners add value to these investments, and why.

Change of context and Chilean responses

Beginning in 1975, Chile embarked upon a process of market liberalization that involved a coherent set of reforms affecting almost every aspect of economic life. These reforms unleashed free market forces that promoted domestic and international competition through the active participation of the private sector in the economy, while retaining only a subsidiary role for the state.[6] In the mid–1980s, other Latin American countries began to implement similar reforms. Bolivia and Mexico launched their liberalization in 1985; Jamaica, Uruguay, and Trinidad and Tobago in 1987; Costa Rica in 1988; Guyana, El Salvador and Venezuela in 1989; Argentina, Colombia, Honduras and Nicaragua in 1990; Paraguay, Peru and Brazil in 1991 and finally, Guatemala and Panama in 1992.[7] Though similar to the Chilean process, the particular characteristics, intensity and scope of the reforms varied from one country to the next (see Edwards 1995).

Chile's liberalization and the similar processes that followed it in other Latin American countries dramatically changed the structure of the industries in which Chilean firms operated. The context changed from a local, regulated and protected government-led environment to a global and highly competitive one. The reforms integrated most of the country's industries internationally through imports, inbound FDI, exports and outbound FDI. These four variables have grown vigorously since the start of the Chilean reforms in 1975 (see Table 8A.1, p. 104).

This process posed serious threats to Chilean companies, but also opened up tremendous opportunities.

Domestic competition grew substantially, as did foreign competition in the form of imports and inbound FDI. However, the availability of inputs also increased while prices declined, not only in terms of raw materials and equipment but also as regards the capital needed to finance new company ventures. Liberalization also brought the expansion of domestic demand, the opening up of domestic industries previously restricted to private firms (such as electricity), and enormous opportunities to compete abroad, export throughout the world and invest in Latin American countries that had implemented reforms similar to those adopted in Chile.

Chilean firms responded to the Chilean and Latin America liberalizations by completely reformulating their competitive strategies (see del Sol 2001). They made a multiple set of choices regarding horizontal and vertical scope, organizational capabilities, assets and resources, alliances and geographic market. They built a variety of world-class tangible and intangible assets, among which management capabilities are particularly worthy of highlight.

Chilean firms radically changed their geographic market, switching their overall focus from domestic to foreign markets (see Table 8A.2, p. 105). Total exports and total imports grew at an average rate of 10 per cent annually from 1975 to 2000. Chilean companies' investments in foreign markets grew from virtually nothing to an outbound FDI peak of US$6.4 billion in 1996, accounting for 9 per cent of GDP. The greater integration of Chile's economy into that of Latin America has come about mainly through outbound FDI, 95 per cent of which has gone to Latin America (see Table 8A.1 and 8A.3, pp. 104 and 105). Chilean exports and imports are geographically diversified (see Table 8A.2). The percentage of Chile's exports destined for Latin America, and the percentages of its imports and inbound FDI originating there, have not changed substantially since the 1980s (see Table 8A.1). Latin America has become very relevant for Chilean firms owing to the unprecedented Chilean direct investments across the region.

Did Chilean investments across Latin America during the 1990s benefit from alliances?

To answer this question, we broke it down into three component queries:

(1) Does investment profitability increase when the firm is *part of a Chilean group*?
(2) Does investment profitability increase when the investment is made *with a partner from a developed country* (DC partner)?
(3) Does investment profitability increase when the investment is made *with a firm located in the country where the investment was made* (local partner)?

Our analysis focused on three types of alliance. These three categories of partners emerge from two previous papers included in our research agenda on outbound Chilean direct investment. Del Sol (2001) analysed investment decisions by applying a logit model to data collected through a survey of 102 chief executive officers (CEOs). The empirical results showed that a firm has a greater tendency to invest abroad if it is a member of a Chilean business group. Del Sol (2002) analysed the response of the electricity generating company Endesa de Chile to the electricity reforms in Chile and other Latin American countries, a response that included investments in privatized power plants in Argentina,

Peru, Colombia and Brazil. To invest across Latin America, Endesa joined with local partners who, in addition to providing money, also supplied knowledge of local and country conditions where the investment was made. Endesa also joined with American partners who were an essential element in the definition of a position on a foreign investment. It was believed, for example, that the American partner, if supported by the American Embassy, might help to prevent arbitrary changes in the rules of the game by the local government. In addition, the American partner provided access to major financing resources.

Del Sol and Duran (2002) analysed these questions empirically (using a sample of 1,214 observations, grouped into 377 different foreign investments of 100 Chilean firms). They showed that foreign investments made by firms affiliated with business groups were (by 7.4 per cent) more profitable than foreign investments made by unaffiliated firms, and that foreign investments made with DC partners were (by 8.3 per cent) more profitable than foreign investments made without DC partners (controlling for destination country, industry, year and size effects). They did not find that foreign investments made with local partners were more profitable than foreign investments made without them.

Del Sol and Duran (2002) also discovered that an increase in the percentage of ownership boosted profitability as long as that percentage was below a certain threshold (55 per cent), and reduced profitability once the percentage was above it. The second part of this result corroborated the finding that the DC partners added value. As Chilean ownership approached 100 per cent of the investment, profitability declined because there was no room for added value from the partners.

This chapter makes new suggestions regarding alliances' motivation and partner roles. Doz and Hamel (1998, p. 45) argue that 'firms that race for the world often need local partners to gain market access and global partners to complement their skills'. Furthermore, they maintain (p. 47) that 'the balance of contributions between local and global partners generally follows this model: the local partner contributes the knowledge and insider skills needed to crack the local market; the foreign partner provides the specialized skills and other resources to serve it efficiently'.

Caves (1996, p. 78) argues that 'joint ventures seem to be more prevalent as Multinational Enterprises proceed toward more unfamiliar host countries...Japanese MNEs at least initially were more prone to joint ventures than are other MNEs...One explanation is that the great cultural distance between Japan and foreign markets induces Japanese firms to seek expertise on local conditions.' Caves (1996, p. 80) also reports that knowledge of the local market and good relations with the host government top the list of qualities that US MNEs value when they seek JV partners in other industrialized countries.

In this chapter we suggest that the DC partner helps overcome institutional voids in the host country in the spirit of Khanna (see, for example, Khanna and Palepu (1997)), a result we believe is new. Our results also suggest that there is no role for partners from the host country (they do not add value). In addition, we introduce a partner from an emerging country (Chile) other than the host country, whose role is difficult to explain in terms of the current literature. Caves (1996, p. 239) argues that the proprietary asset used by third-world MNEs to invest in foreign countries may be their entrepreneurial ability to operate in less developed countries' (LDCs') institutional conditions, but the evidence given to support this hypothesis is indirect.

The result that Chilean profitability on investments across Latin America increases when the investing firm is part of a Chilean group is consistent with the conclusion drawn in recent literature to the effect that *collective action* within groups may be valuable. Belonging to a business group gives firms additional access to financial and managerial resources and capabilities. In particular, the extensive literature published by Khanna and various co-authors shows that while conglomerates are being dismantled in western economies, business groups in emerging economies add value. They argue that emerging country groups help overcome institutional voids in their own countries.[8]

But this result – that emerging markets groups improve the profitability of outbound Chilean FDIs – raises the following question not answered in the existing literature: How do Chilean groups add value in outbound Chilean FDI? Fisman and Khanna (1998) showed that Indian groups helped to obtain international funds for investment in India, but could not obtain corresponding results for Chilean groups. Belderbos and Sleuwaegen (1996) used a logit model to show that in Japan, membership of a group (*keiretsu*) helped to lower barriers faced by Japanese firms investing in Southeast Asia. But of course, these were Japanese groups, not groups from emerging countries.

Can a Chilean firm add value to DC firms when they invest outside Chile?

We have focused above on the question whether partners add value to Chilean direct investments across Latin America. Another question now arises, the mirror image of the one just answered: did Chilean firms add value to FDI in Latin America from developed countries in the 1990s? To put it another way, were direct investments in Latin America during the 1990s with a Chilean firm as partner more profitable than those without a Chilean partner? And if so, why? Four papers growing out of our research agenda suggest some answers to these questions.

First, the result found by del Sol and Duran (2002) – that below a certain threshold, an increase in the percentage of the Chilean firm's ownership boosts profitability – constitutes evidence supporting the hypothesis that the active participation of Chilean firms in the investment adds value. Second, the case of Endesa de Chile (Del Sol 2002) suggests that Chilean firms add value to the partnership (to invest across Latin America) by offering *distinctive management capabilities* acquired through Chile's experience as the first Latin America country to liberalize its economy. This case suggests that these management capabilities constitute one of the competitive advantages of Chilean investments across Latin America. In fact, in addition to money, Endesa offered its partners its own management experience in transforming an inefficient state owned firm into an efficient private one, as well as in operating the firm within the Chilean electrical industry regulatory framework which was similar to the one in which the privatized firm would operate. The evidence that partners recognized these capabilities is that they allowed Endesa to be the operator of the firm. Endesa's competitive advantage thus stemmed from the fact that Chile was the first country in Latin America to reform its electrical sector.

Third, del Sol (2001)[9] shows that a firm's tendency to invest abroad is greater the more strategy changes it has made in dimensions other than investing abroad. One interpretation of this conclusion is that some firms are intrinsically motivated to change more (Ghemawat and Ricart 1993), perhaps because they have better managers or different types of managers. These firms learned locally how to manage firms in the newly liberalized environment, and applied the knowledge and skills so gained to investments abroad as soon as the liberalization process got underway in the rest of Latin America.

Fourth, the result found by del Sol and Duran (2002) that having a local partner did not increase profitability can be interpreted as supporting the Endesa case. A local partner is usually useful because its managers understand the existing environment. In the 1990s, however, the environment had just recently changed so that local partners were not knowledgeable about the new conditions; the Chilean partner did have some knowledge of the new environment and was therefore more valuable than a local partner.

Finally, the hypotheses that Chilean involvement in businesses abroad contributes to profitability and that Chilean participation is beneficial because of their knowledge of reform are supported by the results of del Sol and Kogan (2003). They show empirically that during the period 1994–2002 the foreign affiliates of Chilean companies were more profitable than other companies operating in the same countries, controlling for industry, year and size effects. This difference between the profitability of Chilean affiliates and other companies decreases over time, however, suggesting that the Chilean advantage is transitory. The authors use a database of 165 foreign affiliates of public Chilean firms operating in Latin America during the period 1994–2002 and compare these affiliates with 754 other public Latin American companies.

The liberalization handling knowledge as a competitive advantage is new in the literature of third-world outbound FDI. Most of the existing literature on third-world multinationals has focused on the role of labour-intensive technology (see, for example, Heenan and Keegan 1979; Wells 1983; Caves 1996). This literature argued that the technology used in developed countries is not always appropriate to developing countries because typically the latter have lower labour costs and smaller market size. The competitive advantage of third-world multi-nationals is based, according to this literature, on their superior knowledge of small-scale labour-intensive technology, know-how that is unavailable to firms in developed countries. We do not believe that technology was the primary motivation for outbound Chilean FDI.

Porter (1990b) has argued that a nation may obtain a competitive advantage when it has sophisticated consumers whose needs anticipate those of consumers in other countries. Similarly, we propose that a nation that leads its neighbours in economic reform may also gain a competitive advantage. Even though developing countries, through their economic reforms, may be converging to markets similar to those of developed countries, we argue that there is a period of transition where the strategies employed and lessons learned in the steady states of developed countries are not relevant.

Conclusion

This chapter has focused on the following two questions:

- Do Chilean and foreign partners add value to outbound Chilean FDI?
- Do Chilean firms add value to the outside Chile FDI of its partners from developed countries?

Perhaps not surprisingly, it was shown that being part of a Chilean group and having a partner from a developed country help outbound Chilean FDI. More unexpectedly, we have demonstrated that firms from America and other developed countries can benefit from a Chilean partner even if they are not investing in Chile. The liberalization handling capabilities constitute one of the competitive advantages offered by Chilean firms to investments across Latin America. Chilean firms added value to the partnership by providing distinctive management capabilities acquired by virtue of Chile's experience as the first Latin America country to liberalize its economy.

This results have interesting implications for policy-makers, managers and academics. To gain and maintain a competitive advantage in the region a country must be nurtured by continuing leadership in reform. Our results also imply that business strategy in developing countries adopting free market reforms is different from strategy in developed countries. This explains why Chilean managers had something of value to offer in the 1990s to developed country firms investing in Latin America outside Chile.

Appendix

Table 8A.1 Chilean exports, imports and outbound and inbound foreign investment, 1975–2000 (US$ million)

Year	Exports FOB			Outbound FDI	Imports CIF		Inbound FDI	
	Total (US$, current year)	% non-Copper	% to Latin America	Total (95% to Latin America)	Total (US$, current year)	% from Latin America	Total (US$, current year)	% from Latin America
1975	1,552	43	–		–	–	35	11
1976	2,083	40	–		1,684	33	45	21
1977	2,190	46	–		2,260	33	28	3
1978	2,408	50	26		2,408	29	286	5
1979	3,835	51	25		4,708	25	304	8
1980	4,705	55	24		6,145	28	307	11
1981	3,837	55	22		7,318	22	427	12
1982	3,706	55	19		4,094	21	478	8
1983	3,831	51	12		3,160	26	208	7
1984	3,650	56	15		3,739	26	196	9
1985	3,804	53	15		3,006	26	167	11
1986	4,191	58	17		3,157	23	259	4
1987	5,303	58	17		4,023	24	541	4
1988	7,054	52	13		4,924	28	845	2

Table 8A.1   (Continued)

Year	Exports FOB			Outbound FDI	Imports CIF		Inbound FDI	
	Total (US$, current year)	% non-Copper	% to Latin America	Total (95% to Latin America)	Total (US$, current year)	% from Latin America	Total (US$, current year)	% from Latin America
1989	8,080	50	12		7,505	27	974	2
1990	8,373	54	12	15	7,857	25	1,320	2
1991	8,942	60	14	192	7,686	27	981	5
1992	10,007	61	17	671	9,670	25	1,000	5
1993	9,199	65	20	742	10,869	23	1,728	4
1994	11,604	63	21	2,795	11,412	26	2,518	5
1995	16,024	60	19	4,158	15,348	27	3,041	3
1996	15,405	61	20	6,368	17,353	27	4,824	3
1997	16,663	58	21	4,731	18,888	28	5,230	3
1998	14,830	64	20	2,244	18,779	29	5,973	4
1999	15,616	62	22	1,417	15,143	25	9,086	5
2000	18,158	60	20	1,210	18,089	30	2,977	3

Source: Imports and exports: Central Bank of Chile (Monthly Reports). Inbound FDI: Comité de Inversiones Extranjeras (includes only investments made under DL600, and excludes those made under Chapter XIX, which are approximately 12 per cent of those under DL600). Outbound FDI: Cámara de Comercio de Santiago (2001).

Table 8A.2   Origin of Chilean imports and destination of Chilean exports, 2000

	Origin of Chilean imports (%)	Destination of Chilean exports (%)
Mercosur	24	9
Andean Community	6	7
Nafta	25	23
EU	18	27
Asia, Pacific	17	31
Others	10	3

Source: Central Bank of Chile.

Table 8A.3   Chilean foreign investments, by country of destination and economic sector, 1990–2000

Country	Percentage of total investments	Economic sector	Percentage of total investments
Argentina	52	Energy	43
Brazil	16	Industry	32
Peru	14	Wholesale and retail	10

Colombia	5	Banking and finance	7
Venezuela	5	Pension funds and insurance	2
Bolivia	2	Other	6
Other	6		

Source: Cámara de Comercio de Santiago (2001).

Notes

1. See for example Vodusek (2001) for FDI from European countries to Latin American countries and Enright (2002) for FDI from North American, European and Japanese firms in the Asia-Pacific Region. See also Belderbos and Sleuwaegen (1996). Some exceptions are Louri, Papanastassion and Lantours (2000) who analyse outward FDI of Greek firms, Athukorala and Jayasuriya (1988) who analyse multinationals in Sri Lankan manufacturing, Lecraw (1977, 1993) who examines outward direct investment by firms from Thailand and Indonesia and Ferrantino (1992) who considers Indian and Argentinean multinationals.
2. For a study of strategic alliances between firms from developed countries and Latin American countries, see Kotabe *et al.* (2000). Sim and Ali (1998) examine JVs of developing and developed countries in the Bangladesh context and Luo (1995, 1998) analyses JVs in China.
3. Caves (1996, p. 74), for example, argues that 'pursuing some activity might well require teaming assets that belong to different firms'. Caves (1996, p. 77) also reports that 'joint ventures are also sought by multinational enterprises lacking some capacity or competence needed to make the investment succeed'.
4. See for example Narula (2002), Aggarwal and Agmon (1990) who consider experiences of the Indian, Singaporean and South Korean economies and Büchi (1993), Edwards (1995), Corbo, Lüders and Spiller (1996) and Majluf and Raineri (1997).
5. See also Khanna and Palepu (1997, 1999a, 1999b, 2000a, 2000b), Fisman and Khanna (1998), Ghemawat and del Sol (1998), Ghemawat, Kennedy and Khanna (1998), Ghemawat and Khanna (1998), Ghemawat and Kennedy (1999), Khanna (2000) and Toulan (2002)
6. See Büchi (1993), Corbo Lüders and Spiller (1996) and Majluf and Raineri (1997)
7. Years are approximate, as there exists no non-arbitrary starting point for a liberalization process
8. See, for example, Khanna and Palepu (1997, 1999a, 1999b, 2000a, 2000b), Khanna (2000) and Khanna and Rivkin (2001)
9. Del Sol (2001) analyses outbound Chilean direct investment by applying a logit model to data collected through a survey of 102 CEOs.

References

Aggarwal, R. and T. Agmon (1990) 'The International Success of Developing Country Firms: Role of Government-Directed Comparative Advantage', *Management International Review*, 30(2), 163–80.

Athukorala, P. and S. Jayasuriya (1988) 'Parentage and Factor Proportions: A Comparative Study of Third-World Multinationals in Sri Lankan manufacturing', *Oxford Bulletin of Economics and Statistics*, 50(4), 409–23.

Belderbos, R. and L. Sleuwaegen (1996) 'Japanese Firms and the Decision to Invest Abroad: Business Groups and Regional Core Networks', *Review of Economics and Statistics*, 78(2), 214–20.

Büchi, H. (1993) *La Transformación Económica de Chile: Del Estatismo a la Libertad Económic* (Santafé de Bogotá: Editorial Norma).

Cámara de Comercio de Santiago (2001) *Inversión Detectada de Empresas Chilenas en el Exterior 1990–2000* (Santiago de Chile: Cámara de Comercio), March.

Caves, R. (1996) *Multinational Enterprise and Economic Analysis*, 2nd edn. (Cambridge, MA: University Press).

Corbo, V., R. Lüders and P. Spiller (1996) 'The Foundation of Successful Economic Reforms: The Case of Chile', Working Paper.

Del Sol, P. (2001) 'Investment across Latin America: A Logit Analysis of Chilean Strategies', Working Paper presented at the 21th Annual International Conference of the Strategic Management Society, San Francisco, CA, 21–24 October.

————(2002) 'Responses to Electricity Liberalization: The Regional Strategy of a Chilean Generator', *Energy Policy*, 30(5), 437–446.

Del Sol, P. and P. Duran (2002) 'Responses to Globalization in Asia and Latin America: Chilean Investment Alliances across Latin America', Laeba Working Paper, 5, December.

Del Sol, P. and J. Kogan (2003) 'Global Competitive Advantage Based on Pioneering Economic Reforms: The Case of Chilean FDI', Working Paper presented at the 23rd Annual International Conference of the Strategic Management Society, Baltimore, MD, 9–12 November.

Doz, Y. L. and G. Hamel (1998) *Alliance Advantage: The Art of Creating Value through Partnering* (Boston, MA: Harvard Business School Press).

Edwards, S. *Crisis and Reform in Latin America: From Despair to Hope* (New York: Oxford University Press).

Enright, M. J. (2002) 'Responses to Globalization in East Asia and Latin America: The Activity Locations of Multinational Manufacturers in the Asia-Pacific', Paper presented at the Strategic Management Society Conference, Paris.

Fisman, R. and T. Khanna (1998) 'Intermediation in Global Capital Markets: The Role of Business Groups', Working Paper, Harvard Business School.

Ferrantino, M. (1992) 'Transaction Costs and the Expansion of Third-World Multinationals', *Economical Letters*, 38, 451–56.

Ghemawat, P. and P. del Sol (1998) 'Power Across Latin America: Endesa de Chile', *Harvard Business School Case* N9-799-015.

Ghemawat, P. and R. Kennedy (1999) 'Competitive Shocks and Industrial Structure: The Case of Polish Manufacturing', *International Journal of Industrial Organization*, 17(6), 847–67.

Ghemawat, P., R. Kennedy and T. Khanna (1998) 'Competitive Policy Shocks and Strategic Management', in M. Hitt, J. E. Ricart and R. Nixon, (eds), *Managing Strategically in an Interconnected World* (New York: John Wiley).

Ghemawat, P. and T. Khanna (1998) 'The Nature of Diversified Business Groups: A Research Design and Two Case Studies', *Journal of Industrial Economics*, 46(1), 35–61.

Ghemawat, P. and J. E. Ricart (1993) 'The Organizational Tension Between Static and Dynamic Efficiency', *Strategic Management Journal*, 14, 59–73.

Heenan, D. A. and W. J. Keegan (1979) 'The Rise of Third World Multinationals', *Harvard Business Review*, January–February, 101–9.

Khanna, T. (2000) 'Business Groups and Social Welfare in Emerging Markets: Existing Evidence and Unanswered Questions', *European Economic Review*, 44, 748–61.

Khanna, T. and K. Palepu (1997) 'Why Focused Strategies May be Wrong for Emerging Markets', *Harvard Business Review*, July–August.

———(1999a) 'Policy Shocks, Market Intermediaries, and Corporate Strategy: Evidence from Chile and India', *Journal of Economics and Management Strategy*, 8(2), 271–310.

———(1999b) 'The Right Way to Restructure Conglomerates in Emerging Markets', *Harvard Business Review*, July–August. 125–134.

———(2000a) 'Group Affiliation Profitable in Emerging Markets? An Analysis of Diversified Indian Business Groups', *Journal of Finance*, 55(2), 867–891.

———(2000b) 'The Future of Business Groups in Emerging Markets: Long Run Evidence from Chile', *Academy of Management Journal*, 43(3), 268–285.

Khanna, T. and J. Rivkin (2001) 'Estimating the Performance Effects of Business Groups in Emerging Markets', *Strategic Management Journal*, 22(1), 45–74.

Kotabe, M., P. S. Aulakh, R. J. Santillan-Salgado, H. Teege, M. C. Coutinho de Arruda and W. Greene (2000) 'Strategic Alliances in Emerging Latin America: A View from Brazilian, Chilean, and Mexican Companies', *Journal of World Business*, 35(2), 114–32.

Lecraw, D. (1977) 'Direct Investment by Firms from Less Developed Countries', *Oxford Economic Papers*, 29(3), 442–57.

———(1993) 'Outward Direct Investment by Indonesian Firms: Motivation and Effects', *Journal of International Business Studies*, 24(3), 589–600.

Louri, H., M. Papanastassiou and J. Lantouris (2000) 'FDI in the EU Periphery: A Multinomial Logit Analysis of Greek Firms Strategies', *Regional Studies*, 34(5), 419–27.

Luo, Y. (1995) 'Business Strategy, Market Structure, and Performance of International Joint Ventures: The Case of Joint Ventures in China', *Management International Review*, 35(3), 241–64.

———(1998) 'Joint Venture Success in China: How Should We Select a Good Partner?', *Journal of World Business*, 33(2), 145–66.

Majluf, N. and R. Raineri (1997) 'Competition Through Liberalization: The Case of Chile', Chapter 3 in J. Taulchin and M. Naim (eds), *Regulation, Deregulation and Modernization in Latin America* (Washington, DC: The Woodrow Wilson Center).

Narula, R. (2002) 'Switching from ISI to NEM and the Opportunities for Latin America Industrial Development: A Case of Not Learning from Asia', Paper presented at the Strategic Management Society Conference, Paris.

Ohmae, K. (1989) 'The Global Logic of Strategic Alliances', *Harvard Business Review*, March–April, 143–54.

Porter, M. E. (1990a) 'Competitive Advantage of Nations', *Harvard Business Review*, March–April.

———(1990b) *The Competitive Advantage of Nations* (New York: Free Press).

————(1998) *On Competition* (Boston, MA: Harvard Business School Press).

Sim, A. and Ali, Y. (1998) 'Performance of International Joint Ventures from Developing and Developed Countries: An Empirical Study in a Developing Country Context', *Journal of World Business*, 33(4), 357–77.

Toulan, O. (2002) 'The Impact of Market Liberalization on Vertical Scope: The Case of Argentina?', *Strategic Management Journal*, 23(6), 551–60.

Vodusek, Z. (2001) *Foreign Direct Investment in Latin America: The Role of European Investors* (Washington, DC: Inter-American Development Bank).

Wells, Louis T. (1983) *Third World Multinationals: The Rise of Foreign Investment from Developing Countries* (Cambridge, MA: MIT Press).

9

International Geography and History in Host Market Competitiveness of Foreign Multinational Enterprises: A Research Agenda

*Subramanian Rangan and Aldemir Drummond**

Introduction

Multinational enterprises (MNEs) from Europe, the USA and Japan now operate and compete against one another in a number of third-host markets. While we know a great deal about the foreign direct investment (FDI) patterns of these MNEs, we know much less about the actual relative performance of these enterprises in the foreign markets in which they compete. The fact that region-by-region performance data are not readily available must partly explain this. Also there possibly is an implicit belief that MNE foreign performance outcomes might not represent an interesting pattern. In other words, the putative dependent variable (host market relative performance) might not be well behaved or meaningfully researchable (say, because a whole host of factors might be expected to influence it, not to mention the possibility of unsystematic differences across sectors). Partly, too, there might be a sense that competition is competition and ultimately, at least in free market settings, the more productive MNE should prevail no matter where.

* This chapter draws on our paper 'Explaining Outcomes in Competition among Foreign Multinationals in a Focal Host Market', *Strategic Management Journal*, 2004. We thank John Wiley & Sons for permission.

In this chapter, building on research we conducted in the host market setting of Brazil, we advance a different and perhaps provocative view. We contend not only that the dependent variable is probably well-behaved and predictable, but we also contend that its pattern poses a puzzle worthy of deeper research. *A propos* the first claim, we posit international geography and especially international history as significant and systematic predictors of MNE foreign market relative performance. To flesh out the second claim, we identify seven concrete research questions that follow from the first claim. We shall begin by describing and framing the research gap that is at the core of this chapter.

The emergence, expansion and now re-invigoration of MNEs have all received, and rightly continue to receive, substantial attention in research in international business and international management. Invariably, theories of superior firm-specific knowledge ('technology'), combined with theories of transaction costs, combined now with theories of spatial specialization (regional clusters) play the lead roles in this work. In contrast, there is much less research on the competitiveness and relative performance of MNEs in the host markets in which they operate. The literature that does exist on MNE performance emerges from comparative case studies and rich fieldwork, and mainly posits theories of superior organizational capabilities that foster a networked, think global–act local mindset within employees. In a best practice vein, this work has tended to hold up specific MNEs (including, until recently, such firms as ABB) as role models. Although unintended and perhaps nowhere expressly stated, an implication of this work is that better managed MNEs are in general likely to outperform their foreign rivals no matter where.

Yet the reality appears to be that a very few MNEs uniformly outperform their foreign rivals across the globe. For instance, while Unilever vastly outperforms Procter & Gamble in India, the reverse is the case in Mexico. Similarly, while Wal-Mart vastly outperforms Carrefour in Mexico, the reverse is the case in Brazil. And likewise, while British-headquartered Vodafone is the leading foreign mobile phone service firm in the USA, that position in Mexico is held by Spanish-headquartered Telefónica.

There is an MNE foreign competitiveness puzzle contained in this pattern of host market performance outcomes. If Unilever is the better-managed transnational relative to P&G, why does the former not lead the latter in Mexico (or Germany or Japan)? Or if P&G is the better-managed MNE, why does it not lead Unilever in India (or Brazil or South Africa)? Or if both are equally well managed why is it that they do not hold roughly equal shares in the various host markets (be it Germany, India, Japan, or Mexico) in which they both compete? Similar questions could be posed about rivals GE and Siemens, or Ford and Volkswagen, the Gap and Zara, Philips and Matsushita, and so on.

More formally, the research question can be framed as follows: assume a host market *h* that is open to MNEs from foreign regions. Assume further that there are two foreign regions *j* and *k* from which market-seeking MNEs invest and compete in the same industry in *h*. Taking firms to be profit-seeking, which between *j* and *k* MNEs is likely to be more successful in host market *h*? Is there a parsimonious and testable explanation for outcome patterns in competition among foreign multinationals in a given host market?

As more and more of the world's firms turn to foreign expansion as a route to profitable growth, this question assumes greater significance and merits greater attention. Work by authors such as Tallman (1991), Zaheer (1995), Ghemawat (2001) and Miller and Parkhe (2002) can shed useful light on the question. Drawing on Hymer (1960 [1976]), those authors have highlighted liabilities of 'foreignness' and related handicaps faced by foreign firms operating in a host market. However, with the exception of Tallman (1991), focal comparisons in most such existing work in international strategy have tended to be between foreign and local (that is, host country) firms. Less developed are propositions on behaviour and performance differences between foreign MNEs from two (or more) regions competing in a third host market – propositions that offer clear predictions on the questions stated above.

In Brazil, for instance, while US-based MNEs such as Coca-Cola and IBM lead in their sectors, other leading US MNEs (including Citibank, GE, Otis, Pfizer, Procter & Gamble, and Wal-Mart) are outsold locally by European rivals that appear less competitive globally. This was our finding from an examination of more than thirty-five manufacturing and service sectors. Below we outline a parsimonious framework that promises to explain and predict outcome patterns in such MNE contests in third markets.

An FSA–GHL framework of MNE competition outcomes in a given host market

In international business, there are two ideas that speak to the question at hand. One, premised on firm heterogeneity, emphasizes relative levels of firm-specific advantages (FSAs). As Hymer (1960 [1976:25]) observed long ago, 'firms are very unequal in their ability to operate in a particular industry'. In this view, if firm j has superior capabilities and is, as a result, more productive than k, then, in a steady state, j is likely to lead k in h. However, using, as in Dunning (1980), worldwide revenues per employee as an indicator of FSAs, we found that the pattern in Brazil was not systematically consistent with the predictions of this view (see also Tallman 1991). Broadly, while US MNEs exhibited higher productivity, it was European MNEs that led in Brazil. Apparently, as Hymer (1960 [1976]) (p. 43) himself put it: 'A firm may have advantage in a certain industry, but international operations are concerned with a certain industry in a *particular country*.' Thus, when an MNE enters a particular foreign host market, it might not perform well there.

The second idea, dubbed the liability of 'foreignness' (LOF), now enters the picture. The original LOF idea maintains that, *vis-à-vis* local firms operating in a given host market, the competitiveness of foreign MNEs is weakened owing to lesser relative familiarity with local information, laws and language. Likewise, in relations with local governments, consumers and suppliers foreign MNEs will tend to be at a disadvantage. Last but not least, because communication over distance is costly and often enfeebled, foreign MNEs, in managing remote operations, face yet another disadvantage.

The logic underlying the LOF view would appear to extend quite naturally to the question at hand. Instead of comparing local firms with foreign MNEs, we would, however, take a given host nation and compare a foreign MNE from one home region with a rival from another. Applied this way, this theory would suggest that outcomes in MNE contests might turn on j's and k's relative liabilities of 'foreignness' in h. In coarse terms, if LOF $(j, h) <$ LOF (k, h), then j is likely to lead k in h.

But how might we predict which between j and k will have the lower LOF *vis-à-vis* h? Based on our study in Brazil, we propose bilateral *geography and history links* (GHLs) between home and host nations as a good predictor. Admittedly arbitrarily, we categorize GHLs along five dimensions: geographic links, colonial links, immigration links, linguistic links, and institutional (especially legal system) links. With the exception of immigration, the links correspond one-to-one with items in Hymer's (1976 [1960], p. 28) LOF construct (communication, government, language and law). Importantly, these bilateral links are empirically observable.

While GHLs have been scantly discussed in explaining the relative *performance* of MNEs, they have been shown to predict patterns of affinities in FDI. These patterns 'result from factors that reduce communication and information costs even in the political and social realms...

[For instance] colonial ties offer political protection and lower transaction costs to MNEs' (Caves 1996, p. 52). 'These affinities ... cover factors that reduce [i] the MNE's cost of entering a foreign market or [ii] increase the cost-effectiveness of their internal control mechanisms' (Caves 1996, p. 50).

Similarly, here, we are suggesting that GHLs also influence MNEs' foreign performance outcomes (not just their investment behaviour). GHLs influence competitive outcomes because they probably deliver to MNEs important relative advantages in three realms: *information, consumer tastes* and *ongoing operations*. In economic sociology and international economics it is now well documented that GHLs influence business information flows (see Rauch 2001).[1] GHLs have also been linked to consumer taste advantages, the argument being that in differentiated markets, home varieties come to be demanded in tied host markets (see Head and Ries 1998).

Most importantly, we suspect that GHLs bring advantages in terms of ongoing operations – that is, strategy implementation. For instance, our fieldwork in Brazil suggested that the willingness among linked home country expatriates to both accept a transfer and to make a prolonged stay (of three–four years) in the host market was much greater because the presence of home national immigrant communities or familiar languages made experiences in the host nation less alien. Community, children's schooling and family relocation were all issues that appeared more easy to sort out. Indeed, we would hypothesize that because they are able to mobilize the right senior expatriates for the necessary duration, European MNEs are more willing to commit greater financial and technical resources in Brazil. Likewise, GHLs might help MNEs in the selection of local partners. This to some extent is thought to explain the difficulties encountered in Brazil by GE Capital (whose local partner went bankrupt shortly after their tie-up in 1999). What is more, since Wal-Mart is linked with GE Capital (for its store credit cards), this could not have helped that US retailer's business 'ecosystem' in Brazil.

If host nation inputs (namely, local labour and suppliers) are viewed as complements to home technology, capital and especially management, then the product of such complementarity is likely to be greater for those home–host pairs that are *geographically adjacent* or for which *historic links* are greater. This reasoning is consistent with the transaction cost-based model of multinational management elaborated in Rugman and Verbeke (1992). Using their terminology, GHLs can help an MNE both better exploit its FSAs (by making them less 'location-bound') and better tap into the host nation's 'country-specific advantages'. Accordingly, as a baseline, we would contend that in MNE contests in a given host market, the MNE whose home nation has greater links along geographic, colonial, immigration, linguistic, and institutional dimensions to the focal host nation will lead in that focal host market (and vice versa).

In the case of Brazil, from colonial links to immigration to the (civil code-based) legal system, it is clearly Europe, not the USA, that has relatively greater history links to the host nation. Of course, those links cannot explain the success in Brazil of such US MNEs as Coca-Cola, Gillette and IBM. Since liabilities of 'foreignness' should apply equally to these US MNEs, how can we explain their lead over European rivals in Brazil? This is where the FSA explanation comes in. In Hymer's words, international operations will occur in industries 'where some firms have advantages over other firms' (1960 [1976]: 92). He went on to note that: 'The rarest case will be the one where there is a single firm which has advantages over all other firms in the world in the production of a particular product . . . Wherever the product is produced, the firm will have some part in its production . . . A more prevalent case . . . [is] where there is not just one firm but several firms with advantages.'

Extending this view to contests among MNEs in a given host market, we conjecture that if j leads k in k's home market, then j will also lead k in h. The logic is that, almost by definition, the liability of 'foreignness' of j in k is bound to be greater than that of k in k. If, nevertheless, j leads k in k (for instance, as US-based Gillette leads French rival Bic in France) then, in general, j is likely to lead k in all hs. This is consistent with the success in Brazil (and elsewhere) of US MNEs such as Coca-Cola and IBM. Accordingly, we would propose that GHLs notwithstanding, *if an MNE's firm-specific advantages are so superior that it leads a competitor MNE in the latter's own home market, then it will also lead that competitor in the focal host market.*

Based on the above we can conceptualize an FSA–GHL two-dimensional framework that can predict outcome patterns in MNE contests in third markets. To exercise the framework, it would be necessary to categorize instances of rivalry as dominated or contested. *Dominated* instances would be those where j firms beat k firms in k (that is, in the competitor's home market), or where k firms beat j firms in j. In those cases, the dominant MNE (for example, Intel, Ikea) would be predicted also to lead in the focal host market.

In reality, few industries are dominated, and dominated industries seldom remain that way (think of leadership in memory chips shifting from the USA to Japan to Korea). Most industries, in fact, are what we might refer to as *contested* industries. Here the extent of any relative superiority is limited such that even though MNEs might have 'unequal ability', j firms do not dominate k firms in k nor vice versa. For instance, by some objective measures (such as sales per employee) Procter & Gamble might be the 'superior' firm, yet it does not dominate Unilever in Europe, nor does Unilever dominate P&G in the USA. Thus, in contested industries there is an absence of the massive superiority that characterizes dominated industries, and it is in these instances that outcomes in MNE competition would be predicted by GHLs. Here, the MNE with greater GHLs would be predicted to lead in the focal host market. This explanation can accommodate the varied pattern of outcomes that we observe in competition across various foreign host markets between the same pair of MNEs (for example, between Pfizer and Novartis, or Carrefour and Wal-Mart, or Toyota and Volkswagen).

A research agenda

The hypothesis outlined above predicts systematic variation in the dependent variable and it is falsifiable. At the same time, it raises a multitude of questions rich enough that it would appear to constitute a research agenda. Setting aside as important but obvious the issue of empirical testing of the ideas advanced above, we now outline seven questions that emerge from the central proposition on GHLs offered above. The list is not meant to be exhaustive but indicative of the rich nature of the research opportunity. Importantly, only by addressing these questions can our understanding of any systematic relationship between GHLs and MNE foreign performance be advanced.

(1) *What meaning has history?* In the dictionary, the word 'history' is associated with two different meanings, neither of which appears to fully capture our use of the term here. In one, history signifies the past; in the other it signifies a scientific account (as in natural or medical history). In the current context, which meaning of history is relevant? Does history signify timing (chronology), does it signify prior contact, both, or something else? If the international history–MNE foreign market performance relationship is mediated (that is, explained) via early accumulation of valuable but scarce resources (for example, distribution), then history here signifies a time line in the past – and, correspondingly, *timing of market entry* gains importance as an explanation. To the extent that actors' different levels of confidence and commitment are important in mediating the international history–MNE foreign market performance relationship, then the prior contact meaning of history would gain importance. Perhaps both are important, but at least based on the pattern we observed in Brazil (see Rangan and Drummond 2004), it appears unlikely

that these meanings are equally important (in fact, we found timing of entry to be much less important). From a theory-building point of view, it would be useful to consider which explanation is more consistent with relative performance in domestic settings. After all, it would be comforting (not to mention more persuasive) if a theory of relative performance abroad was also consistent with a theory of market performance at home. For the moment, however, it remains an open question which of the two meanings better satisfies this criterion.

Though abstract, it is important to probe this question if we are to move beyond the usage of 'history' as simply a convenient label. If the causal logic here is not well specified, history will stand as a weakly developed independent variable. The question has implications for the design of empirical tests, and its resolution could have implications for MNEs' reaction strategies.

(2)   *Which is relatively more important: geography or history?* Geography has received considerable attention in international business economics since the 1980s. Like history, geography too is used with at least two meanings, one as a *specific location* (that might be endowed with certain characteristics *à la* regional cluster models), and another as a *spatial indicator* of distance relative to a reference location. Perhaps owing to its easier measurability, in international economics it is the spatial distance meaning that has received greater usage. Here, we would contend, it is the *adjacency* more than the spatial distance meaning that is relevant. In any case, it will be useful to incorporate the adjacency, distance and cluster meanings in empirical tests.

It will also be helpful to sort out which is more important to the relative performance of MNEs: geography or history? To the extent that it is the former, the *costs of distance* become an area to focus on (for both research and practice). That finding would be interesting because presumably since the 1850s advances in transportation and telecommunication have reduced the pure costs of distance. Further advances can be expected, and this would have implications for the durability of geography effects. In fact, to the extent that infrastructural technological advances (as in transport and telecommunication) aid disproportionately more remote actors, and to the extent that such advances are more readily diffused, there will be a catching up if not a convergence in MNE relative performance. (In other words, FSAs will become relatively more important.)

On the other hand if history is more important, then *political factors* (such as foreign power, international influence, colonial contact) rather than technological factors come to the fore. This would have different implications for the durability of patterns influenced by history. It would appear that political power does not diffuse easily and does tend to shift, but typically only slowly. The emergence of regional blocs (such as the EU) generate their own politics and history, and such developments comingle geography and history. These issues merit exploration and research.

(3) *Which is relatively more important: culture or history?* Some observers might regard history and culture as similar, if not the same thing.Yet, if the international history–MNE relative performance relationship is to have theoretical and practical merit, then this issue too will have to be clarified. Not far from the dictionary meaning of 'culture' as the norms and customs of a people, Hofstede defines culture as the *values held by a people*. 'Values' are reasons for acting (in a certain way), and hence Hofstede refers to culture as programming of the mind (assuming not unreasonably that the mind influences people's actions). Like history and geography, culture too can be treated as an exogenous factor. Importantly too, once it has emerged, national culture is propagated from generation to generation, becoming a durable aspect of a nation (hence the *prima facie* validity of terms such as 'Japanese culture', 'American culture' and so on).

Two questions need to be addressed in the culture versus history debate. First, what are the elements of culture, and how distinct are they from history? If Hofstede's five indicators (power distance, uncertainty avoidance, masculinity/femininity, individualism/collectivism and time horizon) are used to define culture, then history and culture can be treated as distinct variables. The concept of *psychic distance* builds on cultural distance but includes language too. Not surprisingly, the concept of psychic distance has been found to have an almost perfect positive correlation with cultural distance. Is there such correlation between cultural distance and GHLs? If cultural closeness and history links are highly correlated, the case for developing a GHL variable will need to be made more clearly.

Considering the cases of Britain and India, Japan and the USA and Brazil and Germany (all of which have history but not culture links), one might expect the two constructs to not be highly correlated. In that case, a second question arises: which is more influential in terms of MNE relative performance? Cultural distance between nations has been used to predict *entry modes* and also the amount of *autonomy* granted to foreign subsidiaries. Its power as a predictor of MNE performance has, at least in partial models, been mixed. This empirical matter should be looked at in a complete model (where both variables are entered simultaneously). If culture is more important than history, managerial focus can turn on national patterns of decision making, greater local recruitment and cross-cultural training. If history is more important, then those avenues (which appear to be receiving a lot of attention in practice) will fall in importance and other avenues will have to be proposed.

(4) *Why does history influence MNE–host market relative performance?* Here there are at least three theoretical avenues that merit exploration: transaction costs, confidence and commitment and power. Transaction costs and commitment have been touched upon above, so we shall turn to power. As an illustration, consider the case of Estonia, the former Soviet controlled state that is now acceding to the EU. Since Soviet times, Russia has had a large influence on Estonia, immigrants were sent there to 'Russify' Estonia, Russian is still widely spoken and the two nations are adjacent. Today, Russian business interest in Estonia (especially in certain sectors such as petroleum) is considerable. To what extent does the Russian MNEs' considerable presence in Estonia reflect the influence of power of both a political and military kind? To what extent is the large presence and success in Germany and Japan of US headquartered MNEs also a reflection of such power? How does macro (national) power influence micro (firm-level) decisions and outcomes? Is it via confidence (that host government actions will be implicitly or explicitly protective of vulnerable investments)? Is it via transaction costs? or both? If we are to understand the 'history hypothesis' fully then an exploration and discussion of the operative role of power is very necessary.

(5)   How durable are GHL effects? If GHLs influence MNE foreign market performance in only a temporary manner, their implications for sustainable competitive advantage will be meagre. If, on the other hand the GHL influence is durable, or is expected to be so, then its implications for MNE strategy and regional resource allocation grow in importance. To be sure, elements of history such as colonial past, language and legal system will appear rather durable. Geography, it would seem, can safely be counted as durable. Does this automatically imply that the consequences will also be so?

Intuitively, one would expect catching up by laggard MNEs. After all, early mistakes (made, say, owing to the absence of GHLs) are likely to be corrected and market knowledge, just like technical knowledge, ought to diffuse. At the same time we are also aware that, perhaps contrary to textbook finance theory, managers allocate incremental resources based not just on future expectations but also on past results (with good results leading to escalated commitment and poor results leading to de-escalation). Illustrative of this, a cover story in the *Wall Street Journal Europe* (7 January 2004) discussed Philips' threat to shut down its loss-making US operations (this despite the fact that the USA remains the largest market for consumer electronics). Last but not least, in industries in which there are 'experience effects' (that is, where once customers choose and experience a satisfactory offer they refrain from switching), early leaders might lock-in sustainable positions unless their customers are confronted with vastly superior rival offers. So, are GHL effects durable, and due to what mechanisms?

(6) *What is the magnitude of GHL effects?* If GHLs matter, they ultimately have to influence unit costs and quality in the focal host market. Setting aside politically influenced markets (markets where governments rather than consumers influence outcomes – for example, the US auto industry), the unit cost–quality dyad has to be the link between factors influencing competitiveness (be they GHLs or FSAs) and actual market performance. The question is: by how much do host market unit costs go down because of GHLs? By how much does host market quality go up because of GHLs? Is it the cost side where GHLs deliver the greater advantage, or is it the quality side? Such understanding will aid the precision of policy prescriptions.

Related to this, what is the substitution quotient between superior technology and GHLs? It is clear that superior FSAs can substitute or compensate for GHLs (otherwise no foreign MNE would outperform a local rival in the host market). The question is: can we estimate the magnitude of the FSA advantage necessary to offset GHLs? The answer to this question will give managers some guidance as to threshold levels of product (that is, quality) and process (unit cost) leadership required to unseat better-linked rivals. In practice, of course, the challenge will be greater because rivals can often and will always try to imitate technological advances. This can turn into an arms race (with gains going mostly to host market customers and relative market positions appearing durable).

(7) *What, if anything, can MNEs do about the absence of GHLs?* What are the managerial implications of GHLs, especially their absence? Should MNEs exit host markets where their rivals have more extensive GHLs? Are there some effective ways to compensate for this relative handicap? Are there MNEs that have surmounted this disadvantage in a credible manner, and do they offer any useful lessons?

Beyond the seven questions sketched above, there are others that merit exploration. For instance, among the various aspects of history links, is there a hierarchy in terms of importance? For parsimony, it would helpful to know whether any single element (for example, colonial links) is the prime indicator. Separately, is the GHL–MNE performance influence a supply – or a demand-side phenomenon? Do GHLs predict specific market entry modes? Are GHLs influences symmetric – are they bi-directional (for instance, US MNEs do well in the UK and UK MNEs do well in the USA)?.

Conclusion

Rumelt, Schendel and Teece (1994) have pointed to the determinants of international success and failure of firms as one of five fundamental questions in strategy. We have explored one angle of this understudied question. In doing so, we have integrated history along with the geography and technology dimensions, and hypothesized the net effects on MNEs' relative performance in foreign markets.

Today, competition has become an unavoidable fact of life for most if not all firms. In avoiding the worst consequences of this development, MNEs have traditionally been helped by superior firm-specific technologies. This has been especially essential in expanding abroad and taking on local firms in their own backyards. Theorists have researched and written a great deal about this. Product cycle theories on the direction of internationalization, internalization theories on optimal entry modes, integration-responsiveness theories of overall MNE performance and even host market learning-knowledge accumulation theories of MNE reinvigoration have been developed.

In contrast, the role of geography and history appears not to have been adequately explored. While some MNEs (such as Gillette, Ikea and Intel) appear to have vastly superior technology than all the others in their sector, empirically most MNEs must be content with sharing technological leadership with one or more rivals from other home nations. As a result – and this is more and more the case (think of Samsung increasingly challenging Nokia in mobile phones) – the vast majority of MNEs have to compete in third host markets against other *equally good* rivals from other home markets. In such competition, where rival MNEs' home technology levels stand almost shoulder to shoulder, it appears that GHLs can play a decisive and durable role in influencing performance outcomes.

We hope the ideas advanced here will provoke renewed interest in the study of international strategy (as in Ghemawat 2001). Eventually, such work could help MNE managers better appreciate, anticipate and address the consequences of international geography and history on their firms' performance abroad.

Note

1. It is important to note however that, in an authoritative review, Portes (1998, p. 3) stipulates that: 'Social networks are *not a natural given* and must be constructed through investment strategies oriented to the institutionalization of group relations, usable as reliable source of other benefits' (emphasis added). If geography and history are treated as givens, the pertinence of GHLs to social capital concepts is not direct.

References

Caves, R. E. (1996) *Multinational Enterprise and Economic Analysis* (New York: Cambridge University Press).

Dunning, J. (1980) 'Toward an Eclectic Theory of International Production: Some Empirical Tests', *Journal of International Business Studies*, 11(1), 9–31.

Ghemawat, P. (2001) 'Distance Still Matters', *Harvard Business Review*, September, 137–47.

Head, K. and J. Ries (1998) 'Immigration and Trade Creation: Econometric Evidence from Canada', *Canadian Journal of Economics*, 31(1), 47–62.

Hymer, S. H. (1960 [1976]) *The International Operations of National Firms: A Study of Foreign Direct Investment* (Cambridge, MA: MIT Press).

Miller, S. R. and A. Parkhe (2002) 'Is There a Liability of Foreignness in Global Banking? An Empirical Test of Banks' X-Efficiency', *Strategic Management Journal*, 23, 55–75.

Portes, A. (1998) 'Social Capital: Its Origins and Applications in Modern Sociology', *Annual Review of Sociology*, 24, 1–24.

Rangan, S. and A. Drammond (2004) 'Explaining Outcomes in Competition among Foreign Multinationals in a Focal Host Market', *Strategic Management Journal*, 25(3), 285–93.

Rauch, J. (2001) 'Business and Social Networks in International Trade', *Journal of Economic Literature*, 39, 1177–1203.

Rugman, A. M. and A. Verbeke (1992) 'A Note on the Transnational Solution and the Transaction Cost Theory of Multinational Strategic Management', *Journal of International Business Studies*, 23, 761–71.

Rumelt, R., D. E. Schendel and D. J. Teece (1994) *Fundamental Issues in Strategy* (Boston, MA: Harvard Business School Press).

Tallman, S. B. (1991) 'Strategic Management Models and Resource-Based Strategies Among MNEs in a Host Market', *Strategic Management Journal*, 12, 69–82.

Zaheer, S. (1995) 'Overcoming the Liability of Foreignness', *Academy of Management Journal*, 38(2) 341–63.

Part III

Organizing MNCs for Value Creation

10

Introduction to Part III

Bruno Cassiman and Giovanni Valentini

Organizational design has always been and still constitutes a fundamental issue in management research and practice. The three chapters
in Part III tackle the problem of organizational design in multinational
enterprises.

Caves (1998, p. 5) maintains that 'international business designates
not a class of decisions but a group of firms that face decision making
problems beyond those that confront single-nation business, or they
encounter the same problems transformed by their international context'.
It therefore appears advisable to start by untangling the factors that
may make the problem of organizational design in a multinational
corporation (MNC) fundamentally different with respect to a domestic
firm. And the obvious response, already contained in Caves' words, is
'foreignness'.

Notwithstanding mass-media proclamations, the world is still far from
being global (Ghemawat 2003a), and 'foreignness' keeps constituting a
'liability' for overseas firms (Zaheer 1995; Zaheer and Mosakowski 1997).
In particular, 'foreignness' may cause additional costs for MNCs due to
spatial distance, host and home country environment-specific factors
and firm-specific variables such unfamiliarity with a given, new market.
Besides these potential perils, each location may offer specific advantages.
A successful MNC is one whose capabilities are strong enough to overcome these liabilities and profit from the differences as well as from the
opportunities offered to create value (Hymer 1976; Hennart 1982;
Ghemawat 2003b). The tension between the advantages and drawbacks
of internationalization is somewhat typical: strategy *is* about tradeoffs
(Porter 1996). Still, the tradeoffs between value creation and the liabilities
of going international are different depending on the organizational
level involved. We will now briefly analyse how 'foreignness' and liabilities

can create tradeoffs in decisions concerning organizational design at the corporate, at the functional and at the subsidiary levels.

At the *corporate* level, an important organizational decision concerns the extent of internationalization itself. Received theory suggests that internationalization is motivated by the desire to exploit firm-specific assets such as technological advantages, management skills and geographical advantages (Hymer 1976; Dunning 1977). In addition, having cash-flows in non-perfectly correlated markets also provides a diversification benefit, lowering firm risk (Rugman 1976). However, the benefits of diversification may be often offset by the liabilities of 'foreignness'. As Kwok and Reeb (2000) highlight, the dominant factor in explaining the overall impact of internationalization on firm risk is the different *risk classes of different countries*, and its effects vary with home and target market economic conditions. Cultural distance is definitely another factor of fundamental importance in determining the right balance of internationalization (Shenkar 2001). On one hand, the risks involved in doing business in a country culturally different appear relevant (Hofstede 1980); but on the other, diversity of cultures means diversity of routines and repertoires, and thus new opportunities to learn and adapt to environmental turbulence (Morosini, Shane and Singh 1998). Cultural distance may also exacerbate the arduous task of multinational coordination.

Along these lines, Chapter 13 by Jeffrey J. Reuer and Tony W. Tong shows how the multinationals' downside risk increases with the average cultural distance between the firm's home base and its foreign subsidiaries and that coordination across firms' foreign subsidiaries, is easier when the firm has foreign subsidiaries in culturally similar locations. Reuer and Tong use a real options approach for the decision of a firm to have operations in different countries. On the one hand, diversification into different geographical areas provides the firm with the option to reallocate different value-chain activities across subsidiaries when external conditions change. On the other, diversifying into different regions increases the coordination and communication costs of the firm. This leads to an optimal organizational design where the firm diversifies into a number of geographical markets depending on the precise tradeoff between the option of risk spreading and coordination costs.

Accordingly, Reuer and Tong find that bankruptcy risk and income stream risk fall as a firm successively invests in different host countries, yet more dispersed foreign direct investment (FDI) elevates downside risk after a threshold is reached.

The tradeoff between the benefits of internationalization and the constraints of 'foreignness' liabilities also plays an important role at the functional level. And more and more importantly over recent years the issue has concerned the *R&D function*. First, innovation is in many ways the *raison d'être* of multinationals (Caves, 1996; Bartlett and Ghoshal 1997). Second, while traditional MNC theories start by assuming some kind of *internal advantage*, which is then exploited through internationalization (Hedlund and Nonanka 1993), it has been recognized that a MNC may invest abroad not only to exploit its advantage but also to obtain access to scientific and technological knowledge located abroad (Kuemmerle 1999). The MNC has been described as a sovereign organizational form for exploring and exploiting technologies, knowledge and markets on a global scale in order to create value (Dunning 1993). Therefore, even in this case, differences and distance related to 'foreignness' may assume a positive meaning. But, again, coordination is crucial.

One perspective on technology transfer holds that the *transfer of knowledge* is facilitated or inhibited by organizational forms and organizational design (Nobel and Birkinshaw 1998). To understand the optimal organizational design, Bengtsson and Soderholm (2002) maintain that firms have primarily to consider (1) what is being transferred and (2) over what distance it is transferred. Distance is a multidimensional concept, but geographical and technological distances appear to be the most important dimensions in the case of R&D.

Within this framework, Chapter 12 by Reinhilde Veugelers and Francesca, Sanna Randaccio analyses the drivers of the decision of an MNC to centralize or decentralize the R&D function – that is, to determine its autonomy. In the Veugelers – Sanna Randaccio model, the key parameters affecting this decision are related to the information transmission within and across firm boundaries. Actually, if investing abroad may provide access to local knowledge through incoming spillovers, it also increases the chances of outgoing spillovers and makes the transmission of knowledge within the MNC – back to the central lab or other subsidiaries – more difficult.

If at a corporate or functional level the numerous tradeoffs, the omnipresent pros and cons that arise with any decision regarding organizational design and internationalization constitute a challenge, it is at the subsidiary level that the liabilities of 'foreignness' are actually and directly experienced. Kostova and Zaheer (1999) stress in particular the importance of *institutional distance*. 'Institutional distance' is the extent of similarity or dissimilarity between the regulatory, cognitive and normative institutions of two countries (Xu and Shenkar, 2002). Institutions may and should have an impact on firms' strategy and design. For instance, Khanna and Palepu (2000) argue that while focus, as opposed to diversification, may be good advice in developed countries, it may not be in countries in which institutions are poorly functioning, and where internal markets may substitute them. The importance of external, institutional forces appears in Chapter 11 by Sunil Venaik, David F. Midgley and Timothy M. Devinney. They relate local pressures to the subsidiaries' strategy and performance. In particular, the chapter focuses on one function, marketing, and two organizational measures – the autonomy of the subsidiary in the MNC structure and its existing network within the MNC. The chapter is particularly innovative insofar as it incorporates the relevant constructs of learning and innovation to assess subsidiary performance.

Given the long history of research in the area of organizational design and MNCs, any claim to comprehensiveness would be foolhardy. Several problems remain out of the analysis; however, we believe that these three chapters do raise important issues and that their contribution is relevant both independently and as a whole. In fact, first, they tackle design problems at different organizational levels, from the corporate headquarter to the subsidiary. And, second, they present different and complementary theoretical frameworks through the lenses of which it is possible to analyse the potential role of 'foreignness', distance and communication in the relationship between organizational design and value creation.

References

Bartlett, C. and S. Ghoshal (1997) 'Managing Innovation in the Transnational Corporation', in M. Tushman and P. Anderson (eds), *Managing Strategic Innovation and Change* (New York: Oxford University Press), 452–76.

Bengtsson, M. and A. Soderholm (2002) 'Bridging Distances: Organizing Boundary-Spanning Technology Development Projects', *Regional Studies*, 36, 263–74.

Caves, R. E. (1996) *Multinational Enterprise and Economic Analysis*, 2nd edn (New York: Cambridge University Press).

———(1998) 'Research on International Business: Problems and Prospects', *Journal of International Business Studies*, 29, 5–19.

Dunning, J. H. (1977) 'Trade, Location of Economic Activity and the MNE: A Search for an Eclectic Approach', in B. Ohlin, P. O. Hesselborn and P. M. Wijkam, *The International Allocation of Economic Activity* (New York: Holmes & Meier), 395–418.

———(1993) *Multinational Enterprises and the Global Economy* (Wokingham: Addison-Wesley).

Ghemawat, P. (2003a) 'Semiglobalization and International Business Strategy', *Journal of International Business Studies*, 34, 138–52.

———(2003b) 'The Forgotten Strategy', *Harvard Business Review*, 81(11), 76–84.

Hedlund, J. and I. Nonanka (1993) 'Models of Knowledge Management in the West and in Japan', in, P. Lorange *et al.* (eds), *Implementing Strategic Process: Change, Learning and Cooperation* (Oxford: Basil Blackwell 117–44).

Hennart, J. F. (1982) *A Theory of Multinational Enterprise* (Ann Arbor: University of Michigan Press).

Hofstede, G. (1980) *Culture's Consequences* (New York: Sage).

Hymer, S. H. (1976) *The International Operations of National Firms: A Study of Direct Investment* (Cambridge, MA: MIT Press).

Khanna, T. and K. Palepu (2000) 'Is Group Affiliation Profitable in Emerging Markets? An Analysis of Diversified Indian Business Groups', *Journal of Finance*, 55, 867–91.

Kostova, T. and S. Zaheer (1999) 'Organizational Legitimacy under Conditions of Complexity: The Case of the Multinational Enterprise', *Academy of Management Review*, 24, 64–81.

Kuemmerle, W. (1999) 'The Drivers of Foreign Direct Investment into Research and Development. An Empirical Investigation', *Journal of International Business Studies*, 30, 1–24.

Kwok, C. C. and D. M. Reeb (2000) 'Internationalization and Firm Risk: An Upstream-Downstream Hypothesis', *Journal of International Business Studies*, 31, 611–29.

Morosini, P., S. Shane and H. Singh (1998) 'National Cultural Distance and Cross-Border Acquisition Performance', *Journal of International Business Studies*, 29, 137–58.

Nobel, R. and J. Birkinshaw (1998) 'Innovation in Multinational Corporations: Control and Communication Patterns in International R&D Operations', *Strategic Management Journal*, 19, 479–96.

Porter, M. E. (1996) 'What is Strategy?', *Harvard Business Review*, 74(6), 61–78.

Rugman, A. (1976) 'Risk Reduction by International Diversification', *Journal of International Business Studies*, 7, 75–80.

Shenkar, O. (2001) 'Cultural Distance Revisited: Towards a More Rigorous Conceptualization and Measurement of Cultural Differences', *Journal of International Business Studies*, 32, 519–35.

Xu, D. and O. Shenkar (2002) 'Institutional Distance and the Multinational Enterprise', *Academy of Management Review*, 27, 608–18.

Zaheer, S. (1995) 'Overcoming the Liability of Foreignness', *Academy of Management Journal*, 38, 341–63.

Zaheer, S. and E. Mosakowski (1997) 'The Dynamics of the Liability of Foreignness: A Global Study of Survival in Financial Services', *Strategic Management Journal*, 18, 439–64.

11
Dual Paths to Multinational Subsidiary Performance: Networking to Learning and Autonomy to Innovation

Sunil Venaik, David F. Midgley and Timothy M. Devinney

Introduction

Both directly and indirectly, the process of globalization is a dramatic determinant of the strategic posture, organizational structure, processes and performance of firms, both multinational and domestic. World Trade Organization (WTO) liberalization, the pervasiveness of communications technology and the advent of regional trading blocs are just a few of the reasons why the global imperative has become relevant for an increasing number of firms whose integration into the global economy requires expanded subsidiary operations and a deeper understanding of the complexities of managing a global organization.

Our study adds to this understanding by relating the market pressures faced by subsidiaries to the decisions about strategy and structure applied in those units to the performance of the subsidiary. We focus on one narrow aspect of subsidiary structure and performance, the *marketing function*, which we pick for two reasons. First, it is generally one of the first functions to be internationalized, and therefore represents the most international aspect of a firm's operations. Second, the final judgement about the success or failure of any strategy is usually delivered at the downstream end of the value chain, making marketing a critical linchpin in determining business performance. Although our approach differs from the seminal study of Johansson and Yip (1994), it is consistent with more recent work (Birkinshaw, Hood and Jonsson 1998), allowing us to make a more concentrated examination of narrower operations with a more direct line between managerial strategy and performance.

Although a number of studies have investigated the characteristics of environmental pressures and the influence of these pressures on firm strategy, structure and performance, none of the these studies incorporate the new concepts of learning and innovation that are increasingly regarded as prerequisites for improving firm performance, nor do they take the broader stance to conceptualizing and measuring the pressures operating at the subsidiary level called for by some (Devinney, Midgley and Venaik 2000; Venaik, Midgley and Devinney 2004). Johansson and Yip (1994) examined the linkages between the globalization drivers, organization structure and decision making and firm performance, but did not consider the constructs of learning and innovation that are regarded as key organizational outcomes that impact on the current and future performance of the firm (Anderson and King 1993). In investigating the effects of environmental pressures on firm strategy, structure and performance, Roth and Morrison (1990), Johnson (1995) and Harzing (2002) do not examine the role of the intermediate constructs of learning and innovation that might mediate the effect of environmental pressures and organizational activities on business unit performance.

On the other hand, the theoretical models that examine the phenomena of organizational learning and innovation often ignore the environmental and organizational antecedents and the performance consequences of learning and innovation. Ghoshal, Khorine and Szulanski (1994) studied the effects of autonomy and networking on interunit learning and innovation, but their model did not include the environmental pressures of global integration and local responsiveness, nor did it test the effects of learning and innovation on overall performance. Tsai (2001) examined the linkage between networking, innovation and performance, but did not show how these are influenced by environmental pressures or the organizational decision making mechanisms used by the firm. Schulz (2001) presents the most comprehensive model, incorporating both environmental and organizational determinants of knowledge flows, although performance, the *raison d'être* of a business, is not included in his model.

Our contribution can be seen in the development and testing of an integrated and comprehensive model that examines the impact of five environmental pressures and organization conduct on the desirable outcomes of learning, innovation and overall performance. The potential benefits of this model are twofold. First, it allows the relative importance of various factors to be established. Second, it reduces the risk of finding spurious relationships due to model misspecification.

The chapter is organized as follows. The next section outlines the theoretical model, followed by a presentation of series of results based upon an empirical variant of this model. Rather than formulate hypotheses, we concentrate on understanding the nature of the empirical findings.

The theoretical model

Our theoretical model follows from a combination of the industry structure–conduct–performance (SCP) paradigm and the resource-based view (RBV) of the firm. According to the SCP framework, industry structure influences firms' conduct which, in turn, impacts on the performance of the industry (Scherer 1996), a viewpoint that regards industry factors as having a greater influence on firm performance than organization factors (Porter 1981). The RBV (Barney 1991) looks on organizational resources, skills and competencies as having far greater impact on firm performance than industry structure.

Our approach applies more focused attention to the *interaction between environmental factors and internal managerial structures* as determinants of performance. In this sense, it is a natural extension of both the SCP and the RBV taken down to the functional level of the firm. We separate the environmental factors – represented by environmental pressures on firms – as well as structural firm factors – such as industry, age, size, location and nationality – from the more strategic choices of autonomy of decision making and the extent of networking within the organization. By taking this approach, we hope to address industry- and firm-level influences on performance – a problem in prior studies (for example, Mauri and Michaels 1998) – as well giving equal emphasis to the role of organization level influences (Bowman and Helfat 2001). The basic model is shown in Figure 11.1.

This model is a natural extension of the earlier work of Johansson and Yip (1994). Like them, we look on environmental pressures as one of the determinants of performance, although we use a greater number of constructs to represent this environment. Similarly, following the strategic management literature, firm conduct is represented by two organizational constructs, autonomy and networking. Finally, the firm outcome is represented by three constructs, the intermediate outcomes of subsidiary interunit learning and marketing innovation and the ultimate performance outcome of market and financial return. We also build on the tradition of Birkinshaw, Hood and Jonsson (1998) with our emphasis on the role of subsidiary autonomy in MNE innovation.

Environmental pressures

MNCs are confronted with diverse and often conflicting environmental pressures as they expand their activities around the globe. Traditionally,

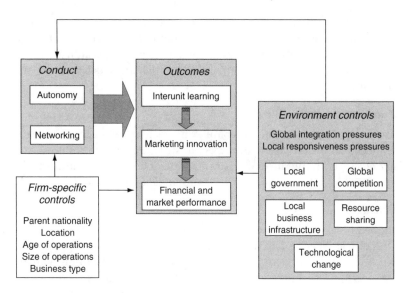

Figure 11.1   The theoretical model

these pressures have (often too broadly) been referred to as the pressures of 'global integration' (GI) and 'local responsiveness' (LR) (Prahalad and Doz 1987). The GI pressures force firms to take an *integrated approach* to their global activities – that is, to coordinate their business units and strategies to attain maximum efficiency and competitive advantage. These pressures might lead to responses such as producing parts in a single location for global use on an efficient scale, or mandating global consistency in brand positioning. Concurrently, firms face a counter-vailing set of pressures to adapt their activities to the *unique circumstances* of the countries in which they operate. These pressures for LR may prompt responses such as producing parts locally to obtain tax incentives or adapting brand positioning to local market circumstances.

Although the literature regards these pressures largely as two-dimensional, Venaik, Midgley and Devinney (2004), in a theoretical reconsideration of the logic of this thinking and a comprehensive replication of most prior studies, show that the diverse environmental pressures confronted by multinational firms, are better represented with at least five dimensions – (1) local government influence; (2) quality of the local business infrastructure; (3) global competition; (4) technological change and (5) resource sharing. However, there is no extant literature that indicates how these five pressures might impact on various facets of the firm, and it is our contention that they pervade the milieu in which the MNC is operating. Hence, one would expect that these pressures would affect not only performance through a direct effect, but also intermediate outcomes and the conduct choices of firms through both direct effects and anticipatory decisions on the part of management.

Conduct → outcome link

The heart of our model are the complex interactions between *conduct* – the choices that firms make with respect to structure and interaction – and *outcomes* – both intermediate, as in the case of learning and innovation, and final, as in the case of financial and market performance.

Conduct

In the case of conduct, one needs to encapsulate the facets of organization structure and decision making. The major dimensions of organization structure are complexity, centralization and formalization (Van de Ven 1976). Here, most studies concentrate on the issue of *centralization* versus *autonomy*, since centralization is regarded as the central construct in organization design (Egelhoff 1988). However, as we normally see MNCs making decisions using multicultural teams and task forces, this approach may not completely capture the wide range of tools and processes that are used by firms, or be an adequate representation of their true organization structure (Ghoshal, Korine and Szulanski 1994). Hence, a network approach to decision making is essential to gain deeper insights into the complexities of the diverse product markets served by large MNCs and to sense and respond rapidly to changes in the product markets.

In our model, we capture these factors by focusing on the *autonomy* of the subsidiary and the extent of *interunit networking* among subsidiaries and between subsidiaries and the headquarters. Prior work suggests that greater autonomy is likely to motivate the local subsidiary managers to take initiatives which may result in marketing innovations that are useful either locally, or leveraged by the MNC on a global basis. For example, Bartlett and Ghoshal (1989) found that subsidiary autonomy is associated with a high level of innovation in multinational firms, and Birkinshaw, Hood and Jonsson (1998) show that autonomy is associated with the subsidiary contributing more toward firm-specific advantages at the global level. Similar results are found with respect to networking. According to Powell, Koput and Smith-Doerr (1996) collaboration enhances organizational learning and aids rapid communication of new market opportunities and risks. MNCs use a network organization structure to facilitate interunit learning and communication among their geographically and culturally dispersed units (Ghoshal, Korine and Szulanski 1994). Teamwork and collaboration among the geographically dispersed units of MNCs are likely to enhance organizational learning in MNCs. In addition, since the MNC's parent and subsidiary managers work in different customer, competitive, and country environments, they bring together a diversity of experiences, resulting in corporate decision making that is superior to that by any individual country manager. Thus, the pooling of MNCs' managerial skills and capabilities also results in better managerial decisions and improved corporate performance.

Outcomes

We examine performance outcomes not only in the context of market and financial performance but also through the *intermediate outputs* of learning and innovation, which might be thought to partially determine market and financial performance. Despite their importance (as noted in the theoretical model of Slater and Narver 1995), there have been few attempts in the academic literature to test environmental and organizational determinants and the consequences of organizational learning and innovation. We concentrate on two intermediate performance outcomes – learning and innovation – both within the marketing context of the firm.

Learning is regarded as an important source of sustainable competitive advantage and one of the key determinants of organizational effectiveness (Nonaka 1994). There is extensive literature in strategic management on *inter*organizational learning and knowledge transfer as mechanisms for gaining competitive advantage and improving firm performance (for example, Inkpen and Beamish 1997). Although the advantages and difficulties of *interfirm* knowledge transfer are extensively discussed in the literature, recent research has increasingly been focused on *intrafirm* learning and knowledge transfer (for instance, Birkinshaw, Hood and Jonsson 1998), the focus of our analysis. Internalizing knowledge by a subsidiary from another subsidiary creates opportunities for generating new knowledge that is fed back into the multinational system, creating a 'spiral of knowledge' in the organization (Nonaka and Takeuchi 1995). It is important to note the distinction between *interunit learning* and *interunit networking*, as already discussed. Learning is a valuable *intermediate output* of the firm, whereas networking is *one* component of organizational conduct that is an antecedent that can increase learning.

While Dunning (1988) focuses on the *parent* company creating and possessing the firm-specific advantages (FSAs) for successful multi-nationalization, more recent work has shifted the focus of attention to MNC *subsidiaries* as sources of FSAs (Gupta and Govindarajan 1994). In addition to developing *inventions* and *innovations* for use in the local subsidiary, the subsidiaries also develop innovations that the MNC can leverage in other markets around the globe. In this way, subsidiary companies contribute to the FSAs of the MNC, and shift the generation of FSAs 'from being the sole concern of the parent company to a collective responsibility for the corporate network' (Birkinshaw, Hood and Jonsson 1998). Such innovation has been shown through repeated studies to have a direct effect on firm performance, independent of the nature of the performance variable chosen. Innovative output has been shown to lead to improved stock price performance (Chaney, Devinney and Wines 1991), increased sales growth (Soni, Lilien and Wilson 1993), greater likelihood of business survival (Banbury and Mitchell 1995), and sustained profitability (Geroski, Machin and Reenen 1993).

Summary

Table 11.1 provides a description of the constructs and their relationship in the model. The logic is that exogenous environmental pressures are antecedents to conduct and outcomes, and that, conditional on this, conduct determines outcomes. In addition, firm-specific factors can account for idiosyncratic conduct and outcomes that would not be explainable otherwise. This is consistent with the RBV and Dunning (1988) with their emphasis on firm-specific resources being a determinant of both conduct and performance.

Early empirical tests

The model in Figure 11.1 was tested using data from 165 subsidiaries of US, UK and Japanese MNCs. A simple breakdown of the sample is given in Table 11.2. The respondents, representative of a cross-section of industries and countries, were sampled from the Dun and Bradstreet Worldbase database of MNCs. The model in Figure 11.1 was estimated using partial least squares. Four of the pressures are formative indices following Venaik, Midgley and Devinney (2004), and the other controls are measured with a single item (for example, age of subsidiary).

To make this estimation, we apply three important criteria. First, we estimate more links than are specifically hypothesized within our model. For example, we argue that the only clear hypothesis we can make about

Table 11.1 Main constructs and their relationship in the model

	Definition	Hypothesized relationships
Conduct		
Autonomy	Extent to which the MNC headquarters allocates marketing mix decisions to the local subsidiary	Affects: innovation (+)
Networking	Extent to which marketing mix decisions in the MNC are taken in groups such as teams, task forces, committees, etc. comprising managers from the corporate and regional headquarters and country subsidiaries	Affects: learning (+) performance (+)
Outcomes		
Interunit learning	Extent to which marketing knowledge and information are shared among the corporate headquarters, the regional headquarters and the country subsidiaries of the multinational firm	Affects: innovation (+) performance (+)
Marketing innovation	Extent to which the subsidiaries seek new ideas for carrying out their marketing activities and improving their marketing mix, including product and service attributes as well as pricing, promotion and distribution	Affects: performance (+)
Performance	Financial performance includes sales growth and profitability; operational (non-financial) performance includes market share, new product introduction, technological efficiency, etc. that improves the firm's financial performance	

autonomy is between it and innovation. This is not to say that there may not be other effects, but within our structure, they are not clearly specified and, *a priori*, the effect directions cannot be determined. However, to estimate the model without these effects may erroneously bias the coefficients for which we have made specific predictions, and lead to false conclusions about our hypotheses. Thus, we estimate these effects without making any hypotheses as to direction. Second, we separate the effects of *structure* – such as environment and firm-specific controls – from *conduct* – such as autonomy and networking – and *intermediate outputs* – such as learning and innovation – from financial and market performance. This will allow us to make specific statements about the role of structure versus the role of conduct and the mediating effect of the intermediate outcomes on performance. Third, in line with many published models of this general type, we have chosen to ignore issues of

Table 11.2   Sample descriptors

Descriptor	Number
Subsidiaries sampled	728
Subsidiaries studied	165
Distinct MNCs represented	103
Geographic representation	
• Unique countries in which subsidiaries operated	36
• Subsidiaries operating in developing countries	51
MNC domicile[a]	
• Japan	40
• USA	66
• UK	40
Employees (mean)	
• In MNC	22,000
• In subsidiary	325
Industry breakdowns	
• Manufacturing (remainder is service operations)	130
• Consumer products (remainder is industrial products)	83

Notes:
a Remainder are from other countries. This is due to ownership change after the sample was created.

feedback loops and simultaneous relationships (for instance, Johansson and Yip 1994). With cross-sectional data, imperfect measures and the current state of structural equation modelling, it is difficult to incorporate these more subtle effects. Each path in the model can be thought of as hypotheses about the net effects that might be observed in cross-sectional data. They also imply a causal order that can clearly be falsified by poor fit of the model to these data, but never conclusively supported by its good fit.

The model and five of the six hypothesized relationships are supported by these data, as presented in summary form in Table 11.3. Indeed, both the conduct constructs and firm performance are well explained with r^2 around, or exceeding, 30 per cent. Only networking is not so well explained with an r^2 of 20 per cent. The only unsupported hypothesis is the relationship between interunit learning and marketing innovation, a finding that has potentially profound implications relating to the interpretation of our results. We thus find *dual paths* to high performance – one through networking and learning, and one through autonomy and innovation. Networking has both a positive direct impact on

Table 11.3 Summary of empirical results

Constructs	Hypothesized relationships	Constructs				
		Autonomy	Networking	Interunit learning	Marketing innovation	Performance
Conduct						
Autonomy	Innovation (+)				+	
Networking	Learning (+)			+		
	Performance (+)					+
Outcomes						
Interunit learning	Innovation (+)				Not significant	
Marketing innovation	Performance (+)					+
Performance	Performance (+)					+
Environmental pressures						
Local government influence			+			–
Quality of local business infrastructure		–		+		–
Global competition		–	+	+	–	+
Technological change		+			+	
Resource sharing			+	+		–
Fit						
R^2 (No controls/environmental pressures)		0.24	0.14	0.32	0.30	0.26
R^2 (With controls/environmental pressures)		0.27	0.20	0.35	0.35	0.30

performance and an indirect impact through interunit learning. Autonomy has only an indirect impact on performance through its relationship with innovation. Because there is no link between either networking and learning or autonomy and innovation, these effects are additive, meaning that they are strategically separable. One implication of this is that firms which are able to somehow utilize both paths – networking → learning and autonomy → innovation – are likely to be better performers than those that can execute only along one or neither of the paths. However, as we will see in our later discussion, this is a difficult proposition to execute in reality.

The effects of global pressure constructs are also interesting, in that different pressures clearly impact on different aspects of conduct, and in different directions. For example, local government influence has a strong negative and direct impact on firm performance, and a negative impact on subsidiary innovation, leading to an indirect lowering of performance. However, this is somewhat offset by the fact that this pressure increases the need for networking which, in turn, leads, indirectly, to higher performance. Similarly, the quality of the local business infrastructure *reduces* subsidiary autonomy (somewhat surprisingly) but *increases* learning. Global competition has strong negative effects on autonomy (as much of the prior literature would suggest) and increases networking, learning and performance (although the latter is a small effect). Technological change impacts positively on one path to improved performance through positive effects on autonomy and innovation. However, it reduces firm performance through another direct effect. Finally, pressures for resource sharing impact on the other path to improved performance through positive effects on networking and learning.

Conclusion

The logic of the model presented has both theoretical and empirical implications. From a theoretical perspective, it attempts to address the issue: 'How do environmental pressures impact on the SCP framework as applied to MNC subsidiary operations?' The argument posited is that environmental pressures act at all three levels in the SCP path, but that different pressures are more important at different points in this chain of effects. More traditional arguments, based upon the GI–LR dichotomy assumed, first, that all pressures could be subsumed into a two-dimensional framework and, second, that GI–LR affected mainly the choices of MNCs with regard to structure and conduct. Most empirical investigations assumed this to be the case, and estimated their models based on this assumption (for example, Roth and Morrison 1990). However, if our logic is correct, violation of this supposition has tremendous empirical implications. If different pressures impact on SCP differentially, one must not only model a more complex mixture of pressures, but also account for the fact that they will have potentially *reinforcing* or *conflicting* effects at different points in the progression from structure, through conduct, to performance. This is exactly what we did, and the results show a more complex picture of the interaction of environment with SCP than is normally considered in the empirical literature.

A somewhat more practically and strategically useful result is the finding of *dual* and *separable* paths to performance. The fact that there is no relationship between networking and learning and innovation is somewhat surprising, but it implies that, at least within our limited sample of MNC subsidiaries, that the paths to performance are distinct. The complexity of this finding is even more interesting when one examines the environmental pressures on these paths. On the networking → learning path, four of the five pressures come in positively – local government influence, quality of the local business infrastructure, global competition and resource sharing. On the autonomy → innovation path, three of these same pressures have a negative influence – local government influence, quality of the local business infrastructure and global competition – one is insignificant – resource sharing – and the one unimportant for networking and learning – technological change – has a strong positive influence. If we believe that firms operate rationally and efficiently with an understanding of the pressures they face, we can come up with a rule for structure and conduct based on this. The networking → learning path is most likely to have a large impact on performance when resource sharing, global competition, local infra-structure and local government influence are greatest. The autonomy → innovation path is more relevant the less influence there is from global competition, local infrastructure and local government influence, and the more there is from technological change. Given the opposing effects seen in our results, while it is possible for firms to choose both paths simultaneously, it is unlikely that it would be rational to do so within the same market. The global presence of the MNC would, however, potentially allow it to choose different paths in different markets, and our results indicate that this would lead to greater overall performance.

All in all, our findings inspire us toward further research. One issue that immediately arises from our results is that the standard prescription found in the literature pushing for a 'transnational solution' based on learning, networking and innovation may not have empirical credence (Bartlett and Ghoshal 1989). The managerial importance of this is that if MNC headquarters force on subsidiaries a mandate that implies that both paths to performance should be pursued, it is likely that profitability or market share may be reduced in those environments where the countervailing environmental pressures identified by us are strong. Hence, following Johansson and Yip (1994), we recognize a need to examine MNC strategy as mandated from headquarters. Second, our results assume that all the subsidiaries in our data can be characterized with one model and its associated total sample coefficients. Through the technique of latent class modelling, we can relax this assumption to look at segments of firms. This would be more in keeping with the literature on firm heterogeneity (for instance, Hatten, Schendel and Cooper 1978) and most relevant, given our speculation that *MNC flexibility* is critical to subsidiary performance.

Both of these issues – multiple MNC models and the role of the headquarters – subsidiary interaction – put us in line with the work of Nohria and Ghoshal (1989, 1994). Their finding that headquarters use two strategies to control subsidiaries – differentiated fit and shared values – is not inconsistent with our own; however, direct comparison is not possible, as we did not examine the issue of headquarters–subsidiary fit. What we are able to do is describe more accurately the environmental correlates associated with different MNC strategic postures and the relationship between structure, conduct and performance. In addition, we go beyond Nohria and Ghoshal in terms of *decomposing the path to performance*. In their case, a single subjective performance measure was shown to be correlated with fit between subsidiary and headquarters orientation. We capture both the multifaceted character of performance as well as a process by which environment and strategic posture interact to determine performance. Our findings potentially imply that even within the same MNC there may be more room for differentiated fit than originally supposed, and that it may be possible, through a better understanding of environmental antecedents to strategic choice, to generate prescriptive measures that allow managers to determine more accurately what such fit means.

References

Anderson, N. and N. King (1993) 'Innovation in Organizations', in C. L. Cooper and I.T. Robertson (eds), *International Review of Industrial and Organizational Psychology*, 8 (New York: Wiley), 1–33.

Banbury, C. M. and W. Mitchell (1995) 'The Effect of Introducing Important Incremental Innovations on Market Share and Business Survival', *Strategic Management Journal*, 16, 1611–82.

Barney, J. (1991) 'Firm Resources and Sustained Competitive Advantage', *Journal of Management*, 17(1), 99–120.

Bartlett, C. A. and S. Ghoshal (1989) *Managing Across Borders: The Transnational Solution* (Boston, MA: Harvard Business School Press).

Birkinshaw, J., N. Hood and S. Jonsson (1998) 'Building Firm-Specific Advantages in Multinational Corporations: The Role of Subsidiary Initiative', *Strategic Management Journal*, 19(3), 221–41.

Bowman, E. H. and C. E. Helfat (2001) 'Does Corporate Strategy Matter?', *Strategic Management Journal*, 22(1), 1–24.

Chaney, P., T. M. Devinney and R. Winer (1991) 'The Market Value of New Product Introductions', *Journal of Business*, 61(4), 573–611.

Devinney, T. M., D. F. Midgley and S. Venaik (2000) 'The Optimal Performance of the Global Firm: Formalizing and Extending the Integration–Responsiveness Framework', *Organization Science*, 11(6), 674–95.

Dunning, J., (1988) 'The Eclectic Paradigm of International Production: A Restatement and Some Possible Extensions', *Journal of International Business Studies*, 19(1), 1–31.

Egelhoff, W. G., (1988) *Organizing the Multinational Enterprise: An Information-Processing Perspective* (Cambridge, MA: Ballinger).

Geroski, P., S. Machin and J. V. Reenen (1993) 'The Profitability of Innovating Firms', *Rand Journal of Economics*, 24(2), 198–211.

Ghoshal, S., H. Korine and G. Szulanski (1994) 'Interunit Communications in Multinational Corporations', *Management Science*, 40(1), 96–110.

Gupta, A. K. and V. Govindarajan (1994) 'Organizing for Knowledge within MNCs', *International Business Review*, 3(4), 443–57.

Harzing, A. W. (2002) 'Acquisitions versus Greenfield Investments: International Strategy and Management of Entry Modes', *Strategic Management Journal*, 23(3), 211–27.

Hatten, K. J., D. E. Schendel and A. C. Cooper (1978) 'A Strategic Model of the US Brewing Industry: 1952–1971', *Academy of Management Journal*, 21(4), 592–610.

Inkpen, A. C. and P. W. Beamish (1997) 'Knowledge, Bargaining Power and International Joint Venture Instability', *Academy of Management Review*, 22(1), 177–202.

Johansson, J. K. and G. S. Yip (1994) 'Exploiting Globalization Potential: US and Japanese Strategies', *Strategic Management Journal*, 15(8), 579–601.

Johnson, J. H., Jr. (1995) 'An Empirical Analysis of the Integration–Responsiveness Framework: US Construction Equipment Industry Firms in Global Competition', *Journal of International Business Studies*, 26(3), 621–35.

Mauri, A. J. and M. P. Michaels (1998) 'Firm and Industry Effects within Strategic Management: An Empirical Examination', *Strategic Management Journal*, 19(3), 211–19.

Nohria, N. and S. Ghoshal (1989) 'Internal Differentiation within Multinational Corporations', *Strategic Management Journal*, 10(4), 323–37.

————(1994) 'Differentiated Fit and Shared Values: Alternatives for Managing Headquarters–Subsidiary Relationships', *Strategic Management Journal*, 15(6), 491–502.

Nonaka, I. (1994) 'A Dynamic Theory of Organizational Knowledge Creation', *Organization Science*, 5(1), 14–37.

Nonaka I. and H. Takeuchi (1995) *The Knowledge Creating Company: How Japanese Companies Create the Dynamics of Innovation* (New York: Oxford University Press).

Porter, M. E. (1981) 'The Contributions of Industrial Organization to Strategic Management', *Academy of Management Review*, 6(4), 609–20.

Powell, W. W., K. W. Koput and L. Smith-Doerr (1996) 'Interorganizational Collaboration and the Locus of Innovation: Networks of Learning in Biotechnology', *Administrative Science Quarterly*, 41(1), 116–45.

Prahalad, C. K. and Y. Doz (1987) *The Multinational Mission: Balancing Local Demand and Global Vision* (New York: Free Press).

Roth, K. and A. J. Morrison (1990) 'An Empirical Analysis of the Integration–Responsiveness Framework in Global Industries', *Journal of International Business Studies*, 21(4), 541–64.

Scherer, F. M. (1996) *Industry Structure, Strategy, and Public Policy* (New York: HarperCollins).

Schulz, M. (2001) 'The Uncertain Relevance of Newness: Organizational Learning and Knowledge Flows', *Academy of Management Journal*, 44(4), 661–81.

Slater, S. F. and J. C. Narver (1995) 'Market Orientation and the Learning Organization', *Journal of Marketing*, 59(3), 63–74.

Soni, P. K., G. L. Lilien and D. T. Wilson (1993) 'Industrial Innovation and Firm Performance: A Re-Conceptualization and Exploratory Structural Equation Analysis', *International Journal of Research in Marketing*, 10(4), 365–80.

Tsai, W. (2001) 'Knowledge Transfer in Intraorganizational Networks: Effects of Network Position and Absorptive Capacity on Business Unit Innovation and Performance', *Academy of Management Journal*, 44(5), 996–1004.

Van de Ven, A. H. (1976) 'A Framework for Organization Assessment', *Academy of Management Review*, 1, 64–78.

Venaik, S., D. F. Midgley and T. M. Devinney (2004) 'A New Perspective on the Integration–Responsiveness Pressures Confronting Multinational Firms', *Management International Review* (Special Issue), 44, 15–48.

12
Decentralization of R&D and Know-How Flows through MNEs: Some Stylized Facts and Insights from Theory

*Reinhilde Veugelers and Francesca Sanna-Randaccio**

Introduction

In the traditional literature on multinational enterprises (MNEs), multi-national expansion originates from the R&D activities of the firm. But rather than seeing the geographic dispersion of MNEs as a *result* of knowledge creation, the emphasis in the literature has shifted towards seeing the geographic dispersion of MNEs as a *source* for knowledge creation (see, among others, the special issue of *Research Policy*, 1999). In the current international environment, innovation strategies require increasingly more global sourcing, thus a need for sensing new market and technology trends worldwide. All this implies a different role for subsidiaries in the innovative strategy of the MNE: subsidiaries become important vehicles to *access (local) external sources*.

This chapter discusses the tradeoffs an MNE faces when it assigns subsidiaries an active role in innovation, organizing its R&D in a decen-tralized versus a centralized manner. The discussion is based on insights from empirical evidence and theoretical modelling. We will use the

* Revised version of the paper prepared for the IESE Conference on 'Creating Value through Global Strategy', Barcelona, 15–17 June 2003. Veugelers acknow-ledges support from PBO99B/024, DWTC(S2/01/08) and VIS/02/001. Sanna-Randaccio acknowledges a travel grant support from the EU Commission (EU MESIAS network).

implications of a game-theory model (Sanna-Randaccio and Veugelers 2002) which analyses how the interplay of internal and external knowledge flows interacts with the nature of host market competition in influencing an MNE's choice to effectively disperse its R&D internationally.

The model highlights the importance of the *intensity of competition* in the local market in determining the size of both benefits and costs to R&D decentralization. It shows that when R&D is undertaken abroad in association with production, the local knowledge base is not unequivocally a 'pulling' factor attracting R&D investments by foreign MNEs, as its effect depends on the level of local competition. The results also illustrate the complementarity between an efficient internal and external knowledge management system and the technology sourcing motive for R&D decentralization. In addition the results suggest that, with a fall in the cost of intracompany technology transfers, relative market size loses importance as a critical factor shaping the pattern of R&D internationalization.

Before presenting the model and its results in the final section we first discuss the related literature. The chapter draws on both the Industrial Organization (IO) literature on spillovers, R&D and FDI, which is reviewed in the next section, as well as on the insights from International Business on R&D decentralisation, discussed in the third section. The empirical evidence on R&D decentralisation and international know-how flows is reviewed in the fourth section. The chapter ends with a brief summary of the main findings.

Spillovers and R&D by MNEs : an industrial organization perspective

The impact of external know-how spillovers on the incentives of firms to innovate has been widely studied in IO (see De Bondt 1996 for an overview). This literature focuses on the importance of the strategic effects of spillovers, stressing the interaction with product market competition. When competing firms are marketing substitute products, high spillovers can lead to fewer incentives for investment in R&D. Some IO models have taken into account that firms can manage these spillovers through organizational decisions. Cohen and Levinthal (1989) pioneered the idea that firms can try to increase incoming spillovers by investing in 'absorptive capacity' – that is, spillovers are more efficient in reducing own costs when the firm is engaged in own R&D (see also Kamien and Zang 2000).

Another related line of research is the *geographical localization* of innovative activities. Innovative activities are found to be highly clustered (Jaffe, Trajtenberg and Henderson 1993; Audretsch and Feldman 1996). The principal explanatory factor revolves around the existence of knowledge spillovers. Since distance hinders the exchange of especially tacit knowledge, firms agglomerate their R&D activities to be able to capitalize on external knowledge spillovers. Gersbach and Schmutzler (1999) present a game-theoretic model of two competing firms, deciding on the location of their R&D and production. They consider two types of external spillovers: external spillovers when rival production units are co-localized with own R&D sites, and knowledge complementarities among co-localized R&D sites. In addition, the firms also need to consider that internal spillovers are required when R&D is located separately from production. They find that an agglomeration outcome, where both firms choose their R&D site in the same location, requires simultaneously internal and external spillovers: not only must firms learn something in agglomeration, they must also be able to transport this know-how internally.

The relationship between the MNEs' choice of international market entry mode and technology transfer has been studied in the theoretical literature. The notion that establishing subsidiaries abroad leads to dissipation of know-how is developed in Ethier and Markusen (1996), who find that MNEs may prefer exports over FDI to be better able to appropriate the benefits. Similarly, Fosfuri (2000) analyses the MNEs choice between FDI, exports and licensing and the vintage of the technology transferred. He finds that if imitation is possible – for instance, because of a lower degree of patent protection in the host country – firms may prefer to choose exports or FDI which avoids imitation or to license the older technology for which there are fewer incentives to imitate. Siotis (1999) develops a game-theoretic model where the MNE, when serving the foreign market through FDI rather than exports, will be generating spillovers to local competitors, but will also be able to learn from local rivals. In a symmetric two-firm, two-country model, he finds that if the technology gap between the firms is wide, the advanced firm may prefer exports if spillovers are large, while the technologically backward firm may prefer FDI, which is motivated by technology sourcing.

A more closely related line of previous research, linking internal and external knowledge flows around MNE subsidiaries, examines whether parent firms will transfer technology to subsidiaries given that local rivals may learn. These models are specifically set up for less developed countries (LDCs). In Das (1987), the subsidiary is non-R&D active, but receives a transfer of technology from its parents, while it is competing as a leading firm facing a competitive fringe of local firms which are non R&D active but can, without costs, learn from subsidiaries. Das finds that despite local learning, it is still profitable for the parent to transfer the better technology. Wang and Blomström (1992) take into account that MNEs face a cost of transferring technology internally, which will be higher for state-of-the-art technologies, and that local firms face a cost of learning. When the subsidiary competes in a differentiated duopoly with the local firm who faces a technology gap, they find that technology transfers via FDI are positively related to the level of host country's firms' learning investment.

The focus of this literature on LDCs implies that only the internal transfers from headquarters to subsidiaries and the external transfers from subsidiaries to local firms are considered, while the competitive structure the subsidiary is facing is one of weaker local rivals. The issue of R&D decentralisation is not at stake here. The decision to decentralize R&D to advanced host countries has not yet been studied theoretically. When FDI is located in developed countries, technology sourcing as motive for FDI becomes an important issue. In addition, the problem of appropriating know-how becomes more critical when local rivals are not technology laggards.

Changing innovative strategies of transnational companies: an international business perspective

In the traditional literature on multinationals, following the seminal work of Dunning (1988), multinational expansion originates out of the R&D activities of the firm. R&D is a central headquarters function, which permits the firm to capitalize on economies of scale from pooling R&D resources. The result is internal transfers of know-how from central R&D labs to subsidiaries. This is the *home-base-exploiting FDI* (Kuemmerle 1997) or the *'centre-for-global'* innovations (Bartlett and Ghoshal 1997) terminology.

The production subsidiaries can be engaged in incremental innovations, adjusting products and processes to (changing) local needs. This leads to decentralized R&D which permits responsiveness to local differences. Subsidiaries create location-specific knowledge, adjusting products and processes to local specificities. These are the demand oriented motives for decentralization of R&D, where it is important to be close to 'lead users' and adapt products and processes to local conditions, often related to host market regulations.

Supply-related motives for R&D decentralization relate to acquiring access to a wider range of scientific and technological skills. Within an international technology sourcing strategy of the MNE, subsidiaries can have different functions, depending on the level of technological capabilities and the strategic importance of the host market. The subsidiary can play a monitoring role, transferring market know-how to direct global innovations elsewhere developed in the company. But when the location holds a high level of technological capability for a particular innovative project, it can even be assigned a leading role as 'centre of excellence', with a 'global product mandate', developing innovations which are implemented worldwide. This is the *home-base-augmenting FDI* in the Kuemmerle terminology, while Pearce and Singh (1992) label such innovations as *internationally interdependent labs*, whose role is in the long-term basic research of the group. These subsidiaries are responsible for sourcing know-how in other units of the MNE (including headquarters), but also accessing external sources, within both their local environment and globally.

Centrifugal forces need to be traded against centripetal forces (see Grandstrand, Hakanson and Sjolander 1992). Besides the economies of scale in R&D already mentioned, centralisation permits better control of R&D, minimizing leaking of information to external parties – that is, to (potential) competitors. The costs of communication and coordination to manage the *cross-unit interactions* also need to be considered. This requires work on effectively linking R&D units, mobility and transfer of people, building long-distance interpersonal communication and providing adequate reward systems and responsibilities (Bartlett and Ghoshal 1997; Westney 1997).

Empirical evidence on the internationalization of R&D

Statistical evidence and survey results on R&D internationalisation suggest that most research still remains at corporate headquarters. For instance, Patel and Pavitt (1992), on the basis of US patent data for 1969–86, found, for large US, German and Japanese firms, that less than 15 per cent of their technological activities were located abroad. But the percentage of R&D carried out abroad is increasing rapidly (Grandstrand, Hakanson and Sjolander 1992; Caves 1996; Reger 2001). Serapio and Dalton (1999) report that the R&D spending by US affiliates of foreign firms increased at a rate of 11.6 per cent between 1987 and 1996, much faster than the R&D done by US firms: the share of foreign owned firms in US R&D spending has increased to 16.3 per cent in 1996.

This R&D internationalisation is mainly an intra-Triad phenomenon with the US and EU as the major locations for foreign R&D while US and EU firms have the largest shares of foreign R&D. Reger (2001) reports that US and EU firms spent, respectively, 30 per cent and 28 per cent of R&D outside home in 1998, while for Japanese firms it was only 7 per cent. The pharmaceutical industry is typically ahead in terms of having the most internationalized R&D (see, for instance, Serapio and Dalton 1999). The rapid growth of non-home R&D is realized through acquisitions of local firms, but the research intensity of foreign-based production has also increased (Dunning 1988).

Several studies indicate that MNEs undertake mostly development rather than research abroad. Von Zedwitz and Gassman (2002) find that foreign R&D is twice as development oriented as domestic R&D. And labs undertaking development are generally operating within (or near) production facilities of the same MNE. Pearce (1999) finds that only 16.7 per cent of R&D labs created by foreign MNEs in the UK indicate that they operate independently of any producing subsidiary.

With respect to motives for R&D decentralisation, Hakanson (1992), from a sample of 150 subsidiaries of twenty Swedish MNEs, found demand-related factors to be more important than supply-related ones. Pearce and Singh (1992) from an international sample, also find limited evidence for supply-side factors such as the local scientific environment and availability of researchers. But more recently Florida (1997), from a sample of 187 foreign R&D labs in the USA, find that although both technology and market-driven motives are important, access to human capital and technological expertise is becoming a major force.

The choice of MNEs on whether to decentralize R&D has implications for the *external know-how flows* between the multinational plants and their environment. In the endogeneous growth literature, FDI has been recognized as a channel for international spillovers, enabling home country R&D to contribute to host country productivity growth (see, among others, van Pottelsberghe de la Potterie and Lichtenberg 2001). Most of this empirical literature derives the existence of technology spillovers through FDI indirectly from the effect that this FDI has on local productivity growth. It has generally failed to find robust evidence of positive knowledge spillovers from multinational investment, often muted by the negative effects from increased competition (see Blomström and Kokko 1998; Mohnen 2001 for a review). But even when abstracting from competition effects, the potential benefits from FDI may not materialize, since a critical factor to exploit spillovers is the *technological capability of indigenous firms* (Blomström and Kokko 1998).

Survey-level evidence provides more direct proof of technology transfers arising through affiliates of foreign firms. In a UK survey, Mansfield and Romeo (1980) found that two-thirds of the sampled firms indicated that their technological capabilities were raised by technology transfers from US firms to their overseas UK subsidiaries. But only 20 per cent felt that this effect was important. More recently, the empirical literature on technology transfers has turned to using patent information to trace knowledge spillovers. The use of patent citation information for measuring knowledge spillovers was pioneered by Jaffe, Trajtenberg and Henderson (1993). They used patent citation data to show that proximity matters and that being close to an external information source increases the impact of citation on the source. Patent citation information can also be used to trace technology transfers from *local sources to foreign subsidiaries* in search of a technology sourcing motivation. Almeida (1996), using USA patent citations counts on a sample of foreign subsidiaries in the US semiconductor industry, finds foreign subsidiaries to cite regionally located firms significantly more. Branstetter (2000) found Japanese firms investing in the USA to have a significantly higher probability of citing other US firms' patents. Frost (1998) also found subsidiaries to be citing local sources. Furthermore, proximity mattered a lot, since patents from subsidiaries cited other entities located in the same state. Simultaneously, these patent citation studies document the *reverse spillovers* from foreign subsidiaries to the local economy. Almeida (1996) for instance, finds that patents belonging to foreign firms investing in the USA are cited more by local USA firms than other foreign firms. Branstetter (2000) also finds a higher probability of USA firms citing Japanese firms when they invest in the USA, supporting positive technology transfers through FDI.

The choice between centralizing and decentralizing R&D also has implications on the *internal know-how flows* between parents and subsidiaries. For centrally developed innovations, know-how flows basically from parents to subsidiaries. When subsidiaries are assigned a role in accessing and developing local specific know-how, this local know-how needs to flow to corporate level within a global innovation strategy. Recent studies can more easily provide evidence for the transfers of know-how from parents to affiliates, but find less conclusive support for the reverse direction – from subsidiaries to headquarters. Frost (1998), using US Patent and Trademarks Office patent citation data for 1980–90, found evidence for the importance of headquarters patents for the innovations of subsidiaries, while patent citation data provided only limited evidence for the transfer of know-how from subsidiaries to headquarters. Fors (1997) finds parent R&D to significantly influence host output growth, while subsidiary R&D fails to influence significantly home output growth (see also Patel and Vega 1999). On the mechanisms used to effectively transfer know-how within MNEs, Reger (2001) reports *personnel transfer* as important.

Veugelers and Cassiman (2002, 2003), using survey data from a sample of Belgian innovation active manufacturing firms rather than patents, directly assess the occurrence of technology transfers between subsidiaries and other external local partners in both directions. Furthermore, they can identify directly internal technology transfers between parents and subsidiaries. These data seem to suggest that, first of all, most manufacturing subsidiaries of foreign companies are R&D active. This R&D decentralisation is associated with important know-how flows (1) internally from headquarters to subsidiaries but also, although perhaps of less importance, (2) from subsidiaries to headquarters. At the same time there are external spillovers (3) from the local economy to the subsidiary, as a technology sourcing motive would suggest, but also reciprocally (4) from the subsidiary to the local economy. But the data also suggest an asymmetry in importance of external knowledge flows, with foreign subsidiaries more likely to be acquiring local know-how than to be transferring know-how to the local economy. It is interesting to note that in comparison to domestic firms, foreign subsidiaries report far fewer cases of know-how transfers through personnel mobility, suggesting that subsidiaries succeed better in keeping their human capital, thus protecting their know-how from spilling out.

A model for the MNE's decision to decentralize R&D

We will describe here the structure and main implications of a game-theory model, developed in Sanna-Randaccio and Veugelers (2002), which allows us to analyse more carefully the drivers of R&D internationalisation. The model considers R&D decentralization as a choice which allows firms to use the specific know-how of the subsidiary and avoids the need to adapt centrally developed innovations to local markets. In addition, R&D subsidiaries can be used to source locally available external know-how. But the MNE has to *organize* the transfer of local know-how internally so as to be able to benefit from this location-specific know-how throughout the organisation. At the same time, decentralisation of R&D to the subsidiary level intensifies the challenge of effectively appropriating core technology know-how, since-locating R&D resources in the foreign market will more easily lead to the spilling over of valuable know-how to local competitors.

The model will be briefly and non-formally described here. We consider two countries. The first country is the home base of a MNE, which is a monopolist in its home market and controls a production subsidiary in the host country, where a local producer also operates. The MNE has to decide whether to concentrate all its R&D at the headquarters or to decentralize part of its R&D activities to the subsidiary. The decentralization decision of multinational R&D is studied in a two-stage game. In the first-stage, the MNE undertakes its R&D location choice. In the second stage the subsidiary and the local producer, competing in production quantities with differentiated products, decide simultaneously how much to produce and sell in the host country, while the parent chooses as a monopolist the output to be sold in its home country. This two-stage setting allows us to emphasize the (local) competitive implications from R&D decentralization decisions. MNEs need to anticipate how their choice – on whether to decentralize R&D or not – will impact spillover patterns and hence competition in the (*local*) *product market*.

The model set-up

Technological innovation

Both the MNE and the foreign competitor are considered to be engaged in product innovation, which results in an improved product[1]. Taking a short-run perspective, we assume a fixed R&D budget at the corporate level. This allows us to focus on the issue of how to allocate the fixed R&D budget between headquarter and subsidiary. Although the MNE's R&D resources are fixed at the corporate level, the R&D resources individually available to the parent and the subsidiary vary according to the MNE's R&D location decision. The MNE can locate all of its R&D resources in the home country. This is the case of *centralization*. Alternatively, it can locate a share of its total R&D resources in the host country, assigning an innovative task to the subsidiary, which is the case of *decentralization*.

The total knowledge which each plant can use for product innovation (defined as *effective* know-how) is not only composed of own R&D resources, but also includes the know-how which the unit absorbs from other plants within the same firm or from other firms. As to *internal knowledge transfer* between subsidiary and parent, the know-how generated by the MNE in each market is transferred to the other unit. These internal transfers are imperfect, not only because of the costs associated with transferring know-how but also because of the need to adapt transferred know-how to local conditions. The more similar the home and the foreign market, the smaller the need for adaptation.

As to *external knowledge transfer* between the MNE and the local competitor, we assume that there is knowledge dissemination only if there is R&D proximity, in this way capturing the fact that external spillovers are geographically bounded. This implies that only when the MNE decides to decentralize its R&D will there be external spillovers with the local competition. These spillovers are two-way. On the one hand, decentralization creates for the MNE the possibility to source local know-how, but on the other hand, locating R&D resources to local market open up these resources for spillovers to local competitors. The assumption of localized spillovers furthermore implies that there is no dissipation to the local firm of know-how developed centrally and not transferred to the subsidiary.

In addition we account for the fact that the extent to which each unit benefits from external spillovers depends on the absorption capacity of the receiver. The own R&D resources serve to develop the absorptive capacity of the plant.

In total, the effective know-how base that a plant has at its disposition to generate innovations is composed of: own R&D resources *plus* R&D resources from affiliated companies which are (at a cost) transferred internally *plus* R&D resources which are absorbed (imperfectly) from firms located in the same geographic market – at least if and to the extent that the plant has own R&D resources to absorb the external know-how.

Market competition

Firms compete in the product market, which represents the second stage of the game. The effective know-how base will lead to product innovations which improve the product characteristics and hence lead to a larger willingness to pay of the customers for the firm's product. While the parent firm is a monopolist in its home market, in the foreign market the subsidiary and the local competitor are engaged in (quantity) competition. In order to evaluate the effect of the intensity of product competition in the host country, we have allowed for the possibility of differentiation between the goods produced by the subsidiary and the local firm.

The costs and benefits of R&D decentralization for the MNE

A MNE will decide to decentralize its R&D activities – that is, to assign a role in its overall research effort to the subsidiary operating in a foreign country – if its overall profitability (the sum of parent and subsidiary profitability) increases as compared to the case of centralization. We should therefore assess the overall effect from R&D decentralisation on MNE profitability, giving due consideration not only to the impact on the subsidiary profitability but also to the effects on parent profitability and to the role of the additional costs due to forgone economies of scale in R&D.

The impact of R&D decentralization on subsidiary profitability

R&D decentralization influences the subsidiary's profitability via three effects:

The benefits from avoiding adaptation of central innovations by the subsidiary (B.1).
A first positive effect is connected to the *adaptation motive* for R&D decentralization. When the MNE allocates R&D resources to the host country instead of devoting them to the parent lab, the foreign lab's innovative effort can be tailored to satisfy local needs since it benefits from proximity with local production. The subsidiary can thus avoid the adaptation costs that it would have to incur if the MNE had chosen to centralize all R&D in the home country. Effect B.1 can also be interpreted as reflecting the ability of the subsidiary to better tailor its products to local requirements (the same amount of R&D has a more powerful market enhancing effect if invested in the host market rather than at the parent level). The benefits of localizing R&D where the market is will be greater the more the knowledge generated centrally by the parent needs to be adapted to local conditions.

The benefits from the incoming external spillovers to the subsidiary (B.2).
The second positive effect reflects the *supply-related motives* for R&D decentralization, connected with the technology sourcing motive. It captures the effect of incoming external spillovers which arise because of the proximity between the subsidiary lab and the local producer lab. By decentralizing R&D, the MNE becomes able to use its subsidiary to absorb know-how from the local firm, benefiting from incoming external spillovers. The positive effect of incoming external spillovers on subsidiary profitability is not affected by product market competition.

The costs for the subsidiary from outgoing external spillovers (C.1). There are also dangers associated to locating R&D resources close to local competitors, since there are also *outgoing external spillovers*. Owing to lab proximity, at least part of the know-how created by the subsidiary will leak to the local competitor. The dissemination of subsidiary's own R&D to the local firm has a negative impact on subsidiary profitability since it increases local firm competitiveness in the host market. The outgoing external spillovers thus affect the firm's profitability via product market competition. The intensity of the negative impact of the outgoing external spillovers depends on the degree to which foreign and local products are differentiated. The more similar the products are and thus the more intense the product market competition, the higher the costs of R&D proximity. The extent to which the local producer can benefit from these spillovers depends on its *absorptive capacity* which in turn is determined by its own R&D resources. Thus the stronger the know-how base of the local competitor, the larger the negative impact on subsidiary profits of the outgoing external spillovers. A weaker local competitor with less absorptive capacity will be able to learn less, in which case the cost of outgoing external spillovers will be smaller for the MNE.

The impact of R&D decentralization on parent plant profitability

R&D decentralization influences the parent's profitability through two effects:

The costs due to lower R&D resources for the parent plant (C.2). Since we consider the total amount of resources devoted to R&D by the MNE as fixed, the choice of allocating R&D abroad implies lower R&D resources at home, at least in the short run. This has a negative impact on parent equilibrium output and hence profitability. This effect is at least partly compensated by the fact that the subsidiary transfers the know-how it creates back to the parent. This transfer is, however, imperfect. The negative effect is thus mitigated by internal transfers, and hence depends on the ability of the subsidiary to transfer know-how to the central level.

The benefits from the incoming external spillovers to the parent (B.3). R&D decentralization has a positive effect on parent profitability because, by innovating in loco, the MNE becomes able to gain access to the *foreign pool of potential spillovers* generated by local producers. The extent to which the parent benefits from the incoming external spillovers depends on how much the subsidiary will learn, which depends on the *absorption capacity* of the subsidiary which is a function of the latter's own R&D resources. However the benefit for the parent depends also on whether the subsidiary transfers back the acquired knowledge to the headquarters.

The results clearly indicate that the ability of the subsidiary to channel back know-how is a crucial determinant of the effect of R&D decentralization on parent profitability, and thus *internal knowledge management* within the MNE has a pivotal role for the success of R&D investment abroad. Our model thus highlights the importance of the interaction between *internal and external knowledge transfer mechanisms*.

The impact of R&D decentralization on MNEs' total profits

To summarize we have in total six effects that form the benefits and the costs from decentralization on the overall MNE profitability: B.1, B.2, B.3 and C.1, C.2 discussed above, to which we should add the costs from forgone economies of scale in R&D (C.3).

When the external spillover parameter is symmetric – for instance, when the intensity of external technological spillovers is sector – or technology-specific – the *subsidiary* profits will certainly increase when R&D is decentralized. This is the case since the positive effect of the incoming external spillovers is direct, while the negative effect of the outgoing external spillovers is mediated via competition in the product market.

On the other hand, even if the intensity of external spillovers is symmetric, the *parent's* profitability does not necessarily rise. This requires internal spillovers from the subsidiary to be sufficiently large. If internal transmission of know-how is low, R&D decentralization leads to a fall in parent plant profits and a rise in subsidiary profits. The size of both effects is increasing with relative market size. We should therefore expect that within this scenario R&D investment abroad is more likely to be undertaken by MNEs based in small countries which invest in larger markets. When internal transmission of know-how is sufficiently effective, R&D decentralization leads to a rise in both subsidiary and parent plant profitability. If this is the case, the tradeoffs between the rise in subsidiary profits and fall in parent's profits vanish.

When we combine both results, we find that relative market size is relevant only when internal transmission of know-how is low. Hence the trend towards increasing efficiency of internal know-how transfers, brought about through (for instance) improvements in Information and Communication Technology and a greater awareness of the importance of know-how management, would be predicted by our model to lead to a reduction in importance of relative market size as a factor explaining R&D decentralization patterns.

The drivers of the R&D decentralization decisions by MNEs

Rather than evaluating the conditions required for decentralization of R&D, we will concentrate here on discussing factors that can promote R&D decentralization by analysing the effects of *exogenous drivers* for the overall net profit evaluation from R&D decentralization. Of particular interest as factors influencing the R&D decentralization decision by MNE from a technology sourcing perspective are the *local know-how base* and the *mechanisms to transfer know-how* internally and externally.

Local know-how base

A first important factor affecting the R&D decentralization decision, is the local know-how base. We know that a strong local know-how base is positive from a technology sourcing perspective, since it increases the benefits from incoming external spillovers for both the subsidiary and the parent (B.2 and B.3). But at the same time it enlarges the cost of outgoing external spillovers (C.1), since the local rival will have a stronger absorptive capacity.

When evaluating the overall effect, it turns out that due to the cost of outgoing external spillovers, the local know-how base is not a unequivocally positive factor for R&D decentralization. This will happen when the cost of outgoing external spillovers becomes very important. These cost will start to dominate when the learning is asymmetric (the intensity of outgoing external spillovers is high, while that of incoming external spillovers is low) and competition is strong. To understand this result, it should be noted that while the positive effect of the incoming external spillovers is direct, the negative effect of the outgoing external spillovers is mediated via competition in the product market. The latter effect is thus more intense the greater the substitutability between the goods produced by the MNE's subsidiary and by the local producer.

The model thus predicts that a large local know-how base is more likely to attract the location of R&D activity from foreign firms operating in different industries than from direct competitors. This result is in line with Cantwell and Kosmopoulou (2002) who, studying the R&D activity undertaken abroad by the 792 world largest industrial firms, find that 'inward penetration in location of technological excellence tends to be low in the same industry, but attract to a greater extent the investments of stronger firms from other industries' (p. 26).

Whether a strong local know-how base works as a factor attracting R&D FDI depends on (local) competition. In the special case when the MNE subsidiary and the local firms are not direct competitors in production the negative effect for the MNE of the involuntary dissemination of its subsidiary know-how to local producers vanishes. In this case, the local know-how base is a unequivocal positive factor for decentralizing R&D. Two cases come to mind where there are external spillovers with no interaction in product market:

- The subsidiary and the local firms use related technologies but are *unrelated in the product market*. This may be due to vertical relationships between producers such as in the case of a producer of a complex good with its components suppliers or of the producer of a discrete product with a process equipment supplier (interindustry spillovers)
- When the local party is a *public research institution* (universities or government labs), the local source of know-how has no production activities. In this case the subsidiary and local partners relate also only at the technological level. Note that in this case it is less likely that the know-how relates to development activities, but rather to fundamental research.

Internal transfer of know-how

Another important factor determining the size of both benefits and costs to decentralization is the process of *internal transfer of know-how* within the MNE. We find that a more efficient internal know-how transfer process within the MNE *from the subsidiary* to the parent unequivocally acts to promote R&D decentralization. A better internal transfer of know-how from subsidiary to parent results in lower costs of decentralization (lower C.2) and in larger benefits from incoming external spillovers to the parent (higher B.3).

But on the other hand, a more efficient transfer of know-how *from the parent* to the subsidiary makes the motive for avoiding adaptation by the subsidiary less important. Nevertheless, it does not always discourage the MNE from investing abroad in R&D.

External transfer of know-how

Since both parent and subsidiary enjoy higher profits in decentralization when there are more spillovers *from the local source* (see (B.3) and (B.2)), we have that higher spillovers *from* the local source to the MNE unequivocally acts as an incentivator for R&D decentralization. But, of course, since subsidiary profits will decrease with higher spillovers *to* the local source (see C.1), a rise in the intensity of external spillovers from subsidiary to local producers will disincentivate decentralization. Hence, being able to prevent spillovers to the local source unequivocally improves the case for R&D decentralization, as well improving the ability to learn more efficiently from external sources.

Size of R&D resources decentralized

A final important factor to consider as a complementary force for technology sourcing is the amount of R&D resources allocated to the subsidiary. These resources serve as *absorption capacity* for external know-how acquisition. However, at the same time, we have to take into account that the amounts of R&D resources which are decentralized to the local market are open for *appropriation by local competition.*

A higher external spillover level from local sources and a better ability to use subsidiary know-how at corporate level will push the MNE, when deciding on the optimal amount of decentralizing of R&D resources, to allocate more resources to the subsidiary level. On the contrary, a high level of outgoing external spillovers – that is, a low level of appropriability – will lead the MNE to allocate fewer R&D resources to the subsidiary. A sufficiently large incoming external spillover level, while having weak competition or high enough appropriability of subsidiary know-how, are sufficient conditions for the size of the local know-how base to act as a stimulus for allocating more R&D resources to the subsidiary.

A summary of the main findings

This chapter provides a theoretical framework to discuss the tradeoffs which a MNE faces when it assigns a foreign subsidiary an active role in innovation, thus organizing its R&D as decentralized instead of centralized. The proposed model, building further on stylized facts on R&D internationalisation, analyses how the interplay of internal and external knowledge flows interacts with the nature of host market competition to influence a MNE choosing whether to disperse its R&D internationally. The chapter focuses on cases in which R&D activities are undertaken abroad in association with production.

The model highlights the importance of the intensity of competition in the local market in determining the size of both benefits and costs to R&D decentralization. In the absence of local competitors in production, the subsidiary will always profit from R&D decentralization in our model. But even if there is local competition to worry about, the cost from outgoing external spillovers is typically outweighed by the benefit from incoming external spillovers at the subsidiary level, at least when external spillovers are symmetric. In this case, R&D decentralization becomes more profitable the larger is the know-how base in the local economy that can be sourced. However, when competition is strong and the external spillovers are asymmetric, and sufficiently in disfavour of the MNE, a strong local know-how base is no longer a motive for R&D decentralization. While it increases the benefits from incoming external spillovers for both the subsidiary and the parent, it at the same time enlarges the cost of outgoing external spillovers, since the local rival will have a stronger *absorptive capacity*.

Hence, when R&D is undertaken abroad in association with production, the local knowledge base is not unequivocally a 'pulling' factor attracting R&D investments by foreign MNEs, depending on the level of competition in local markets. The model thus predicts that a strong local knowledge base is more likely to attract inward R&D FDI by foreign firms operating in different industries than by direct competitors.

We also find that a more efficient internal know-how transfer process within the MNE from the subsidiary to the parent unequivocally acts to promote R&D decentralization. It will increase the benefits from incoming external spillovers to the parent. But, on the other hand, a more efficient transfer of know-how from the parent to the subsidiary makes the motive for avoiding adaptation by the subsidiary less important. Nevertheless it does not always discourage the MNE from investing abroad in R&D. The results clearly illustrate the *complementarity* between an efficient internal and external knowledge management system and the technology sourcing motive for R&D decentralization. A better internal know-how transfer process within the multinational increases the efficiency of mechanisms used to source external know-how and vice versa. Another important complementary force increasing the efficiency of technology sourcing is the decentralized know-how base of the subsidiary, which serves to absorb local know-how.

In addition, the results suggest that, when internal know-how transfer mechanisms are not very efficient, R&D investment abroad is more likely to be undertaken by MNEs based in small countries which invest in larger markets. With a fall in the cost of intracompany technology transfers – due, for example, to the technological developments in ICT or more attention devoted to know-how management – relative market size loses importance as a critical factor shaping the pattern of R&D internationalization.

While the model allows us to discuss the forces driving the costs and benefits of R&D decentralization within MNEs, a full characterization of the decentralization choice of the firm is bounded by the complexity of the setting. Our future research will move towards obtaining predictions from the model which can be tested against data on R&D decentralization. Extending the theoretical model, such as to allow for endogeneous R&D resources, or local competitors reciprocally locating R&D abroad, will encourage model results which are closer to most empirical settings.

Note

1. The model can easily be adjusted to include the case of process innovations, improving the efficiency of production.

References

Almeida, P. (1996) 'Knowledge Sourcing by Foreign MNEs: Patent Citation Analysis in the US Semiconductor Industry', *Strategic Management Journal*, 155–65.

Audretsch, D. and M. Feldman (1996) 'R&D Spillovers and the Geography of Innovation and Production', *American Economic Review*, 86, 630–40.

Bartlett, C. and S. Ghoshal (1997) 'Managing Innovation in the Transnational Corporation', in M. Tushman and P. Anderson (eds), *Managing Strategic Innovation and Change* (Oxford: Oxford University Press), 452–76.

Blomström, M. and A. Kokko (1998) 'Multinational Corporations and Spillovers', *Journal of Economic Surveys*, 12(3), 247–77.

Branstetter, L. (2000) 'Is FDI a Channel of Knowledge Spillovers? Evidence from Japanese FDI', NBER WP, 8015.

Cantwell, J. A. and E. Kosmopoulou (2002) 'What Determines the Internationalisation of Corporate Technology?', in M. Forsgren, L. Hakanson and V. Havila (eds), *Critical Perspectives on Internationalisation* (Oxford: Pergamon Press).

Caves, R. (1996) *Multinational Enterprise and Economic Analysis* (Cambridge: Cambridge University Press).

Cohen W. and D. Levinthal (1989) 'Innovation and Learning: The Two Faces of R&D', *Economic Journal*, 99, 569–96.

Das, S. (1987) 'Externalities and Technology Transfer through Multinational Corporations', *Journal of International Economics*, 22, 171–82.

De Bondt, R. (1996) 'Spillovers and Innovative Activities', *International Journal of Industrial Organisation*, 15, 1–28.

Dunning, J. (1988) 'The Eclectic Paradigm of International Production: A Re-statement and Some Possible Extensions', *Journal of International Business Studies*, 19, 1–31.

Ethier, W. and J. Markusen (1996) 'Multinational Firms, Technology Diffusion and Trade', *Journal of International Economics*, 41, 1–28.

Florida, R. (1997) 'The Globalisation of R&D: Results of a Survey of Foreign Affiliated R&D labs', *US Research Policy*, vol. 26, 85–103.

Fors, G. (1997) 'Utilization of R&D Results in the Home and Foreign Plants of Multinationals', *Journal of Industrial Economics*, 45, 341–55.

Fosfuri, A. (2000) 'Patent Protection, Imitation and Mode of Technology Transfer', *International Journal of Industrial Organisation*, 18, 1129–49.

Frost, A. (1998) The Geographic Sources of Innovation in the Multinational Enterprise: US Subsidiaries and Host Country Spillovers, 1980–1990, PhD dissertation, Sloan School of Management, MIT.

Gersbach, H. and A. Schmutzler (1999) 'External Spillovers, Internal Spillovers and the Geography of Production and Innovation', *Regional Science and Urban Economics*, 29, 679–96.

Grandstrand, O., L. Hakanson and S. Sjolander (eds), *Technology Management and International Business* (New York: Wiley).

Hakanson, L. (1992) 'Locational Determinants of Foreign R&D in Swedish Multi-nationals', in O. Grandstrand, L. Hakanson and S. Sjolander (eds), *Technology Management and International Business* (New York: Wiley) 97–116.

Jaffe, A., M. Trajtenberg and R. Henderson (1993) 'Geographic Localisation of Knowledge Spillovers as Evidenced by Patent Citations', *Quarterly Journal of Economics* 108(3), 577–98.

Kamien, M. and I. Zang (2000) 'Meet Me Halfway: Research Joint Ventures and Absorptive Capacity', *International Journal of Industrial Organization*, 18(7), 995–1012

Kuemmerle, W. (1997) 'Building Effective R&D Capabilities Abroad', *Harvard Business Review* 75(2), 61–70.

Mansfield, E. and A. Romeo (1980) 'Technology Transfer to Overseas Subsidiaries by US Based Firms', *Quarterly Journal of Economics,* 95(4), 737–50.

Mohnen, P. (2001) 'International R&D Spillovers and Economic Growth', in M.Pohjola (ed.), *Information technology, Productivity and Economic Growth* (Oxford: Oxford University Press).

Patel, P. and K. Pavitt (1992) 'Large Firms in the Production of the World's Tech-nology: An Important Case of Non-Globalisation', in O. Grandstrand, L. Hakanson and S. Sjolander (eds), *Technology Management and International Business* (New York: Wiley), 53–74.

Patel, P. and M. Vega (1999) 'Patterns of Internationalisation of Corporate Techno-logy: Location versus Home Country Advantages', *Research Policy*, 28, 145–56.

Pearce, R. (1999) 'Decentralized R&D and Strategic Competitiveness: Globalised Approaches to Generation and Use of Technology in MNEs', *Research Policy*, 28, 157–78.

Pearce, R. and S. Singh (1992) 'Internationalisation of R&D among the World's Leading Enterprises: Survey Analysis of Organisation and Motivation', in O. Grandstrand, L. Hakanson and S. Sjolander (eds), *Technology Management and International Business* (New York: Wiley), 137–62.

Reger, G. (2001) 'Differences in the Internationalisation of Research and Technology between Western European, Japanese and North American Companies', University of Brandenburg, Mimeo.

Sanna-Randaccio, F. and R. Veugelers (2002) 'Multinational Knowledge Spillovers with Centralised vs Decentralised R&D: A Game-Theoretic Approach', CEPR Discussion Paper, 3151.

Serapio, M. and D. Dalton (1999) 'Globalisation of Industrial R&D: An Examination of FDI in R&D', *US, Research Policy*, 28, 303–16.

Siotis, G. (1999) 'Foreign Direct Investment Strategies and Firm Capabilities', *Journal of Economics and Management Strategy*, 8, 251–70.

Van Pottelsberghe de la Potterie, B. and F. Lichtenberg (2001) 'Does FDI Transfer Technology across Borders?', *Review of Economics and Statistics*, 83, 490–7.

Veugelers, R. and B. Cassiman (2002) 'Innovative Strategies and Know-How Flows in International Companies: Some Evidence from Belgian Manufacturing', in R. Lipsey and J. L. Muchielli (eds), *Multinational Firms and Impact on Employment, Trade and Technology* (London: Routledge).

———— (2004) 'Foreign Subsidiaries as a Channel of International Technology Diffusion: Some Direct Firm Level Evidence from Belgium', *European Economic Review*, 48, 455–76.

Von Zedwit, M. and O. Gassmann (2000) 'Market versus Technology Drive in R&D Internationalization: Four Different Patterns of Managing Research and Development', *Research Policy*, 31, 569–88.

Wang, J. and M. Blomström (1992) 'Foreign Investment and Technology Transfer: A Simple Model', *European Economic Review*, 137–55.

Westney, E. (1997) 'Multinational Enterprises and Cross-Border Knowledge Creation', Sloan Working Paper, edited by MIT 159–97.

13

Multinational Investment and Organizational Risk: A Real Options Approach

Jeffrey J. Reuer and Tony W. Tong

Introduction

Real options theory ascribes unique advantages to the multinational corporation (MNC). By straddling distinct environments determined by country borders, the MNC is positioned to shift value-chain activities across its network of operations in response to changes in foreign exchange rates, factor and product market conditions and so forth (Kogut 1989; Kogut and Kulatilaka 1994). The basic premise is that the MNC possesses a portfolio of *switching options*, which are not available to rivals maintaining purely domestic operations. Relative to other perspectives on foreign direct investment (FDI), real options theory therefore highlights several unique advantages that accrue to the firm, including dynamic production efficiencies, downside risk reduction and the ability to seize opportunities that may materialize over time. Many scholars have noted the MNC's operational flexibility and have pointed out the need to understand better the obstacles to realizing value from multinational operation (for example, Dunning and Rugman 1985; Kogut 1985; Ghoshal 1987; Buckley and Casson 1998).

Existing empirical findings in the international strategy literature paint a somewhat mixed picture for the core predictions of real options theory, however. One the one hand, evidence exists that MNCs do shift sourcing decisions in response to foreign exchange rate movements (Rangan 1998), though such shifts tend to be fairly modest. FDI also reduces firms' economic exposures (for instance, Miller and Reuer 1998; Pantzalis, Simkins and Laux 2001), and clearly there are many studies that have found positive performance and risk outcomes associated with multinational investment (for example, Doukas and Travlos 1988; Morck and Yeung 1992; Kim, Hwang and Burgers 1993; Allen and Pantzalis 1996; see Caves 1996 for a comprehensive review). On the other hand, many studies have produced inconsistent results or have challenged a simple linear relationship between multinationality and either firm performance or risk (for example, Mitchell, Shaver and Yeung 1992; Caves 1996; Reeb, Kwok and Baek 1998; Kotabe, Srinivasan and Aulakh 2002).

In this chapter, we attempt to identify some of the obstacles that firms face in realizing the benefits held out by real options theory and to disentangle some of these mixed findings. We believe that such an effort can help to advance the theory and its application in international strategy and management research more broadly by clarifying the theory's boundary conditions. Our analysis does this by explicitly accounting for unobserved capabilities that lead firms to go global, by incorporating coordination costs that also can attend FDI dispersion and the development of a portfolio of switching options and by including features of the MNC network that determine such costs. For example, as a firm develops extensive operations throughout the world, not only may the marginal benefits of switching options decline, but the firm may face increased marginal costs from greater *coordination complexity* (Roth, Schweiger and Morrison 1991) and from *information processing* loads borne by top managers (for instance, Jones and Hill 1988). In the parlance of options theory, such costs may be seen as *carrying costs* that reduce the benefits of holding a portfolio of options.

In the empirical analysis that we conducted, we focused on the implications of multinationality for different dimensions of firms' downside risk. Although related empirical predictions might be made for other organizational outcomes, our emphasis on downside risk reduction is attractive for several reasons. Perhaps most importantly, the downside conceptualization of risk used in this study aligns well with the basic theoretical arguments of real options theory. Formally stated, a real option confers the right, but not the obligation, to take some specified future action. Real options theoretically can reduce the downside risk of an uncertain project because the option investment is sunk and future investment is discretionary. As McGrath states, 'the distinguishing characteristic of an options approach lies in firms making investments that confer the ability to select an outcome only if it is favorable' (1997, p. 975). If firms can limit downside losses to initial investments (Kogut 1991), avoid future outlays in the event of negative signals and position themselves to seize upside opportunities in individual projects in a selective manner, then firms' downside risk levels will decline as they build portfolios of real options (Bowman and Hurry 1993). Miller and Reuer (1996) discuss other reasons why researchers might find it valuable to adopt downside measures of risk rather than the traditional measures used in finance and strategy research.

The remainder of the chapter proceeds as follows: in the next section, we identify three important contingencies that can adversely affect the net benefits that firms derive from multinationality – the complexity of the multinational network, the coordination challenges stemming from cultural differences across foreign operations and incentive misalignments arising from shared ownership with local parties in foreign subsidiaries. We then highlight some of the key findings of our empirical study. Four main findings stand out from our analyses:

(1) MNCs do not generally experience lower levels of *downside risk* than domestic firms. In fact, after accounting for the endogeneity of FDI, we note that bankruptcy risk is positively affected by FDI. In other words, part of the relationship between FDI and risk observed in prior research might be due to unobserved firm capabilities and other factors that led firms to go global, rather than the FDI decision *per se*.

(2) When we allow for non-monotonic effects of multinationality, we find that the relationship is *U-shaped*. Bankruptcy risk and income stream risk fall as a firm successively invests in different host countries, yet more dispersed FDI elevates downside risk after a threshold is reached. The fact that the relationship between FDI dispersion and risk is contingent upon the firm's level of multinationality speaks to the initial benefits of globalization, the declining marginal benefits of acquiring switching options and the coordination challenges that arise as firms enter many foreign locations.

(3) Also consistent with the view that coordination costs are important sources of carrying costs, we find that downside risk increases with the *average cultural distance* between the firm's home base and its foreign subsidiaries. Coordination across firms' foreign subsidiaries, and hence the implementation of switching options, is easier when the firm has foreign subsidiaries in culturally similar locations.

(4) The effects of *subsidiary ownership* are insignificant, which is consistent with offsetting growth options available through partial ownership. This finding could also imply that there is a lack of a need for full ownership for effective systemwide management of switching options.

The chapter concludes with a discussion of some of the implications of these findings for future research on real options and international strategy.

Background theory

One of the main implications of the real options view of the MNC as a portfolio of switching options is that the firm's downside risk should decline as the firm invests in foreign subsidiaries that are geographically dispersed. As noted above, the switching options acquired by the firm confer the right, but not the obligation, to shift value-chain activities across its foreign subsidiaries as market conditions change. Such shifts may be triggered by changes in local demand, labour expenses, other input costs, competitors' actions and so forth. For example, Kogut and Kulatilaka (1994) model a MNC's decision to shift production across countries in response to changes in exchange rates. Firms with options to shift production across countries are able to achieve a lower overall cost structure than firms embedded in a single-country environment and subject to its uncertainty. However, empirical research provides no evidence that multinationality reduces different dimensions of firms' downside risk (Reuer and Leiblein 2000), which suggests that significant obstacles exist for firms to actually realize the benefits that real option theory emphasizes. Below we identify several such obstacles.

It is worth beginning with the general observation that firms are likely to bring their distinctive strengths, as well as their shortcomings, into their international operations (for instance, Hymer 1976). These may include not only intangible assets and monopoly power, but particular *administrative heritages and control systems* (Rangan 1998). This suggests that the relationship between FDI and risk may be confounded by many unobserved firm characteristics. For example, firms may experience lower downside risk when they go global, not because of the decision to engage in FDI *per se* but because of the unobserved capabilities that led them to go global in the first place, perhaps for reasons other than obtaining real options. Thus, in order to examine the effects of decisions concerning FDI dispersion, we wish to account for the possibility of self-selection in order to address potential biases in interpreting the effects of the FDI decision. Shaver (1998) illustrates the importance of this issue in an investigation of firms' foreign market entry mode decisions. However, even after one accounts for factors other than obtaining real options that propel firms to global, the relationship between FDI dispersion and organizational downside risk might not be negative and linear for several reasons, to which we turn next.

The first issue that we wish to explore is whether the relationship between FDI dispersion and risk is *constant at different levels of multi-nationality*. We suspect that it may not be for two reasons. First, as firms successively enter foreign countries, the marginal benefits of obtaining more switching options are likely to decline at some point. For example, in Kogut and Kulatilaka's (1994) model of production switching options and foreign exchange rate movements, firms can exploit the movements of different currencies by entering new locations. Nevertheless, while the number of currencies is quite large, they can effectively be reduced to a small set of underlying factors due to their co-movements (Miller and Reuer 1998), which limits the marginal benefits of obtaining more options as multinationality becomes large.

Second, as the firm enters more and more foreign countries, this implies greater *complexity and coordination costs* for managers attempting to manage a portfolio of subsidiaries (for example, Jones and Hill 1988; Roth, Schweiger and Morrison 1991). For instance, not only do managers need to perceive latent options in international networks, they also must monitor *external cues* to make decisions concerning the exercise of options and design appropriate organizational systems to facilitate the shifting of value-chain activities (for example, Kogut 1985). These factors suggest that firms may not fully reap the flexibility benefits of FDI dispersion. More-over, combined with the likely declining marginal benefits of switching options as multinationality increases, these coordination costs may outweigh the benefits of FDI into new countries at high levels of multi-nationality. In other words, the relationship between multinationality and downside risk may not only be curvilinear but *non-monotonic*, with firms' risk levels increasing beyond some threshold of FDI dispersion.

There are many specific, and different, sources of coordination costs that can influence the net benefits that firms derive, or fail to derive, from their portfolios of foreign subsidiaries. One that has been heavily emphasized in the international literature is *national cultural differences* and the resulting internal uncertainty that arises for the firm. Such differences have been related to diverse outcomes such as the lower survival of ventures abroad (Barkema, Bell and Pennings 1996); limits on the leveraging of brands, technology, and other know-how (Davidson and McFetridge 1985; Hennart 1991); and post-merger integration costs in international acquisitions (for example, Kogut and Singh 1988).

Cultural differences throughout a firm's portfolio of foreign subsidiaries can reduce the benefits the firm attains from its latent options, for several reasons. Because managers may be uncomfortable with, or even disagree with, the operating values and procedures of the host country, they are likely to rely more heavily on local parties for management systems rather than use a standard control system (Gatignon and Anderson 1988). Marketing strategies are similarly likely to be adjusted significantly to the local environment. The local tailoring of systems and even strategies implies that the uniformity required for operating flexibly and shifting value-chain activities across locations is likely to be constrained. Even if firms attempt to exercise greater control over their foreign operations, transaction costs are likely to be higher due to encoding and decoding gaps in communication (Root 1987), problems that encourage country managers to look after local objectives and resources (for example, Ghoshal and Nohria 1989) and also make it more difficult for the firm as a whole to manage option exercise decisions appropriately.

The final contingency that we examine is the *ownership structure* of the firm's portfolio of subsidiaries abroad. We suspect that a firm's ability to achieve operational flexibility and actually reduce downside risk through switching options will not only turn on the level of uniformity or tailoring of systems and functional policies across foreign subsidiaries, but also the distribution of control rights throughout the firm's network of operations. For instance, firms that maintain control over a foreign subsidiary will tend to be able to manage the operation based on the interests of the corporation as a whole, whereas local interests will become much more salient when local parties have a greater stake in decision making.

The international literature has long emphasized the relationship between the MNC's ownership of foreign affiliates and the firm's ability to make decisions based on global objectives. For example, Stopford and Wells (1972) noted that firm's ownership decisions for their foreign subsidiaries reflected a tradeoff between the firm's desire for control and its desire for resources. Firms will give up ownership and control of a foreign subsidiary when local parties offer valuable resources (see also Teece 1986).

Sharing ownership with local parties therefore has two effects on the firm's ability to operate flexibly by shifting value-chain activities across borders. First, it increases the likelihood of *value-chain incompatibilities* with other foreign operations due to the reliance on local resources. Second, it puts control rights in the hands of parties in the host countries, whose objectives are more likely to be *local*, or *country-specific*, rather than consistent with the MNC's global interests. The resulting conflicts will be reduced if the multinational firm entering the country with jointly owned facilities aimed at local market access, but the scope for integrated action with other foreign subsidiaries will be limited in this case. When the MNC instead has global objectives and a desire for operational flexibility across borders, the provision of local resources and the sharing of control rights with owners in the host country potentially obstructs the appropriate development and exercise of switching options. We therefore predict that firms with significant local ownership of their foreign subsidiaries will probably not have formed such foreign subsidiaries in order to achieve operational flexibility through switching options. Even if they had, the adverse effects of local ownership for the conformity of value chains across foreign subsidiaries and for the alignment of incentives potentially constrain the benefits of operational flexibility by reducing the opportunities for switching or increasing the costs of doing so.

Key findings

We tested the above predictions on a sample of 244 manufacturing firms based in the USA, 188 of which had investments in at least one foreign country. A more detailed discussion of the research methodology is available on request from the authors. In order to test the implications of FDI on organizational risk, we relied upon two measures of downside risk that reflect the firms' income stream risk and bankruptcy risk (see Miller and Reuer 1996 for technical details). We then regressed this measure of risk on firm-level factors such as the number of countries the firm had invested in, the average national cultural distance between the firms' home bases in the USA and their foreign subsidiaries and the percentage of wholly owned or majority owned subsidiaries in order to characterize the ownership structure of the firms' subsidiary networks, in addition to a number of control variables. Moreover, in order to account for unobserved factors that might influence the firms' decisions concerning FDI as well as their risk consequences, we employed a two-stage model that accounts for such unobserved heterogeneity and self-selection by firms expanding overseas.

Our first-stage FDI model indicated that more R&D intensive firms and larger firms were more likely to invest in foreign subsidiaries, and industry effects were also highly significant. This set of findings is consistent with prior research in the area (for example, Horst 1972; Buckley and Casson 1976; Hennart 1982; Grubaugh 1987; Caves 1996). For the full sample of firms, we found that FDI modestly increased the firm's bankruptcy risk and had no apparent effect on income stream risk in general. We also found that the term used to account for self-selection was significant, indicating that part of the FDI–risk relationship was due to unobserved capabilities and other factors that led firms to go global, rather than the FDI decision *per se*. For the sample of MNCs, we found that organizational risk first declined and then increased as firms progressively entered into more countries. This finding is consistent with the declining marginal benefits of multinationality as well as the increasing coordination complexity that arises as the firm's subsidiary network becomes more dispersed. Also supporting the significant coordination costs that MNCs' face, the firm's downside risk is positively related to the average cultural distance between its home base and the national cultures represented by its foreign subsidiaries. Firms operating in culturally similar countries are more apt to realize downside risk reduction from FDI dispersion than firms with foreign operations in culturally distant locations. Finally, we did not find that the ownership structure of foreign subsidiaries had an impact on the downside risk levels experienced by the MNC.

Discussion of results

One distinctive characteristic of MNCs relative to purely domestic firms is the movement of domestic operations to international contexts involving heterogeneous external environments. A natural question raised by the spatial dispersion of value-chain activities across these environments, therefore, is how multinationality influences MNCs' outcomes such as performance or risk. Indeed, this fundamental question has been a central pursuit of scholars of international strategy (for example, Grant, Jammine and Thomas 1988; Lee and Kwok 1988; Kim *et al.* 1993; Hitt, Hoskisson and Kim 1997; Reeb, Kwok and Baek 1998). Continuing this line of research, our study tested the downside risk implications of multinationality by explicitly accounting for *potential endogeneity problems* that have been neglected in prior econometric analyses of the multinational firm and by considering real options predictions and the role of potential coordination costs in order to develop a more contingent view of real options in the multinational firm.

To our knowledge, this study is among the first that has recognized the potential biases in models examining the organizational outcomes of the dispersion of FDI. Our results suggest that endogeneity does exist, and unobserved heterogeneity (for instance, firm-specific capabilities and managerial experiences) affecting firms' FDI decisions also affects their downside risk levels. These results bear a similarity to prior findings by

Mitchell, Shaver and Yeung (1992), who report that although MNCs tend to have a lower risk of business failure, the probability of survival is jeopardized by increasing and decreasing international presence. Thus, being a multinational may confer a number of advantages, but becoming multinational without the requisite capabilities and deliberation may be risky. In broad terms, the approach taken in this study offers a useful way of reconciling some of the mixed findings to date concerning the risk implication of FDI and multinational operations (for example, Lee and Kwok 1988; Kim, Hwang and Burgers 1993; Qian 1996; Reeb, Kwok and Baek 1998).

The U-shaped relationship between multinationality and downside risk we observed points to the double-edged role of multinationality in influencing downside risk. Consistent with real options theory, MNCs beginning to disperse their operations across country borders do enjoy advantages over their domestic counterparts. However, the marginal benefit of investing in more countries is likely to decline, and the marginal coordination costs are likely to increase, the net result being that risk levels increase beyond some value of multinationality.

We have also used the national cultural distance between the firm's home base and its foreign affiliates to understand the role of coordination costs in predictions from real options theory. More specifically, coordination costs increase not only with the sheer number of host countries in which the firm has operations (see for instance, Porter 1990), but also with the cultural differences across the businesses in the firm's portfolio due to complexities in transferring management practices abroad and the corresponding need to achieve local adaptation in the firm's value chain. Based on our findings concerning the non-monotonic relationship between multinationality and downside risk as well as the relevance of cultural heterogeneity in the firms' portfolio of foreign operations, we suspect that factors such as global strategy, organizational structure and management systems all are likely to influence individual firms' coordination costs and, as a consequence, their threshold values and ability to take on more culturally distant foreign operations. Future research on factors such as these that shape firms' capabilities to implement real options and limit carrying costs associated with coordinating multinational networks would be valuable. Viewing coordination costs as *carrying costs* associated with real options, therefore, helps to delineate the boundary conditions of real options theory in the international context.

Of course, alternative views can be developed. For example, an argument might be made that coordination costs should be considered in their own right and not be brought into the real options framework. One might also argue that the reason why real options predictions may not hold in the case of MNCs in general is that firms' motives for FDI are heterogeneous, acquiring switching options being only one of them. However, both of these arguments point to the challenge of systematically identifying and developing contingencies to delineate more precisely the boundary conditions of real options theory as applied to the multinational firm.

Our predictions regarding the effects of subsidiary ownership were not supported, and we suspect that there are several potential explanations for the insignificance of this contingency. It may also be the case that the firm's ability to manage effectively the switching options conferred by FDI does not hinge upon the ownership of foreign affiliates. It may also be plausible that foreign subsidiary ownership facilitates systemwide optimization, but centralized decision making also involves non-trivial costs and rigidity in changing environments. Along similar lines, it is possible that MNCs with significant ownership are still not able to institute effective organizational mechanisms and/or incentive systems conducive to the exercise of real options. For example, while the network nature of MNCs requires a heterarchy (Hedlund 1986) or transnational structure (Bartlett and Ghoshal 1989), many MNCs still rely on an 'M-form' organizational structure couched in dyadic relationships between headquarters and subsidiaries. Future research considering the role of organizational structures and other coordination mechanisms to manage switching options would therefore be valuable.

Finally, the insignificance of subsidiary ownership may also be interpreted in terms of other options available through partial ownership. While minority subsidiaries may not confer switching options to the extent that fully owned operations do, such investments can confer growth options instead. For instance, a firm can increase its ownership in minority foreign subsidiaries in the event of positive developments such as unexpected local demand growth, but the firm is not compelled to expand in the case of a negative turn of events (see for example, Kogut 1991). The insignificant results may thus reflect offsetting growth options available from such investments and the reduced ability to shift value-chain activities into and out of that location. Future research therefore needs to give attention to other types of options possessed by MNCs, addressing questions such as whether growth options in emerging markets pay off, whether option considerations affect location and partner choices and whether strategic considerations affect other options (for instance, deferral, learning and abandonment options).

In other research, we are investigating the value of growth options available to MNCs.

Other theories might also help to identify coordination problems in MNCs and help bound some of the predictions of real options theory. As one example, previous research has suggested that agency problems common in large diversified firms may be exacerbated with increasing international presence, in part because internal monitoring of international managers becomes more difficult and the market for corporate control becomes less effective due to international market imperfections (for example, Lee and Kwok 1988; Reeb, Kwok and Baek 1998). This implies that these managers' interests may not coincide with the optimal option exercise policies from equity holders' perspective. Theories concerning organizational inertia and escalation of commitment may also inform applications of real options theory to MNCs and begin to shift the attention away from investments in real options to the implementation of real options. Research in directions such as these may advance the application of real options approaches in the international strategy arena.

References

Allen, L. and C. Pantzalis (1996) 'Valuation of the Operating Flexibility of Multinational Corporations', *Journal of International Business Studies*, 27, 633–53.

Barkema, H. G., J. H. J. Bell, Jr. and J. M. Pennings (1996) 'Foreign Entry, Cultural Barriers, and Learning', *Strategic Management Journal*, 17, 151–66.

Bartlett, C. A. and S. Ghoshal (1989) *Managing across Borders: The Transnational Solution.* (Boston, MA: Harvard Business School Press).

Bowman, E. H. and D. Hurry (1993) 'Strategy through the Options Lens: An Integrated View of Resource Investments and the Incremental-Choice Process', *Academy of Management Review*, 18, 760–82.

Buckley, P. J. and M. Casson (1976) *The Future of the Multinational Enterprise* (London: Macmillan).

———(1998) 'Models of the Multinational Enterprise', *Journal of International Business Studies*, 29, 21–44.

Caves, R. E. (1996) *Multinational Enterprise and Economic Analysis*, 2nd edn (New York: Cambridge University Press).

Davidson, W. H. and D. G. McFetridge (1985) 'Key Characteristics in the Choice of International Technology Transfer Mode', *Journal of International Business Studies*, 16, 5–21.

Doukas, J. and N. G. Travlos (1988) 'The Effect of Corporate Multinationalism on Shareholders' Wealth: Evidence from International Acquisitions', *Journal of Finance*, 43, 1161–75.

Dunning, J. H. and A. Rugman (1985) 'The Influence of Hymer's Dissertation on Theories of Foreign Direct Investment', *American Economic Review*, 75, 228–32.

Gatignon, H. and E. Anderson (1988) 'The Multinational Corporation's Degree of Control over Foreign Subsidiaries: An Empirical Test of a Transaction Cost Explanation', *Journal of Law, Economics, and Organization*, 4, 305–36.

Ghoshal, S. (1987) 'Global Strategy: An Organizing Framework', *Strategic Management Journal*, 8, 425–40.

Ghoshal, S. and N. Nohria (1989) 'Internal Differentiation within Multinational Corporations', *Strategic Management Journal*, 10, 323–37.

Grant, R. M., A. P. Jammine and H. Thomas (1988) 'Diversity, Diversification, and Profitability among British Manufacturing Companies, 1972–1984', *Academy of Management Journal*, 31, 771–801.

Grubaugh, S. G. (1987) 'Determinants of Direct Foreign Investment', *Review of Economics and Statistics*, 69, 149–52.

Hedlund, G. (1986) 'The Hypermodern MNC – A Heterarchy', *Human Resource Management*, 25, 9–25.

Hennart, J.-F. (1982) *A Theory of Multinational Enterprise* (Ann Arbor, MI: University of Michigan Press).

————(1991) 'The Transaction Costs Theory of Joint Ventures: An Empirical Study of Japanese Subsidiaries in the United States', *Management Science*, 37, 483–97.

Hitt, M. A., R. E. Hoskisson and H. Kim (1997) 'International Diversification: Effects on Innovation and Firm Performance in Product-Diversified Firms', *Academy of Management Journal*, 40, 767–98.

Horst, T. (1972) 'Firm and Industry Determinants of the Decision to Invest Abroad: An Empirical Study', *Review of Economics and Statistics*, 54, 258–66.

Hymer, S. H. (1970) *The International Operations of National Firms: A Study of Direct Investment* (Cambridge, MA: MIT Press).

Jones, G. R. and C. W. L. Hill (1988) 'Transaction Cost Analysis of Strategy–Structure Choice', *Strategic Management Journal*, 9, 159–72.

Kim, W. C., P. Hwang and W. P. Burgers (1993) ' "Multinationals'" Diversification and the Risk–Return Tradeoff', *Strategic Management Journal*, 14, 275–86.

Kogut, B. (1983) 'Foreign Direct Investment as a Sequential Process', in C. P. Kindleberger and D. Audretsch (eds), *The Multinational Corporation in the 1980s* (Boston, MA: MIT Press), 62–75.

————(1985) 'Designing Global Strategies: Profiting from Operational Flexibility', *Sloan Management Review*, 27, 37–38.

————(1989) 'A Note on Global Strategies', *Strategic Management Journal*, 10, 383–9.

————(1991) 'Joint Ventures and the Option to Expand and Acquire', *Management Science*, 37, 19–33.

Kogut, B. and N. Kulatilaka (1994) 'Operating Flexibility, Global Manufacturing, and the Option Value of a Multinational Network', *Management Science*, 40, 123–39.

Kogut, B. and H. Singh (1988) 'The Effect of National Culture on the Choice of Entry Mode', *Journal of International Business Studies* 19, 411–32.

Kotabe, M., S. Srinivasan and P. S. Aulakh (2000) 'Multinationality and Firm Performance: The Moderating Role of R&D and Marketing Capabilities', *Journal of International Business Studies*, 33, 79–97.

Lee, K. and C. C. Y. Kwok (1988) 'Multinational Corporations vs. Domestic Corporations: International Environmental Factors and Determinants of Capital Structure', *Journal of International Business Studies*, 19, 195–217.

McGrath, R. G. (1997) 'A Real Options Logic for Initiating Technology Positioning Investments', *Academy of Management Review*, 22, 974–96.

Miller, K. D. and J. J. Reuer (1996) 'Measuring Organizational Downside Risk', *Strategic Management Journal*, 17, 671–91.

———(1998) 'Firm Strategy and Economic Exposure to Foreign Exchange Rate Movements', *Journal of International Business Studies*, 29, 493–514.

Mitchell, W., J. M. Shaver and B. Yeung (1992) 'Getting There in a Global Industry: Impacts on Performance of Changing International Presence', *Strategic Management Journal*, 13, 419–43.

Morck, R. and B. Yeung (1992) 'Internalization: An Event Study Test', *Journal of International Economics*, 33, 41–56.

Pantzalis, C., B. J. Simkins and P. A. Laux (2001) 'Operational Hedges and the Foreign Exchange Exposure of US Multinational Corporations', *Journal of International Business Studies*, 32, 793–812.

Porter, M. E. (1990) *The Competitive Advantage of Nations* (New York: Free Press).

Qian, G. (1996) 'The Effect of Multinationality Measures upon the Risk-Return Performance of US Firms', *International Business Review*, 5, 247–65.

Rangan, S. (1998) 'Do Multinationals Operate Flexibly? Theory and Evidence', *Journal of International Business Studies*, 29, 217–37.

Reeb, D. M., C. C. Y. Kwok and H. Y. Baek (1998) 'Systematic Risk of the Multi-national Corporation', *Journal of International Business Studies*, 29, 263–79.

Reuer, J. J. and M. J. Leiblein (2000) 'Downside Risk Implications of Multinationality and International Joint Ventures', *Academy of Management Journal*, 43, 203–14.

Root, F. R. *Entry Strategies for International Markets* (New York: Lexington Books).

Roth, K., D. Schweiger and A. Morrison (1991) 'Global Strategy Implementation at the Business-Unit Level: Operational Capabilities and Administrative Mechanisms', *Journal of International Business Studies*, 22, 361–94.

Shaver, J. M. (1998) 'Accounting for Endogeneity when Assessing Strategy Performance: Does Entry Mode Choice Affect FDI Survival?', *Management Science*, 44, 571–85.

Stopford, J. M. and L. T. Wells (1972) *Managing the Multinational Enterprise* (New York: Basic Books).

Teece, D. J. (1986) 'Transaction Cost Economics and the Multinational Enterprise: An Assessment', *Journal of Economic Behavior and Organization*, 7, 21–45.

Part IV

Global Alliances and Networks

14

Introduction to Part IV

Africa Ariño

Globalization is one of the drivers of the explosion in alliance formation that has been experienced since the mid-1980s. Gone are the days when companies seeking multinational expansion formed equity joint ventures (JVs) with the main – and at times, sole – purpose of fulfilling governmental requirements that demanded local ownership. Little more than a 'passport' was expected from partners. On the contrary, in today's alliances companies seek contributions from their partners which are deemed as valuable as their own. Globalization enhances the value of some existing capabilities and diminishes that of others, creating the need for a new set of *capabilities* (Nohria and García-Pont 1991). In this context, *alliances and networks* become a valuable means to gain access to the desired capabilities in a prompt manner, thus contributing to creating value through global strategy.

Some argue that very few industries, if any, deserve to be characterized as 'global' industries. Rather, they contend (Rugman 2003), that industries are becoming *regional*. Whether global or regional, international strategic alliances and networks play an active role in transforming the geographical scope of many industries, and the way to compete in them. The automotive industry is but one example. As articulated by García-Pont and Nohria (2002), alliance formation was triggered in this industry by the oil shocks of the 1970s. European and US firms realized that in order to remain competitive they had to ally with Japanese firms to acquire new capabilities, or else they had to pool together their own resources as a protection against Japanese competitors. Consequently, even if competition in the automotive industry was already international, the new alliances formed transformed the industry into a global one. This is the same as for the airline industry. Once a fragmented industry, the airline business became a truly global one. Alliances have allowed airline companies to expand their geographical scope. This has let them serve customers worldwide in some cases, and contain costs in others.

The evolution of these industries shows that they were not global at the beginning, but their globalization potential was achieved by means of strategic alliances. An industry's 'globalization potential' refers to the opportunities it offers to gain benefits from using globally integrated strategies. Companies in an industry will create and capture value to the extent that their degree of globalization matches the industry's globalization potential. In his Chapter 15, Ring argues that professional service industries entail a globalization potential yet to be realized. It is by forming networks among themselves that professional service organizations (PSOs) may compete internationally, and achieve the benefits of larger scale and scope. To the extent that they engage in this type of activities, their respective industries may become global in fact.

The actual formation of alliances depends on the existence of partners' *prior ties*, among other things. The incidence of organizational ties on alliance formation has been studied in the past (Gulati 1995). Prior ties and common ties to third parties at the organizational level increase the partners' awareness of potential opportunities for collaborating, and provide in-depth information about each other, thus favouring the creation of new ties. However, the role that personal ties play in creating alliances has received scarce attention. Chapter 16, by Olk, Gabbay and Chung, explores the impact of personal and organizational ties on the formation of high-technology alliances in multiple countries. Olk *et al.*'s findings suggest that personal ties are related to the type of alliance formed in terms of scope, and to the kind of contributions partners make.

But the mere creation of an alliance is no guarantee that it will enhance *value creation*. Typically, an alliance's realized value is lower than its potential value (Madhok and Tallman 1998). 'Potential value' refers to the 'theoretical synergies arising from the ideal combination of complementary resources and capabilities', while the realized value 'has more to do with the effectiveness of the actual management of the alliance' (Madhok and Tallman 1998, p. 328).

Implicitly, the chapters in Part IV suggest four key sources of global alliance and network potential value:

(1) *Scope expansion*: Ring suggests that as customers expand their geographic scope and go international, PSOs may need to follow suit in order to serve those customers properly. Forming networks with counterparts of *similar professional competence* is a valuable way for a PSO to expand its geographic scope.

(2) *Flexibility*: Ring implies that PSOs place value in the flexibility derived from forming a global network, as this allows PSOs to maintain their *independence and autonomy* while enabling them to work as a global firm.

(3) *Learning*: Prior work (Doz, Olk and Ring 2000) shows that networks formed by *emergent processes* lead to greater learning relative to those formed by engineered processes. Olk *et al.* here set themselves the task of investigating whether personal and organizational ties have an influence on the kind of process by which a network is formed in terms of who initiates the alliance. Their results indicate that personal ties lead to emergent alliance formation processes, and will result in greater learning consequently. As Ring points out, networks expose companies to the *best practices* of their fellow member organizations, providing a space for learning and capacity enhancing that may spill over to home-based operations.

(4) *Relationship leverage*: Olk *et al.* examine whether *personal and organizational ties* have any impact on the performance of research networks. They find that personal ties have such an effect, suggesting that companies leverage this kind of relationships.

These are some of the ways in which alliances and networks may create value. However, as said earlier, an alliance's realized value depends on the effectiveness of the *management of the alliance*. Its difference to potential value 'can be largely attributed to the quality of the relationship between the parent firms' (Madhok and Tallman 1998, p. 328). *Relational quality* is a function of prior ties, among other things (Ariño, de la Torre and Ring 2001). As was the case with the influence that prior ties have on alliance formation, we know little about the *differential impact* that organizational and personal ties may have on relational quality. Interestingly, Olk *et al.* find that alliances started from a personal tie tended to have better performance than other alliances. Personal ties may diminish the relational risk that an alliance entails (Das and Teng 1999), and results in a more satisfactory pattern of interactions that strengthen relational quality, thus increasing the alliance's realized value.

In conclusion, global alliances and networks are an important element of global strategy, and their use has an impact on the extent to which particular industries achieve their globalization potential. In part, their creation depends on the existence of prior partner ties, both personal and organizational. Alliances and networks may contribute to create value through global strategy in a number of ways, including scope expansion, flexibility, learning and relationship leverage. Typically, their potential value exceeds their realized value. The higher the partners' relational quality, the higher will be the realized value. Prior personal ties seem to add to relational quality, enhancing realized value.

References

Ariño, A., J. de la Torre and P. S. Ring (2001) 'Relational Quality: Managing Trust in Corporate Alliances', *California Management Review*, 44, 109–31.

Das, T. K. and B.-S. Teng (1999) 'Managing Risks in Strategic Alliances' *Academy of Management Executive*, 13, 50–62.

Doz, Y., P. M. Olk and P. S. Ring (2000) 'Formation Processes of R&D Consortia: Which Path to Take? Where Does it Lead?', *Strategic Management Journal*, 21, 239–66.

García-Pont, C. and N. Nohria (2002) 'Local vs. Global Mimetism: The Dynamics of Alliance Formation in the Automobile Industry', *Strategic Management Journal*, 23, 307–21.

Gulati, R. (1995) 'Does Familiarity Breed Trust? The Implications of Repeated Ties for Contractual Choice in Alliances', *Academy of Management Journal*, 38, 85–112.

Madhok, A. and S. B. Tallman, (1998) 'Resources, Transactions, and Rents: Managing Value through Inter-Firm Collaborative Relationships', *Organization Science*, 1998, 9, 326–39.

Nohria, N. and C. García-Pont (1991) 'Global Strategic Linkages and Industry Structure' *Strategic Management Journal*, 12, 105–24.

Rugman, A. M. (2003) 'Regional Strategy and the Demise of Globalization', *Journal of International Management*, 9, 409–17.

15

Globalizing Professional Services: Are Networked Organizations an Answer?

Peter Smith Ring

Introduction

As industries and firms globalize, the issue of organizing wide spread economic activity assumes added importance. One approach has been to rely on *networks and alliances,* and this has provoked a significant amount of academic interest in the topic. In this chapter, I will put forth the case for further exploration of networked organizations (Ring 1996)[1] involving professional services, arguing that they have been underrepresented in academic research, that the professions are a growing part of the global economy and that by exploring the conditions under which professional services providers (PSPs)[2] are likely to form networked organizations we can expand our understanding of the roles that various kinds of networked organizations play in governing global economic exchanges.

Based on an extensive review of the literature on networked organizations at the industry or the firm level, I initially offer three observations about that research. First, industry-focused studies of the conduct of manufacturing firms provide the foundation for much of our knowledge about the networks embedded in networked organizations. Greenwood, Hinings and Brown (1994, 1991), Koza and Lewin (1999) provide seminal exceptions in the field of professional services. Second, codified (Winter 1987) and tacit (Teece 1987) know-how transfers, increasingly, are viewed as providing primary motivations behind the creation (or evolution) of networked organizations (see Ahuja 2000; Hansen 2002). The weight of the research on networks, however, has been associated with governing exchanges of raw materials, intermediate products and/or finished goods.

Third, when service industry networked organizations are the focus of research they involve services (for example, fast foods, airlines, hotels, banks, etc.) that have many of the characteristics of industrial or con-sumer goods networked organizations (for instance, production activ-ities involving clearly defined, logically sequential, value adding steps).

Have these studies provided us with a comprehensive picture of the motivations behind a choice of networked organizations as a means of governing economic exchange? Do they provide us with a full range of the design characteristics and structures of networked organizations? And do they answer the question whether networks are an economically efficient way to govern economic exchanges that occur on a global basis? I believe that they do not, and that research focusing on networked organizations comprised of PSPs will expand our understanding of the roles that various kinds of networked organizations can play in govern-ing global economic exchanges. This chapter seeks to move the research on networked organizations in that direction.

The kinds of conditions generally described in the management literature as sources of globalization among firms in manufacturing industries include:

(1) Similarity of *needs*.
(2) More mobile and informed *buyers*.
(3) Rising *economies of scale* and *geographic scope*.
(4) Greater mobility of *service personnel*.
(5) Greater ability to interact with *remote buyers*.
(6) Wide disparities in nations among *service providers*, in terms of cost, quality, and availability.

There is some evidence that these conditions also apply to professional services (it is an empirical question not well researched), and this pro-vides additional support for the importance of studying the cooperative behavior of PSPs. Porter's research (1990, p. 250) also provides some evidence that PSPs are using alternatives to markets and hierarchies in governing exchange relationships. Porter notes that service firms some-times form alliances, citing engineering as an example. Beyond this brief discussion, however, his work provided little evidence as to how the nature of a profession might affect the incidence of reliance on networked organizations among professional services firms.

PSPs, as I have observed, have largely been ignored in industry studies of networked organizations. This may be due to a failure to conceptualize professions as 'industries', or PSOs as 'firms'. PSPs therefore frequently fall outside the scope of industry-based, and/or firm-based research on networked organizations.

Assuming this to be the case, let me note that the concept of an 'industry' is usually defined in two ways that are directly related to the arguments set out in this chapter. First, an industry is usually defined as an 'aggregate of manufacturing or technically productive enterprises'. It can, however, be viewed as 'any general business field'. Admittedly, the aggregate of PSPs in a specific profession (for example, lawyers, doctors) may not have been viewed as being a part of a technical enterprise, as the concept of 'technical' is usually employed. But law firms and medical groups (or other aggregates of PSPs) are productive enterprises, and the law and medicine are technologies. Moreover, all the professions are part of a general business field.

Professions can thus be thought of in the same terms that are traditionally employed in studies of industries. As with many industries these days, moreover, the boundary lines for many professional services are blurring. This is especially so in the cases of consulting, accounting and engineering; probably less so for the law, medicine and architecture.

The accumulating evidence suggests that professional services are an important part of the global economy and that PSPs appear to be reacting to the globalization of the economy in ways that parallel the approaches of manufacturing firms and other service firms (see, for example, Koza and Lewin 1999). There thus appears to be some merit in exploring whether differences that can be associated with PSPs should alter our current ways of thinking about networked organizations.

Networked organizations

It is not necessary for the development of my arguments to comprehensively review the extensive, and growing, literature related to networked organizations. Others have tackled this task (see, for instance, Gautam 2000; Gynawali, Devi and Madhaven 2001; Human and Provan 2000; Kenis and Knoke 2002; Rangan 2000).[3] Researchers operating in the disciplines that are most frequently used to explore networked organizations, generally, point to their governance structures as being a function of the embeddedness of transactions, or to the kinds of resources exchanged. A networked organization perspective also highlights the positive contributions of learning and social capital (Uzzi, 1997; Rosenkopf, Metia and George, 2000).

This literature also suggests that the networked organizations that are found among manufacturing firms (or in service segments of the economy comprising firms such as banks, food services, or airlines), come into being and are designed with the objective of solving a number of business challenges. Networked organizations can be used to establish *standards* in an industry. This was accomplished in the case of VCRs with the VHS standard. Efforts are under-way to establish similar kinds of standards in a number of wireless communication environments. Networked organizations can also be used by a small group of firms relying on common norms of behaviour to bring to bear *specialized resources* in competition with large firms, as is seen in the Italian packaging, knitting and motorcycle industries, or the garment industry in New York City. Firms such as ARM, SAP, Mips and PixTech have used networked organizations to establish and *grow their businesses*. Some have succeeded (ARM, SAP), while others have failed (PixTech and Mips). Third, a wide variety of firms have used networked organizations as a means of learning from each other to fill *competency gaps* and to internalize that learning (Cal (IT)2, Sematech and MCC are good examples). What appears to be common in all these cases is that the individual participants needed access to resources that they were not able produce organically and could not buy through arms'-length market-based transactions. In each of these broadly defined areas, networked organizations occurred when the relatively small number of firms that joined them either recognized that they were interdependent, had similar interests and could agree on a common action agenda; or when a triggering entity brought them together by demonstrating their common interests and defining an action agenda (Doz, Olk and Ring 2000).[4]

There is also a well-established stream of research on organizations (see, for example, Gerlach 1992; Boisot 1995; Hansen 2002) suggesting that greater access to information, as well as enhanced use of information, can flow from an ability to rely on networked organizations. The research on networked organizations also reveals that trust can be established through them – or, when it already exists, relied upon more easily in these settings (see, for instance, Lazerson 1995; Ring 1996). For example, Kumon (1992, p. 118) argues that the main reasons actors join a network is to share useful information/knowledge with other members, to achieve better mutual understanding and to develop a firm base for mutual trust that may eventually lead to collaboration to achieve the actors' individual as well as collective goals (Gerlach 1992; Lazerson 1995, 1988; Uzzi 1997).

Summarizing the discussion to this point, transactions conducted within networked organizations are likely to entail interwoven, recurring, trust-based exchanges. A relatively small number of economic actors, linked by norms as well as common business objectives, are usually the participants in a networked organization. These economic actors are likely to have experienced long-term relationships with each other, sometimes as intense competitors. The transactions in these networked organizations may involve a sharing of many different kinds of resources or capabilities. These resources may include knowledge-based, financial, human, or tangible goods and services. Capabilities may relate to learning, innovation, managing cooperative relationships and managing trade in tacit forms of knowledge. Non-economic aspects of exchanges within networked organizations also appear to be important to our understanding of their dynamics. Coleman (1988) describes one of them as 'social' capital. Social capital can take the form of obligations and expectations, information channels, or social norms (see also Larsen 1992; Nahapiet and Goshal 1998), and the ability to create social capital can be seen as an important capability in the management of networked organizations.

An ability to create networked organizations of PSPs depends, in my view, on dealing with additional antecedent conditions. Here the antecedent conditions are a function of the nature of the professions, and ability to rely on trust and whether the professional is a sole practitioner or employed by a PSO.

Professions

Abbott (1988, p. 8) defines 'professions [as] exclusive occupation groups applying some abstract knowledge to particular cases'. Similarly, Freidson (1994, p. 10) asserts that a profession 'refers to an occupation that controls its own work, organised by a special set of institutions sustained in part by a particular ideology of expertise and service'. Professions are viewed in differentiated ways.[5] For example, forms of work engaged in by persons of a particular educational status have been described by Elliott (1972) as 'status professions'. These can be traced back to medieval days, when the universities of Europe gave birth to the learned professions of law, medicine and the church. Social and economic conditions meant that there were small numbers of professions in any given area. Their education and their status contributed to a relatively high level of trust being invested by society in those who provided these professional services.

Freidson (1994) argues that this group of professionals should be distinguished from more recent 'occupational professions', which he describes as arising out of a desire of 'newly reorganized or newly formed middle-class occupations to seek the title of "profession" because it was connected with the gentlemanly status of the traditional learned professions'.[6] Abbott (1988, p. 95) points out that

> any occupation can obtain licensure (for example, beauticians) or develop a code of ethics (for instance, real estate). But only a knowledge system governed by abstractions can redefine its problems and tasks, defend them from interlopers, and seize new problems – as medicine has recently seized alcoholism, mental illness, hyperactivity in children, obesity, and numerous other things.

The expertise that flows from an ability to manage the application of an abstract knowledge base to particularized cases appears to have implications for the ways in which professions organize. First, it is possible for individuals to create significant *economic value*, particularly in status professions. Second, in many of the status professions the knowledge base, increasingly, is highly specialized and this leads to the opportunity to differentiate professional service delivery along a continuum that ranges from 'boutique' PSPs to 'full-service' PSPs. Third, because of their historical roots in political systems, the knowledge base of some status professions (for instance, the law) is itself differentiated. Fourth, there are professions in which the skills and knowledge of the profession are applied to the service of individual clients. In such cases (for example, law or medicine) the professional, if she desires, may become a sole practitioner (In Ireland, for example, a barrister can function only as a sole practitioner). In other cases, such as engineering or public accounting, a PSP in all likelihood will work for a PSO, especially if she wishes to work with clients that are large business firms. In still other cases, PSPs will have to work for a PSO in order to deal with individual clients. This is almost universally the case with the clergy, and is increasingly becoming the case within the medical profession.

Some professions will thus be dominated by organizations, while in others individuals can survive. Individual survival, however, will involve one of three basic strategies. In the first case, an individual professional may be able to survive, and even thrive in economic terms, as a *general practitioner*. Such cases are likely to involve locational affects such as rural settings or strong kinship influences. In the second strategy, the sole practitioner will have to develop significantly high levels of *competence* in a narrowly specialized area of professional practice. This competence must be coupled with equally strong *reputation* effects. These kinds of differentiation strategies are, of course, quite common in other industries. The third strategy involves reliance on *networked organizations* comprising

PSPs who retain their autonomy, but cooperate in serving an individual client with diverse needs. As the specialized knowledge base of professions increases, and as the global complexity of business increases, specialization in the professions becomes more attractive. Specialization also provides opportunities for cooperative efforts. Networks of specialists in a profession provide access to economies of scale and scope in areas such as marketing, billing and logistics that are beyond the reach of the individual PSP.

Summarizing this discussion of professions as they relate to elements that can be used to define networked organizations, I draw the following conclusions. Both networked organizations and PSOs frequently comprises small numbers of individuals and/or firms. Members of professions engage in frequent and localized transactions, as do the members of networked organizations. Members of both networked organizations and professions experience mutual orientations, reciprocal relationships and reliance on trust. Complicated norms are found in both networked organizations and among PSPs. PSPs and networked organizations both employ formal as well as informal controls. Knowledge creation and sharing occurs at high levels within networked organizations and by professions. Exchanges within networked organizations and professions frequently lead to both collective and individual outcomes. We ought thus to expect that many PSPs in many professions might find networked organizations as an attractive form of organizing governance structures.

Forms of networked organizations in professions

The foregoing discussion suggests that if PSPs decide to employ networked organizations as a strategy, they are likely to go about designing them in a variety of ways. Initially, status PSPs may approach the issue in ways that differ from those employed in occupational professions. Individual practitioners may take approaches that differ from those employed by PSOs. And the extent to which PSPs can rely on trust (and its associated norms of *reciprocity*) is also likely to have an impact on the ways in which networked organizations are designed by PSPs. In Figure 15.1, this design space is illustrated; the types of networked forms that I wish to discuss are outlined in Table 15.1.

I will discuss these various forms of networked organization in relation to the ability of the participants to *rely on trust* in governing their relationships within the networked organization in question. The literature on networked organizations has demonstrated that an ability to rely on trust reduces the costs of governing, and increases the opportunities

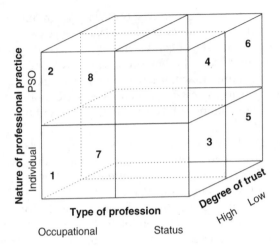

Figure 15.1   The design space

Table 15.1   Forms of networked organizations in professions

Cell no.	Dimensions	Type of networked form
1	Individual, occupational, high trust	Guilds
2	PSO, occupational, high trust	Associations
3	Individual, status, high trust	Clans
4	PSO, status, high trust	Clubs
5	Individual, status, low trust	Associations
6	PSO, status, low trust	Constellations
7	Individual, occupational, low trust	Associations
8	PSO, occupational, low trust	Federations

open to the participants to provide goods and services to their customers/ clients (see, for example, Ring and Van de Ven 1992). Cells 1–4 in Figure 15.1 reflect instances in which the participants in networked organizations involving PSPs are able to rely on a high degree of trust in dealing with each other.

Networked organizations that emerge within Cell 1 (sole practitioners engaged in occupational professions relying on high levels of trust) may look very much like *guilds* (see, for instance, Boisot and Child 1996). They are likely to be localized and designed to facilitate access to scale or scope economies that the individual PSPs could not generate acting alone. Because they are able to rely on a high degree of trust in dealing with each other, moreover, these individual occupational PSPs (for example, accountants, business school management professors who engage in consulting, consulting engineers) may also be able to retain clients who seek expertise that the individual professional does not have by suggesting to the client that another member of the guild can be trusted to offer the service sought with the same degree of competence, reliability and integrity that the professional in question has always provided to the client seeking additional services. More importantly, the occupational professional occupying Cell 1, because she can rely on trust, is not concerned that the professional to whom she is referring her client will act opportunistically by trying to convince the client to remain with him thereafter.

Occupational PSPs who have organized themselves as a PSO (for example, an accounting firm) may participate in a networked organization for similar reasons as their colleagues who function as sole practitioners. I describe these kinds of networked organizations, occupying Cell 2 in Figure 15.1, as *associations*. The dynamics in this case are virtually identical to those just described in Cell 1 for sole practitioners. The difference is that the individual members of the PSPs that make up these associations may be able to operate as *partnerships* (as opposed to corporations) because they trust each other in dealing with their client base and with each other. Similar dynamics will be found in the case of status PSPs occupying Cells 3 and 4 of Figure 15.1, which I have described as *clans* and *clubs*.

To the extent that the PSPs in all four of these cells develop *trust-based relationships* with each other (as sole practitioners or PSPs) they may be able to follow their clients into new geographic markets without having to grow organically. The amount of economic capital that can be generated by PSPs acting as sole practitioners, or practising in small or medium-sized (SME) PSPs, is likely to vary considerably across the professions, and across the industries on which professions may rely for business. In general, these kinds of PSPs will experience severely limited access to sources of economic capital. SMEs–PSPs may intentionally limit the sources of economic capital open to them, or may have limits imposed exogenously. Sources of economic capital that can be available to corporations are usually accompanied by the loss of the kinds of control that can be achieved through resort to partnerships, for example, as a formal governance mechanism. But partnerships usually will gain this autonomy at the expense of access to sources of significant economic capital.

Sole practitioners in occupational professionals who cannot rely on trust (Cell 7) may also gain access to scale or scope economies by forming *associations.* They will incur the higher costs of transacting that will come with the formation of the association (which will employ a small staff that provides some assurance to all the members that none gains 'favours'), in contrast to those who belong to guilds and can rely on trust and the transactional efficiencies it provides. Sole practitioners in status professions (those occupying Cell 5 in Figure 15.1) who cannot rely on trust in dealing with each other, may nonetheless also be able to gain access to scale or scope economies by belonging to an *association* (for instance, a local bar association). But the inability to rely on trust will limit the extent to which they will be able to retain clients whose needs for the services of status PSPs are expanding beyond the 'reach' of the sole practitioner. Because large numbers of sole practitioners and PSOs join these associations, the entry fees they pay in the form of annual dues sustain the staffs required to run the associations and provide the services that the association offers to its members. Needless to say, these services tend to be of a generalized nature.[7]

Occupational PSPs organized as PSOs may cooperate through networked organizations in pursuit of serving clients who demand worldwide reach. Nexia International, a networked organization of accounting firms described by Koza and Lewin (1999), reflects such an approach. These forms of networked organizations occupy Cell 8 in Figure 15.1, and I describe them as *federations*. The firms that belong to a federation will retain a significant amount of local autonomy, but will cede a degree of their autonomy to the central 'government' of the federation (as well as providing the resources required to sustain it). Status PSPs organized as PSOs that cannot rely on trust in dealing with other PSOs of status professionals (Cell 6) may form networked organizations that I will call *constellations*.

These kinds of PSOs are likely to have already grown large enough to benefit from scale and scope economies and to have expanded geographically by either organic growth or by mergers and/or acquisitions. They may also belong to associations and obtain the variety of benefits that can flow from such memberships (legitimacy, certification, etc.). There may be occasions when these PSOs find is useful to cooperate on a short-term or ad hoc basis in the face of some form of crisis, or competitive pressures. The source of the crisis or competitive pressure may not affect all PSOs within the status profession in the same way. In such circumstances, similarly affected PSOS may form a constellation. The constellation's membership may be of a semi-permanent nature. It will not have a central authority (as in a federation), but one or more of the PSOs that make up this form of networked organization is likely to shine more brightly by assuming a leadership role in dealing with the problem of the moment.

Reflecting on the resources available to the professions, Freidson (1994, p. 40) observes that: 'professions have no intrinsic resources other than their command over a body of knowledge and skill that has not been appropriated by others'. However, cultural or human capital has no intrinsic material resource, so professions are dependent on economic capital as well as political power for their very survival, let alone their level of material and social comfort. I have already addressed the role of economic capital in the formation of networked organizations in the professions. I will also take issue with this 'sociological' view of cultural and human capital. The economics and management disciplines have demonstrated that these forms of tacit resources may be the most significant sources of competitive advantages available to firms. But the trade of these kinds of tacit resources among and between PSPs is dependent upon an ability to rely on trust. As such, only those networked organizations in Cells 1–4 will be able to rely on access to these kinds of resources.

Political power also is likely to vary across the professions. For some professions (for example, lawyers) overt political activity may be second nature. For others, it simply may be unwise (for instance, the clergy, architects). Other PSPs may discover that their competencies provide little in the way of preparation for political activities, as is likely to be the case with engineers. Thus, it seems likely that some professions will be better positioned to use political capital to influence entry conditions, the nature of competition within the profession, or regulatory control over professional activities. Observing how this happens in the context of professional service provides may permit researchers to isolate political strategies as a dependent variable while controlling for much more in the way of exogenous or endogenous forces than would be possible in looking at a traditional firm and of group of firms in a more typical industry or cross-industry setting.

Conclusions

In this chapter I have sought to demonstrate that the industry from which a network emerges, or in which a network is embedded, will affect the nature of collaborations among economic actors engaged in that industry. In addition, I have attempted to make the case that research on networks has so far systematically ignored the professional services sector of the economy.

My own efforts suggest that these shortcomings are understandable. Public data on professional service networks is almost impossible to uncover, especially in those services most related to business. I suspect that this result is a consequence of the fact that the vast majority of professional service firms are private – usually partnerships. Thus, there are few demands on these firms to provide the kinds of data with which we are used to dealing for publicly owned corporations. There is both empirical and anecdotal evidence that networks among these firms do exist. How common they are, their antecedents, their scope and scale, are empirical questions.

Given this, what can we say about networked organizations in professional services? First, they are experiencing explosive growth. This is the case in both domestic and in global markets. Second, the dynamics of change appear to be felt in different ways by the various professions. They appear to be less dramatic in the so-called 'status professions', although medicine does appear to provide an exception in that case in the USA. Third, governance issues are becoming more pronounced among some of the professions. This appears to be particularly so in accounting, especially in the aftermath of the Arthur Andersen meltdown.

Finally, existing models of industry studies have provided us with little insight into the professions. Porter's so-called 'national diamond model' provides a good illustration of the point I wish to make. Porter (1994, p. 74) asserts that 'companies achieve competitive advantage through acts of innovation'. There is a real question whether this is the case with the professions. With the professions, competitive advantage would appear to reside in an ability of a privileged individual to apply abstract knowledge to a particular case in ways that solve a client's problems.

The factor conditions that are one of the four elements of the 'national diamond' – labour, land, natural resources, capital, or infrastructure – appear to be much less salient to understanding industry dynamics in the professions. Most professional services firms are not attracted to a nation because of its geographic location, climate, or natural resources. Until recently, capital resources were rarely an issue for professional service firms and access to capital is not likely to be a determining factor in a decision of a professional service firm to locate in France over Germany or the UK. There also appears to be nothing in the way of competitive advantage to be derived from the specialized knowledge base, for example, of the legal profession in France, or the USA.

Demand conditions, however, do appear to be extremely relevant to our understanding of the professions. The robustness of a profession in a home country is almost certainly a function of demand for services. The ability of individuals to engage the services of PSPs is a function of either affluence or governmental policy. We might expect that, in more affluent societies, demand for professional services would be greater and thus expect those countries to have developed PSPs that would be prepared to 'go global'.

Globalization of a profession is also clearly a function of demand factors. Accounting remains that leading profession for the study of these kinds of demand factors and their impact on professional service firms, but the legal profession is becoming more global by the day. Law firms in England and the USA are leading this change because of the prominence of US and UK firms in FDI activities globally and because London and New York are two of the world's three leading financial markets. Japanese law firms are not global, in large measure because of language, the roots of their legal system, a very highly regulated profession that severely limits entry (even in Japan) and, perhaps, an aversion to litigation, contracts, etc.[8] Indeed, Hong Kong has developed as the centre of the legal community in Asia, in some measure because of its roots in English common law.

Until very recently, related and supporting industries did not appear relevant to the development of competitive advantages in a profession. In a more global professional environment, this may change. Information and communication technologies are increasingly critical to success in the professions, at home or abroad, for example. Excellent graduate schools, on the other hand, are critical to the development of the professions.

Finally, until very recently firm strategy and structure were irrelevant issues for most professions. The nature of a *professional relationship* tended to govern structure. Most professional firms looked very much alike because whatever structure existed was designed to preserve as much autonomy as possible for each individual member of the firm. The concept of 'strategy' and the term 'professional service' would not have been uttered in the same breath until the 1980s. Even today, most professional service firms do not think formally about these issues (Beaton 1994). Domestic rivalry, on the other hand, is likely to be an important determinant in the globalization of professional services and in a resort to networks as a means of collaboration among professional service firms. Overall, Porter's 'national diamond' model does not seem to be capable of providing fine-grained analyses of professional service industries.

Notes

1. By a 'networked organization' I mean that more than two economic actors are engaged in ongoing exchanges of resources with each other over an extended period of time. An 'economic actor' can be a firm or an individual, a non-profit organization, or an agency of a state. A 'networked organization' can take the form of a consortium, an equity joint venture (JV), or it may simply involve an set of informal agreements by the participants to pursue a set of common and individual objectives of an economic or non-economic nature. One or more networks may actually be found within a networked organization as a result of empirical examination of the relationships among and between members of the organization. Since, in my view, networks can be established only by empirical examination, the informal use of the term 'networks' that currently dominates much of the management literature is inappropriate. In fact, empirical examination of one of these 'networks' may reveal that there is no network at all, or that more than one network exists.
2. A 'professional service provider' (PSP) can be a sole practitioner, a not-for-profit organization, a partnership, a governmental agency, or a corporate entity. Those not referred to in this chapter as 'sole practitioners' will be discussed as professional services organizations (PSOs).
3. I have consciously ignored the extensive literature dealing with social networks.
4. The action agenda, at a minimum, will include agreement on value creation and value capture, resource contributions and duration and managment of the networked organization on a day-to-day basis.
5. Not surprisingly, the effort to understand the professions in systematic ways is of very recent origin. Nearly all the studies have been undertaken in the late 1980s–1990s (for example, Abel and Lewis 1988; Cocks and Jarausch 1990).
6. Abbott's work appears to demonstrate that 'the nineteenth century professions were important but particular creatures. With the exception of accounting, *they stood outside the new commercial and industrial heart of society'* (Abbott 1988, p. 3, emphasis added). It thus seems likely that newer professions will be more business-like in their structures, objectives and practices.
7. In the manufacturing sector, or in manufacturing-like services, one frequently observes these kinds of so-called 'peak' associations (National Association of Manufacturers, American Bankers Association and so on). In general, these kinds of networked organizations have not been the subject of study by management scholars.
8. The Foreign Lawyers Practice Act (passed in May 1986 and effective in 1987), has only just begun to ease the problem of entry. This is largely because the Act did nothing to lift the ban on the hiring of Japanese lawyers or forming partnerships with Japanese firms.

References

Abbot, A. (1988) *The System of Professions* (Chicago, IL: University of Chicago Press).
Abel, R. and P. S. Lewis (1988) (eds) *Lawyers in Society* (Berkeley, CA: University of California Press).
Ahuja, G. (2000) 'Collaborative Networks, Structural Holes, and Innovation: A Longitudinal Study', *Administrative Science Quarterly*, 45, 425–55.

Beaton, G. (1994) 'Mission Statements in Professional Firms', *Journal of Professional Services Marketing*, 11, 173–88.

Boisot, M. H. (1995) *Information Space* (London: Routledge).

Boisot, M. and J. Child, (1996) 'From Fiefs to Clans: Explaining China's Emergent Economic Order', *Administrative Science Quarterly*, 41, 600–28.

Cocks, G. and K. H. Jarausch (eds) (1990) *German Professions, 1880–1950* (New York: Oxford University Press).

Coleman, J. S. (1988) 'Social Capital in the Creation of Human Capital', *American Journal of Sociology* 94, Special Supplement, S95-S120.

Doz, Y., P. M. Olk and P. S. Ring (2000) 'Formation Processes of Research and Development Consortia: Which Path to Take? Where Does it Lead?', *Strategic Management Journal*, 21(3), 239–66.

Elliott, P. (1972) *The Sociology of the Professions* (London, Macmillan).

Freidson, E. (1994) *Professionalism Reborn: Theory, Prophecy, and Policy* (Chicago, IL: University of Chicago Press).

Gautam, A. (2000) 'Collabaration Networks, Structural Holes, and Innovation: A Longitudinal Study', *Administrative Science Quarterly*, 45: 425–55.

Gerlach, M. L. (1992) *Alliance Capitalism* (Berkeley, CA: University of California Press).

Greenwood, R., C. R. Hinings and J. Brown (1990) 'The P2 Form of Strategic Management: Corporate Practices in the Professional Partnership', *Academy of Management Journal* 33, 725–55.

Gnyawali, Devi R. and R. Madhavan (2001) 'Cooperative Networks and Competitive Dynamics: A Structural Embeddedness Perspective', *Academy of Management Review*, 26, 431–45.

————— (1994) 'Merging Professional Service Firms', *Organization Science*, 5, 239–57.

Hansen, M. T. (2002) 'Knowledge Networks: Explaining Effective Knowledge Sharing in Multiunit Companies', *Organization Science*, 13, 232–48.

Hinings, C. R., J. L. Brown and R. Greenwood (1991) 'Change in an Autonomous Professional Organization', *Journal of Management Studies*, 28, 375–94.

Human, S. E. and K. G. Provan (2000) 'Legitimacy Building in the Evolution of Small-Firm Multilateral Networks: A Comparative Study of Success and Demise', *Administrative Science quarterly*, 45, 327–66.

Kenis, P. and D. Knoke (2002) 'How Organizational Field Networks Shape Inter-organizational Tie-Formation Rates', *Academy of Management Review*, 27, 275–95.

Koza, M. P. and A. Y. Lewin (1999) 'The Coevolution of Network Alliances: A Longitudinal Analysis of an International Professional Service Network', *Organization Science*, 10, 638–53.

Kumon, S. (1992) 'Japan as a Network Society', in S. Kumon and H. Rosovsky (eds), *The Political Economy of Japan* (Stanford, CA: Stanford University Press). 109–42.

Larson, A. (1992) 'Network Dyads in Entrepreneurial Settings: A Study of the Governance of Exchange Relationships', *Administrative Science Quarterly*, 37, 76–104.

————— (1995) 'A New Phoenix: Modern Putting-Out in the Modena Knitwear Industry', *Administrative Science Quarterly*, 40, 34–59.

Nahapiet, J. and S. Ghoshal (1998) 'Social Capital, Intellectual Capital, and the Organizational Advantage', *Academy of Management Review*, 23, 242–66.

Porter, M. E. (1990) *The Competitive Advantage of Nations* (New York: The Free Press).

Porter, M. E. (1994) 'The Role of Location in Competition', *The Journal of the Economics of Business*, 1: 35–9.

Rangan, S. (2000) 'The Problem of Search and Deliberation in Economic Action: When Social Networks Really Matter', *Academy of Management Review*, 25, 313–28.

Ring, P. S. (1996a) 'Fragile Trust and Resilient Trust and Their Roles in Cooperative Interorganizational Relationships', *Business & Society*, 35(2), 148–75.

Ring, P. S. and A. H. Van de Ven (1992) 'Structuring Cooperative Relationships Between Organizations', *Strategic Management Journal*, 13, 483–98.

Rosenkopf, L., A. Metia and V. George (2001) 'From the Bottom Up? Technical Committee Activity and Alliance Formation', *Administrative Science Quarterly*, 46, 748–72.

Teece, D. E. (1987) 'Profiting from Technological Innovation: Implications for Integration, Collaboration, Licensing and Public Policy', in D. E. Teece (ed.), *The Competitive Challenge* (Cambridge, MA: Ballinger), 185–220.

Uzz, B. (1997) 'Social Structure and Competition in interfiler networks', *Administrative Science Quarterly*, 42, 37–69.

Winter, S. (1987) 'Knowledge and Competence as Strategic Assets', in D. E. Teece, (ed.), *The Competitive Challenge* (Cambridge, MA: Ballinger), 159–84.

16

The Impact of Personal and Organizational Ties on Strategic Alliance Characteristics and Performance: A Study of Alliances in the USA, Israel and Taiwan

*Paul Olk, Shaul M. Gabbay and Tsungting Chung**

Introduction

Companies creating value through global strategies increasingly use *alliances* in the 'race for the world' (Doz and Hamel 1998). In order to achieve global success, managers benefit from creating effective alliances. Research into the determinants of strategic alliance characteristics and performance has examined various factors, including motives and organizational characteristics of the partners (Contractor and Lorange 1988; Sakakibara 1997), technology (for example, Williamson 1991), industry characteristics (for instance, Harrigan 1986), and partnering organizations' countries of origin (for example, Gomes-Casseres 1989). While these explanations offer many insights into designing more effective alliances, this research has generally not considered the role of *interpersonal relationships* in creating international partnerships (Olk and Earley 1996). Overlooking this dimension is important because alliances are considered to be a 'relational contract' (Williamson 1985) – a mixture of formal, legal provisions and interpersonal exchanges (Ring and Van de Ven 1994) – and an *exchange-based explanation* underlies most theoretical accounts

* Funding for this study was provided by the National Science Foundation Grant 0120781 – 'SGER: Interpersonal and Interorganizational Networks for Strategic Alliance Development in the High Technology Sector: A Comparative Study of Israel and Colorado', NSF (Innovation and Organizational Change Program). The authors would like to thank Jon Levy, Tyles Entwistle, Eric Frank, Suresh Janarthan, T. J. Stewart and Brianna Tom for their assistance with data collection.

of alliances. Given that there are culturally different approaches toward the concept of an exchange (Fiske 1991), how well a company manages these various exchanges will undoubtedly affect the success of its strategic alliances and its global strategy.

Understanding this issue will also benefit research into strategic alliances. Case studies of the alliance formation process often portray it as a mix of interpersonal and interorganizational activities. These descriptions emphasize the need to appreciate the underlying relational dynamics and social processes (for example, Doz 1996; Ariño and de la Torre 1998), including the importance of interpersonal relationships (Gray 1989). This research has shown that relationships among the founders can influence alliance formation, but has generally been limited to single case studies, simple measures of personal social networks (for instance, Eisenhardt and Schoonhoven 1996), or laboratory studies (for example, Olk and Elvira 2001). Absent from this research is a careful explication of how personal ties interact with organizational ties, and how these relationships affect strategic alliance outcomes.

This chapter begins to fill this gap by exploring the importance of *multilevel ties* for strategic alliances. After providing more details about the motivation for the research question, we present a general model of personal and organizational ties' influence on strategic alliance characteristics and on performance. We then report data on high-technology alliances involving small companies based in the USA, Israel and Taiwan. The findings reveal that interpersonal and interorganizational relationships have separate but significant effects on alliance structure and strategy, as well as on alliance performance.

A multilevel approach towards strategic alliances

Research into strategic alliances has revealed multiple reasons why personal and organizational ties may affect an alliance's characteristics: the respective contributions these ties each bring to an alliance, the strength of multiplex relationships and the increasing prevalence of individual discretion in developing company strategy. We review each of these before turning to our model of these ties' impact on alliances.

One reason for considering both interpersonal and interorganizational levels in forming alliances is that these represent different types of ties and will probably have unique effects on an alliance. Explanations for the formation of alliances draw attention to the nature of the exchange, between either individuals or organizations. The exchanges at the different levels, however, are not identical. For example, trust operates differently between individuals than it does between organizations (Zaheer, McEvily and Perrone 1998). The interpersonal and the interorganizational levels may have different effects on an alliance.

In a study that explored some of these effects, Olk (1998) compared the strategy and structure of R&D consortia that emerged from strong personal ties to those that emerged from organizational relationships. He examined the respective influence on when the alliance was formed as well as on the alliance's strategy and structure. The analysis found that alliances stemming from personal ties tended to occur when there was an environmental problem not related to any one company's particular interest. Alliances emerging from organizational-based ties tended to form when there was a simpler issue that was of interest to all of the companies. In examining the consequences of the personal ties, the findings showed that these alliances had more complex goals, brought together companies with a more disparate product or knowledge domain, had a more decentralized structure and had fewer policies governing technology transfer than organizational-based alliances. In findings that counter the expectation that personal ties will lead to more friendly relationships, alliances formed from personal ties did not influence the power balance among the partners and, during negotiations, reported the same if not even higher levels of conflict than alliances formed from organizational ties. Finally, there were several dimensions – company motives for entering, legal structure of the alliance, budget level of the alliance – for which there was no difference between the two types of ties. These exploratory findings suggest that personal and organizational ties may be related to one another but are not identical, and that each can influence the characteristics of an alliance. Considering both, as well as the absence of either, will provide additional understanding into how these ties affect an alliance.

A second reason for taking a multilevel perspective comes from the value of having several types of ties between alliance partners. The presence of multiple ties enhances the likelihood of forming, and the structure of, an additional alliance (Gulati 1995). Further, multiplex relations serve as a deterrent for breaking an existing tie. Companies tend to not jeopardize the other relationships and will keep an existing tie (Aldrich and Whetten 1981). Although, drawing from the above argument, the importance of a relationship at the interpersonal level may not be identical to one at the interorganizational level, the presence of both will probably lead to a stronger relationship and affect the type of alliance created.

A final reason to consider personal and organizational ties is their enhanced role in developing a company's strategy. Both practitioners and researchers have argued that since the 1980s there has been an increase in *individual-level discretion* in organizations (Galbraith 1994). Unlike in 'command and control' structures, these increasingly flatter and 'boundaryless' organizations rely more upon individual initiative and relationships both within and across organizations to develop and implement a strategy. For example, Doz, Santos and Williamson (2001) argued that as knowledge becomes more dispersed not only within organizations but across various countries, successful companies will be able to locate, harness and exploit the various pools of knowledge. For a firm to become a 'metanational', it needs to make several changes in its structure, including viewing the corporate centre not as the fount of knowledge or the natural leader but letting the 'peripherals lead' in order to incorporate new knowledge created from their entrepreneurial insights. As companies continue to implement these organizational changes and to pursue strategic alliances, we are more likely to see individual-level factors influencing the development of an alliance.

In summary, personal and organizational ties appear to have a unique and increasingly larger impact on company strategies. To understand the determinants of a strategic alliance's characteristics and performance will require incorporating multilevel ties.

The general model

Even though the argument so far suggests that interpersonal and interorganizational relationships need to be considered in understanding alliance strategy, structure and performance, these relationships are generally outside the scope of most explanations of strategic alliances. To provide some empirical evaluation of this argument and to augment existing accounts, we turn to our study of alliances formed in three different countries. Figure 16.1 present a model of the relationships we examined in these alliances.

Our model begins by considering alliances as *exchange-based relationships*. Since exchanges reflect underlying cultural values (Fiske 1991) and typically vary with national culture of the individuals (for example, Hofstede 1991) and of the organizations (for instance, Hamel 1991; Parkhe 1993), we anticipate there will be differences in the experiences found in the USA, Israel and Taiwan. These exchanges create two types of relationships – personal and organizational ties – which represent the starting points for network formation processes reported by Doz, Olk and Ring (2000). These authors argued that networks emerge from either an *emergent* or an *engineered* process. In the former, companies

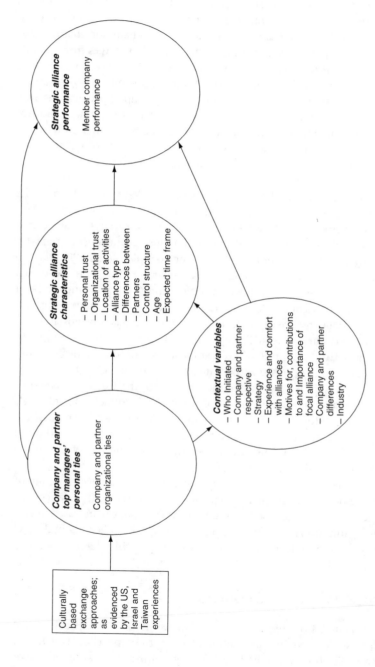

Figure 16.1 Model of the proposed study

that work in the same environment, who have common interests and prior relationships join together to solve a recognized problem. In this formation, there is no triggering entity or champion that oversees the development of the network: the relationship emerges from *existing organizational network ties*. In contrast, the engineered process begins when a champion (typically an individual, but on occasion an organization) initiates discussions with others, often by drawing upon personal network ties, to create a linkage between organizations that previously did not have one. These two formations were associated with different network outcomes, with emergent processes leading to a more formal structure and greater learning while engineered processes leading to informal structures and less learning.

While Doz, Olk and Ring (2000) provided evidence of different paths for network formation, the relevance of variations in personal and organizational networks was not evaluated. Other research has associated prior ties with more informal alliance governance characteristics and with a tendency to form additional alliances (for example, Gulati 1995) but the impact of personal ties on alliances has generally only been speculated upon (for instance, Olk and Earley 1996), and the importance of both of these two types of relationships for strategic alliances remains unexamined. Consequently, we examine interorganizational relationships, in terms of prior and current relationships, and interpersonal relationships, in terms of both formal, role-based relationships and informal, friendship ties and their relationship with strategic alliance characteristics.

In our analysis, we also attempt to account for the variety of *contextual factors* that prior research has revealed will probably influence an alliance's characteristics (for example, who initiated it, the strategic interests of the company and the partner, company and partner differences, the industry). Finally, we examine if these ties have a direct and indirect effect on the performance of the strategic alliance.

In summary, the central theme of the integrated framework we adopt is that global strategy increasingly relies upon strategic alliances. In practice, but not understood theoretically, these alliances are based in part upon organizational and individual relationships. By collecting multilevel data, we attempt to evaluate these ties as possible determinants of successful alliances.

Research locations and methods

The data come from high-technology alliances formed by entrepreneurial companies located in three different countries: the USA, Israel, and Taiwan. We chose small, high-technology companies because the role of interpersonal relationships is likely to be stronger in these organizations than in larger ones. If we are to begin to understand the effect these relationships have on alliance characteristics, these companies are a good place to begin. We focused on these countries, in part, because regions within each country share the commonality of a fast-growing, high-technology community.

We conducted case studies because information on formation processes is typically not found in archival databases or is difficult to capture in survey questionnaires. In each location, we therefore interviewed the company founder, and if necessary other top managers, about the company's overall strategy and its approach towards strategic alliances, and then focused in depth on a particular alliance. The interviews followed a semi-structured process where we asked a series of questions to ensure that we received the necessary information but also permitted the interviewee to discuss other issues about the company or alliance. These interviews generally lasted about 1.5 hours and often included follow-up interviews with other managers in the company, when they were available, or when it was deemed they might have a different perspective. Often, however, because the companies were relatively small, only one interview was conducted. On occasion we also interviewed managers in the partnering company for their perspective. But because our focus was on the focal company, and how it viewed alliances, we did not do this for every case. Finally, we collected data from websites and archival sources to supplement the interview data.

Our data collection efforts resulted in information on forty-three companies and their alliances in the USA, ten companies in Israel and eight in Taiwan. Each interview was tape recorded (if the interviewee permitted). Their responses were coded for each of the key variables in the model.

To analyse these data, we transformed the open-ended responses into categorical or Likert-type responses. We conducted two types of analyses. First, we compared the three samples for differences. Since these are not random samples, we wanted to examine whether the samples varied by which companies were willing to be interviewed. We then controlled for these differences when we analysed all of the data using PLS, a structural equation-modelling programme designed for exploratory analyses with small sample sizes.

Results

The results from these analyses revealed the following significant findings. First, an analysis of variance examining cross-country differences among the samples revealed the following. The companies sampled in the USA tended to be younger and were more likely to be in the computer industries (mostly software and services) while the Israeli and Taiwanese companies were older and likely to be engaged in manufacturing high-technology products. The Taiwanese companies were also larger than either the US or Israeli companies. In terms of the alliances formed by these companies, the Israeli alliances were older than the US alliances while the US alliances were more 'virtual', arrangements that did not create a separate entity. As noted, because these are not random samples, we do not believe these differences reflect overall country-based differences in alliances and will examine their impact in our subsequent analysis. Also important to note for our next analysis is that the samples did not differ in terms of whether the alliance was formed from a personal or an organizational tie, the importance of alliances for the focal company, the levels of personal and organizational trust, or the overall performance of these alliances.

We then combined the data from the three countries and conducted a PLS analysis of the proposed relationships in Figure 16.1. The combined data revealed that 46 per cent of the companies had had neither personal or organizational ties with the partner prior to the alliance; 37 per cent had had personal ties but no organizational ties, 6 per cent had had an organizational tie but not an personal tie, and 11 per cent had had both ties. In an iterative process, we first examined each set of relationships separately (for example, country differences on the use of personal and organizational network ties; the effect of personal and organizational network ties on strategic alliance characteristics; the effect of personal and organizational ties on performance). We then trimmed the non-significant relationships and simultaneously examined the remaining relationships. This produced an overall model evaluating the impact of personal and organizational ties. Table 16.1 summarizes the key findings.

Several interesting relationships emerge from this analysis. First, as was indicated by the ANOVA, there was no difference among the three samples in terms of the presence of a personal or organizational tie. These samples had relatively similar percentage of alliances started via personal ties (approximately 40–67 per cent) and via organizational ties (approximately 15–33 per cent). Because these are not random and fairly small samples, we cannot infer that these percentages are representative of the entire countries. What one can conclude from this analysis is that in each of these countries one could expect to see alliances formed from both prior organizational and personal ties.

We also found that personal ties had an effect on alliance characteristics as well as on performance. Personal ties were related to: the company

Table 16.1 Summary of results

Predictor variable	Dependent variable	Interpretation of relationship
Country	Personal or organizational ties	No differences among the three countries in the likelihood of an alliance emerging from a personal or an organizational tie
Personal tie	Who initiated alliance	Alliances started from a personal tie tended to be initiated by the company rather than encouraged by a third party
Personal tie	Partner's contributions to alliance	Alliances started from a personal tie tended to be associated more with a partner contributing technology or legitimacy and less with contributing advice and money
Personal tie	The type of alliance formed	Alliances started from a personal tie tended to be formed between a small and a large company either to create a value add-on product to the larger company's product or to provide services to the larger company's product; they were not likely to be co-specialization agreements between a large and small company, and these ties were not related to alliances formed between two small companies
Personal tie	Alliance performance	Alliances started from a personal tie tended to have better performance
Organizational tie	Why the company entered alliance	Alliances started from an organizational tie tended to be entered in by a company in order to access technology but not to access customers or to enhance visibility
Organizational tie	Level of personal trust	Alliances started from an organizational tie tended to have higher levels of personal trust
Organizational tie	Expected future time frame of alliance	Alliances started from an organizational tie tended to be expected to last longer
Comfort in managing an alliance	Alliance performance	Alliances formed by company managers more comfortable with managing alliances tended to have better performance

Table 16.1   (Continued)

Predictor variable	Dependent variable	Interpretation of relationship
Comfort in managing an alliance	Expected future time frame of alliance	Alliances formed by company managers more comfortable with managing alliances were expected to last longer
Company's contributions to alliance	Alliance performance	Alliances in which the company contributed technology and sales had better performance than alliances in which the company contributed money or credibility
Who initiated the alliance	Age of alliance	Alliances initiated by third parties tended to be older than those initiated by the company

initiating the alliance, what the partner contributed, the type of alliance created and improved alliance performance. Organizational ties, meanwhile, were associated with: why a company entered into an alliance, personal trust and an expected longer time frame for the alliance. Contextual variables were also found to be associated with alliance characteristics and performance. Specifically, a company's comfort with managing an alliance was associated with an expected longer time frame for the alliance, as well as with better performance. The resources contributed by a company were also associated with better performance.

Discussion

Strategic alliances play a progressively greater role in global strategies. Underlying these collaborative arrangements are exchanges – at both the interpersonal and interorganizational level – that can vary by country. This study set out to contribute to our understanding of strategic alliances by exploring how personal and organizational ties affect the characteristics and performance of strategic alliances. The analysis of data collected on the formation of strategic alliances located in the USA, Israel and Taiwan revealed that the presence of these ties not only affects features of the structure and strategy of an alliance, but also its performance. This supports the general contention of the study: personal and organizational ties present at the time of formation have an influence on strategic alliance characteristics and performance.

Several relationships are worth highlighting. First, an alliance created from a personal tie was reported to perform better than other alliances.

While one explanation might be that personal ties led to greater trust and, therefore, fewer governance costs and enhanced performance, this does not appear to apply to this sample. Personal ties were not associated with enhanced trust nor were either individual or organizational trust related to performance. Future research into personal ties should consider the mechanisms by which these ties improve alliance performance.

These personal-level ties also were related to the type of alliance. As noted, personal ties led to alliances that added-on value to a larger company's product. These personal ties were negatively associated with alliances that were co-specialization arrangements between a large and a small company, and were not related to arrangements between two small companies. This last finding was surprising, given that one might anticipate a greater impact of personal ties in smaller companies. Future research should further explore why these select large company–small company alliances were related to personal ties. One explanation, besides a sampling bias, was found in instances where companies formed alliances with former employees or contractors who set up a new company. The prior personal relationship – perhaps due to either enhanced knowledge about reliability of working together or about opportunities that were mutually beneficial to each party – appeared to provide the basis for a new business relationship.

Turning to the organizational ties, of interest is the fact that these ties were strongly related to personal trust, while personal ties were not. This suggests that in these alliances, personal trust is a consequence of a strong relationship forming first at the organizational level. Without this support, it may be difficult for individuals to overcome organizational differences and create a trusting relationship.

Finally, it is worth noting two findings that were not significant. First, while there were significant differences in the types of alliances formed among the three countries, they were not associated with the presence of personal or organizational ties. Second, many of the contextual factors in this study – for example, industry, company strategy – were not related to either alliance characteristics or to performance. In small, high-technology companies, comparative country differences may not be as important for alliance characteristics as are other factors (for instance, comfort in managing alliances, resources contributed). While these non-significant findings may reflect the limitations of the geographical scope of the study – we focused on only three countries, each having strong high-technology sectors – and of the non-random samples collected in each country, they are worth exploring in future research.

The primary limitations of this research stem from its exploratory nature. The samples were not randomly selected, came from only three countries and we did not consider cross-cultural differences in individuals' attitudes towards personal exchanges. Further, this study did not examine international alliances, where a company is entering into a foreign country. Nonetheless, as an exploratory study this chapter opens up interesting insights into the formation and management of strategic alliances. Besides earlier suggestions, future research should continue to explore these issues by expanding data collection to include additional countries besides the USA, Israel and Taiwan, and to include international strategic alliances that involve individuals and companies from different countries. Further, exploring the context in which each or both of these ties might exert a stronger influence on alliance structure and on performance will also enhance our understanding of how to create effective alliances that help to create value for global strategies.

References

Aldrich, H. and D. Whetten (1981) 'Organization Sets, Action Sets, and Networks: Making the Most of Simplicity', in P. Nystrom and W. Starbuck (eds), *Handbook of Organization Design*, 1 (London: Oxford University Press), 385–408.

Ariño, A. and J. de la Torre (1998) 'Learning from Failure: Towards an Evolutionary Model of Collaborative Ventures', *Organization Science*, 9, 306–25.

Contractor, F. and P. Lorange (1988) 'Why Should Firms Cooperate? The Strategy and Economics Basis for Cooperative Ventures', in. F. J. Contractor and P. Lorange (eds), *Cooperative Strategies in International Business* (New York: Lexington Books), 3–31.

Doz, Y. (1996) 'The Evolution of Cooperation in Strategic Alliances: Initial Conditions or Learning Processes', *Strategic Management Journal*, 17, 55–83.

Doz, Y. and G. Hamel (1998) *Alliance Advantage: The Art of Creating Value Through Partnering* (Boston, MA: Harvard Business School Press).

Doz, Y., P. Olk and P.S. Ring (2000) 'Formation of Research and Development Consortia'. 'Which Path to Take? Where Does it Lead?', *Strategic Management Journal*, 20, 239–66.

Doz, Y., J. Santos and P. Williamson (2001) *From Global to Metanational* (Boston, MA: Harvard Business School Press).

Eisenhardt, K. M. and C. Schoonhoven (1996) 'Resource-Based View of Strategic Alliance Formation: Strategic and Social Effects in Entrepreneurial Firms', *Organization Science*, 7, 136–50.

Fiske, A. (1991) *Structures of Social Life: The Four Elementary Forms of Human Relations* (New York: Free Press).

Galbraith, J. (1994) *Competing with Flexible Lateral Organizations* (Reading, MA: Addison-Wesley).

Gomes-Casseres, B. (1989) 'Firm Ownership Preferences and Host Government Restrictions: An Integrated Approach', *Journal of International Business Studies*, 21, 1–22.

Gray, B. (1989) *Collaborating: Finding Common Ground For Multiparty Problems* (San Francisco, CA: Jossey-Bass).

Gulati, R. (1995) 'Does Familiarity Breed Trust? The Implications of Repeated Ties for Contractual Choice in Alliances', *Academy of Management Journal*, 38, 85–112.

Hamel, G. (1991) 'Competition for Competence and Inter-Partner Learning within International Strategic Alliances', *Strategic Management Journal*, 12, 83–103.

Harrigan, K. (1986) *Managing for Joint Venture Success* (Lexington, MA: Lexington Books).

Hofstede, G. (1991) *Culture and Organizations: Software of the Mind* (London: McGraw-Hill).

Olk, P. (1998) 'A Knowledge-Based Perspective on the Transformation of Individual-Level Relationships into Interorganizational Structures: The Case of R&D Consortia', *European Management Journal*, 16, 36–49.

Olk, P. and P. C. Earley (1996) 'Rediscovering the Individual in the Formation of International Strategic Alliances', *Research in the Sociology of Organizations*, 223–61.

Olk, P. and M. M. Elvira (2001) 'Friends and Strategic Agents: The Role of Friendship and Discretion in the Formation of Organizational Alliances', *Group and Organization Management*, 26, 124–64.

Parkhe, A. (1993) 'Partner Nationality and the Structure-Performance Relationship in Strategic Alliances', *Organization Science*, 4, 301–14.

Ring, P. S. and A. H. Van de Ven (1994) 'Developmental Processes in Cooperative Interorganizational Relationships', *Academy of Management Review*, 19, 90–118.

Sakakibara, M. (1997) 'Heterogeneity of Firm Capabilities and Cooperative Research and Development: An Empirical Examination of Motives', *Strategic Management Journal*, Summer, 143–64.

Williamson, O. (1985) *The Economic Institutions of Capitalism: Firms, Markets, Relational Contracting* (New York: Free Press).

————(1991) 'Comparative Economic Organization: The Analysis of Discrete Structural Alternatives', *Administrative Science Quarterly*, 36, 269–96.

Zaheer, A., W. McEvily and V. Perrone (1998) 'Does Trust Matter? Exploring the Effects of Interorganizational and Interpersonal Trust on Performance', *Organization Science*, 9, 141–59.

Part V

Internationalization, Complexity and Organizational Transformation

17

Introduction to Part V

Joan E. Ricart

We live in a world of change. Companies have to renew to cope with the changes in an increasingly interconnected world and with the impact of increasing levels of competition (Hitt, Ricart and Nixon 1998). This increasingly interconnected world, bred by the development of technological innovations (Bettis and Hitt 1995), and also by the lowering of barriers and deregulation (Walker, Madsen and Carini 2002), is creating a new *competitive landscape* in which companies interplay.

To meet this challenge, companies have to decide to renew in an *incremental* or in a *radical* way (Meyer, Brooks and Goes 1990). When the change is incremental, responses may be adaptive. Nevertheless, more and more companies are facing radical, disruptive or even an avalanche of sudden changes (Suarez and Oliva, 2003) that compel them to carry out more sweeping transformations (Audia, Locke and Smith 2000). *Geographical diversification* is one key corporate transformational strategy to address organizational renewal.

Matsusaka (2001) formulated how a highly competitive environment may stimulate diversification. But geographical diversification is not necessarily the right strategy for all companies, nor will it always deliver positive results. Firms engage in international markets with the objective of generating above-average returns on their investments. It is the responsibility of the corporate level to select and manage its industrial and geographical positioning in order to first gain and then sustain its competitive advantage.

The two chapters in Part V deal with sectors – wireless telecoms and car component manufacturing – that have gone through radical transformation. The transformation of these industries has been characterized by a fast, deep and multidimensional change. At the same time, lowering barriers in both industries intensifies the levels of competition towards what some authors have defined as 'hypercompetition' (D'Aveni 1994). To respond to these profound changes, firms must transform in multiple dimensions simultaneously, and internationalization cannot be forgotten.

In the Introduction to the book (Chapter 1), and based on Ghemawat (2003), we parsed the field of strategy into four domains defined by the *level of location* and *business specificity*. The cases in Part V move the focus from the interaction among locations in the international business strategy domain to the so called International corporate strategy domain (box D in Table 1.1, p. 10). This domain combines considerations of business- and location-specificity into an international corporate strategy.

What operating in multiple countries, even a small number of them, implies in practical terms is the imposition of *additional complexity* in the form of the need to pay attention to variations in the macroenvironment. Corporate strategy making can be complex even in the single-country case in the sense of demanding choices along a number of policy dimensions that are distinct but richly interrelated and must therefore be made with some attention to internal consistency. International corporate strategy has, in addition, to confront the extra external complexities associated with operating across borders and the challenges, thereby exacerbated, of achieving the requisite degree of consistency with presumably more varied environments.

The cases studied in Chapters 18 and 19 develop a subtler way to integrate the corporate and international business components of strategy and to confront the increased complexity. In fact, both chapters are essentially a single business case where the corporate strategy insight and influence are fundamental to drive the international dimension of strategy. They integrate the international dimension as a key factor in the corporate transformation to face the radical changes suffered by their respective industries.

The car component manufacturer industry (Chapter 18) is a good example of a turbulent environment. Caldart and Ricart study the evolution of corporate strategy in a longitudinal case study of one successful firm. The authors highlight three key roles for corporate strategy in turbulent environments:

(1) *Driving*, by developing a cognitive representation of the corporate landscape.
(2) *Pacing*, or setting the pace of the company's evolution in a balance between 'long jumps' and 'local searches'.

(3) *Framing*, by developing the organizational architecture that promotes recombination of self-organized units with intraorganizational collaboration initiatives.

Globalization of the car manufacturer industry is a fundamental driver in the environmental change the company is facing. The response is therefore based on the degree and form of internationalization. As the industry landscape evolves, the corporate response adapts this key dimension to the emerging new reality.

The telecoms industry has lived through one of the fastest periods of change created by technological innovations. Koza, Svejenova and Vives (Chapter 19) develop four different strategic profiles as responses to disruptive change in the cellular industry. 'Technological apostles', 'global emperors', 'culture-based regionalists' and 'mighty locals' emerge as different responses to the same drivers of change. They represent different corporate strategies that make different choices within the scope of geographic competition.

Koza *et al.*'s model is sustained by three main theoretical streams. First, it draws on studies that emphasize *path dependencies and imprints* in firms' development (Nelson and Winter 1982). History matters, as it is embedded in routines, resources and capabilities. Second, it uses a *resource and capability-based* views of global competition (Barney 1991). The two key processes it emphasizes are the capability-leverage or exploitation of current capabilities, and capability-building, or development of new competitive resources. These two processes emphasize a key tension between static and dynamic efficiency (Ghemawat and Ricart 1993), exploration and exploitation (March 1991) and different pacing, as explained in Chapter 18. Third, it overviews the literature in co-evolutionary processes (Koza and Lewin 1998), where the interaction between the development of capabilities and the effect of competition is fundamental to understanding such transforming industry.

This descriptive framework permits the identification of characteristic strategy profiles that combine different degrees of technological development and of internationalization. Each profile supports a distinctive competitive position and, as such, it also limits the capacity of adaptation to new changes in the industry. Carving a consistent positioning limits future exploration.

Overall, Part V develops two different situations, two different changes, two different transformations. Both of them, though, are driven by corporate strategy and with international strategy as the key component in the transformational process. The drivers of de-regulation, privatization, globalization and technological change explain the turbulent, hypercompetitive, avalanche of environmental change. A transformation is necessary and, in re-thinking corporate strategy, *internationalization* is one key transformational driver: a fundamental value-creation move through global strategy.

From a theoretical point of view, both chapters draw on the perspective provided by behavioural evolutionism (March and Simon 1958: Nelson and Winter 1982). Furthermore, Caldart and Ricart's Chapter 18 uses *complexity theory*, the application of the work of Kauffman (1993) in the field of biology to organizational theory (Levinthal, 1997; McKelvey 1997, 1999). This perspective provides a fresh view of corporate strategic decisions. Alternatively, Koza *et al.*'s Chapter 19 uses a co-evolutionary lens (Koza and Lewin 1998; Lewin and Volberda 1999) to identify strategic profiles in an evolving industry.

Both perspectives nicely complement each other. One provides a more normative view, the other a more positive one. Together they provide a dynamic view of corporate strategy as it faces key decision in the internationalization process. Overall, the two chapters define corporate strategy as an ongoing action of continuously crafting businesses in a rapidly changing competitive environment. As usual, there is no unique answer. Each firm has to decide how to respond to the technological and globalizing drivers of change that are shaping their industries. In making these key choices at the corporate level they create corporate value through internationalization, a key component of any global strategy.

References

Audia, P., E. Locke and K. Smith (2000) 'The Paradox of Success: An Archival and Laboratory Study of Strategic Persistence following Radical Environmental Change', *Academy of Management Journal*, 43, 837–53.

Barney, J. B. (1991) 'Firm Resources and Sustained Competitive Advantage', *Journal of Management*, 17, 99–120.

Bettis, R. A. and M. A. Hitt (1995) 'The New Competitive Landscape', *Strategic Management Journal*, 16 (Special Issue), 7–20.

D'Aveni, R. (1994) *Hypercompetition* (New York: Free Press).

Ghemawat, P. (2003) 'Semiglobalization and International Business Strategy', *Journal of International Business Studies*, 34(2), 138–52.

Ghemawat, P. and J. E. Ricart (1993) 'The Organizational Tension between Static and Dynamic Efficiency', *Strategic Management Journal*, 14, 59–73.

Hitt, M. A., J. E. Ricart and R. D. Nixon (1998) *The New Frontier. In Managing Strategically in an Interconnected World* (New York: John Wiley).

Kauffman, S. (1998) *The Origins of Order* (New York: Oxford University Press).

Koza, M. P. and A. Y. Lewin (1998) 'The Coevolution of Strategic Alliances', *Organization Science*, 9(3), 255–64.

Levinthal, D. (1997) 'Adaptation in Rugged Fitness Landscapes', *Management Science*, 43, 934–50.

Lewin, A. Y. and H. W. Volberda (1999) 'Prolegomena on Coevolution: A Framework for Research on Strategy and New Organizational Forms', *Organization Science*, 10(5), 519–34.

March, J. (1991) 'Exploration and Exploitation in Organizational Learning', *Organization Science*, 2, 71–87.

March, J. and H. Simon (1958) *Organizations* (New York: John Wiley).

Matsusaka, J. G. (2001) 'Corporate Diversification, Value Maximization, and Organizational Capabilities'. *Journal of Business*, 74(3), 409–31.

McKelvey, B. (1997) 'Quasi-Natural Organization Science', *Organization Science*, 8, 352–80.

———(1999) 'Avoiding Complexity Catastrophe in Coevolutionary Pockets: Strategies for Rugged Landscapes', *Organization Science*, 10, 294–321.

Meyer A. D., G. R. Brooks and J. B. Goes (1990) 'Environmental Jolts and Industry Revolutions: Organizational Response to Discontinuous Change', *Strategic Management Journal*, 11, 93–110.

Nelson, R. and S. Winter (1982) *An Evolutionary Theory of Economic Change* (Cambridge, MA: Bellknap Press).

Suarez, F. and R. Oliva (2003) 'Avalanche Environmental Change and Organizational Transformation', Working Paper, OTM 03–014, London Business School.

Walker, G., T. L. Madsen and G. Carini (2002) How Does Institutional Change Affect Heterogeneity Among Firms?', *Strategic Management Journal*, 23(2), 89–104.

18

The Roles of the Corporate Level in the Internationalization Process of the Firm

Ádrian Atilio Caldart and Joan E. Ricart *

Introduction

After many years of abundant research in corporate strategy, the issue of whether and how the corporate level contributes to competitive advantage still raises strong controversies. An important stream of work aims at identifying the *sources of corporate performance* by isolating company, industry and corporate effects on this variable (Schmalensee 1985; Rumelt 1991; McGahan and Porter 1997). These contributions concluded that corporate effects appeared to be negligible. However, this 'truth' of strategic management has been challenged by recent findings (Brush and Bromiley 1997, Chang and Singh 2000; Bowman and Helfat 2001), leading to the conclusion that studies within this tradition appear to be strongly affected by apparent and difficult to fix sampling biases and methodological flaws (Brush and Bromiley 1997; Chang and Singh 2000; Bowman and Helfat 2001).

The persistence of mixed results in such important lines of research suggests that new approaches to the study of the field would be welcome. The creation of corporate advantage may be a phenomenon of a subtlety that cannot be captured by cross-sectional database statistical studies (Bowman and Helfat 2001). Addressing the need of approaching corporate strategy under innovative perspectives, the purpose of this chapter is

* We gratefully acknowledge support for this research from IESE Business School's Anselmo Rubiralta Center on Globalization and Strategy.

to explore specifically whether, and how, the corporate level of a firm contributes to the development of its internationalization strategy. This issue has not been addressed by the international business literature., so this study could constitute a way to build bridges between these two closely related but poorly communicating areas of the field of strategic management.

From a theoretical standpoint, we draw on the perspective provided by behavioural evolutionism (March and Simon 1958; Cyert and March, 1963; Nelson and Winter 1982) and complexity theory, particularly, in the application of the work of Kauffman (1993) in the field of biology to organization theory (Levinthal, 1997; McKelvey 1997, 1999; Brown and Eisenhardt, 1998; Gavetti and Levinthal, 2000; Galunic and Eisenhardt, 2001). These theoretical insights led our exploratory fieldwork, performed in a car component manufacturing firm that engaged in an aggressive process of internationalization during the period 1986–2001.

The firm's evolution: fitness Landscapes

Metaphorically, firms have long been viewed as organisms, gathering resources from, and adapting to, their environment. More recently, organizational ecologists have imported models from biology to explain the forces and variables underlying organizational founding, change and mortality. As a result, the notion of *organizational fitness* is now well accepted (Hannan and Freeman 1977). Though typically associated with selection arguments and what is referred to as the 'Environmental School' of strategy (Mintzberg, Ahlstrand and Lampel 1998), the notion of 'fit' is also found in the 'Design School' of strategy (Mintzberg, Ahlstrand and Lampel 1998), which emphasizes strategic choice and views firms as actively seeking strategic fit. Levinthal (1991) stated that the opposition of these two arguments is artificial. The exploration of the managerial issues related to adaptation and strategizing, connecting both approaches, can be done by drawing on Kauffman's *NK* model (Kauffman 1993).

Kauffman's contribution

Kauffman (1993) challenged the universal applicability of selection theory by suggesting that in sufficiently complex systems, selection cannot avoid the order exhibited by organisms as a result of their *self-organizing properties*. In such situations, order is present 'not because of selection but despite it' (Kauffman 1993). To explain the relationship between selection and self-organizing, Kauffman, used the 'fitness landscape' metaphor. A 'fitness landscape' consists of a multidimensional space in which each attribute of the organization is represented by a dimension of the space and a final dimension indicates the fitness level of the organization.

Following Levinthal (1997) and McKelvey (1999), we will accept the premise that Kauffman's assumptions apply equally well to firms. Organizations adapt by modifying their existing form in an attempt to enhance their fitness in a *payoff surface* or *fitness landscape* (Sewell Wright 1931, cited in Levinthal 1997). The character of adaptive evolution depends on the structure of such a fitness landscape. Increasing the density of interdependencies affects the complexity of the landscape and, consequently, the emergent patterns of behaviour.

The NK model

Kauffman (1993) characterizes fitness landscapes by, essentially, two structural variables: N, the number of elements that characterize the entity (actions or policy choices in the context of organizations) and K, the number of elements of N with which a given attribute interacts. When there is no interaction ($K = 0$), the landscape tends to assume a single-peak configuration. As the contribution of each attribute is independent of that of others, there is an optimal behaviour independent of others' behaviour. In this situation, the collective fitness of the firm is improved by improving each attribute's contribution to fitness through local search. However, as interactions increase, the landscape becomes more rugged or multipeaked. Multiple peaks are the direct result of interdependencies among a set of policy choices. In a rugged landscape, incremental search will lead only to the local peak closest to the starting point of the search process, regardless of its height relative to other peaks in the landscape. As a result of this locking-in to the first available solution, a strong form of *path dependence* is observed and, on average, modest performance ('competency traps'). One mechanism to overcome such 'traps' is to engage in 'long-jumps', random explorations of more distant portions of the landscape.

The international expansion of Lujan SA[1]

This section provides an insight into what roles the corporate level plays during the internationalization process of a firm. Given the lack of a comprehensive framework for understanding the impact of the corporate-level initiatives in an internationalization strategy over a long period, we chose to develop a longitudinal case study research. Concretely, this section narrates briefly how Lujan SA, a car component manufacturer based in Barcelona, evolved from being a 'Spanish Champion' in the mid-1980s to a positioning in eighteen countries located in all the key geographical 'centres of gravity' of the car industry worldwide by 2001. During this period, Lujan achieved a tremendous success, illustrated by an annual increase in sales averaging 23 per cent from 1985–2000. The company increased its number of employees from 703 in 1985 to 6,121 in 2000. The purpose of this study was to identify how the company's corporate strategy contributed to Lujan's extraordinary and successful internationalization process during the period under study. It is the result of extensive fieldwork at Lujan from summer 2001–summer 2002.

The evolution of Lujan, 1986–2001

After the end of the Second World War, Spain suffered an international economic embargo against the Franco regime. Lacking an local automobile industry of its own, isolation led to a severe shortage of spare parts for cars. In this context, in 1949, Lujan was founded by two cousins, Pere Feliu and Joan Roig with the purpose of supplying brake, clutch and speedometer cables for used cars. As it was in close contact with its customers, Lujan noticed the car manufacturer's additional needs and expanded its product line beyond the cable business. In this way, the small firm became a group of companies producing many products such as cables, windscreen wipers, rearview mirrors, sunvisors and window handles.

The organization was strongly centralized, with CEO Roig making all the strategic and marketing decisions concerning the different businesses, with only operational management being decentralized. By 1976, as a consequence of the firm's growth, Roig decided to delegate all business decisions to the managers of the different companies, who from then on operated with a high degree of autonomy. Consequently, Lujan became a holding company, acting as the corporate centre of a multibusiness group, to which it provided commercial, financial, administrative, legal and economic services.

Becoming European, 1986–95

The first major shift in Lujan's corporate strategy began in 1986 and lasted for nearly a decade. On 1 January 1986, Spain entered into the EEC. Besides this regulatory breakthrough, Lujan's industrial sector also had also been undergoing important changes since the late 1970s and early 1980s. Car manufacturers began to centralize component development in their regional headquarters, making Lujan's strong local commercial relationships in Spain no longer critical. In the light of these events, Lujan's top management realized that, from then on, the natural market space for 'tier 1' European companies was no longer their home countries, but the whole of the EU. Lujan had barely had commercial relations with the car makers' European headquarters in the past. The controlling shareholders decided to engage in a European expansion plan aimed at positioning the company as a major European component manufacturer. The tactic was to open engineering centres in each target country, led by native engineers hired 'ad hoc', with the purpose of building the company's reputation as an innovative European manufacturer. The purpose of the engineering centres was to establish strong relationships with the car manufacturers' R&D centres. Only once this process was successful and contracts with the customer had begun to be agreed would Lujan consider beginning operations at the site. Lujan thus opened an engineering centre in London in 1987 and a factory in Birmingham a year later. In 1988 Lujan opened its second engineering centre in Germany, to conduct dealings with the German manufacturers. That same year Lujan opened a third engineering centre in France and bought 50 per cent of a local rearview mirror manufacturer, as French customers particularly appreciated suppliers with operations in the country.

After less than two years, Lujan was already present in three out of four key European areas (the exception was Italy) and had operations in two of them.

Going global, 1995–2000

In 1995, new developments taking place in the car and component industries gave rise to new challenges. Since the beginning of the 1990s, competition among car manufacturers had been tough. In the aftermath of excessive capacity-building came a huge wave of industry consolidation that left the world market in the hands of a very few firms. As components accounted for between 60 per cent and 70 per cent of the cost of a new car, trimming the cost of supplies became the manufacturers' central concern. This issues put pressure on component manufacturers to acquire a presence in all the high-volume or high-growth regions of the car business, in order to obtain scale economies in purchases and R&D.

Despite the fact that its European expansion was not yet complete, Lujan's management realized that *global presence* was the only way to hold on to its 'tier one' status, a central strategic objective of the company, and so decided to embark on a new geographical expansion plan in order to follow their existing customers' global expansion and win new customers worldwide. Lujan's repositioning was aimed at developing a presence in the two geographical areas that made up the 'heart' of the car industry besides Europe – NAFTA and Japan – and in markets with strong growth potential such as Mercosur, India, Korea and China.

After assessing several alternatives for positioning within NAFTA, Lujan in 1995 opened a small sales office in Detroit, USA and began its operations by renting a small plant in Monterrey, Mexico, the NAFTA country with the lowest production costs and highest market growth potential. In 1997 significant business growth persuaded the company to build its own plant and convert the Detroit sales office into an engineering centre. In 1999 a second plant was opened in Monterrey and the engineering centre was further expanded.

In India, Lujan entered into a joint venture (JV) with a local holding company in 1997, hoping to exploit the huge market potential that an emerging India offered. The JV was expected to supply components to a division of the Indian holding company and to international manufacturers operating in India.

In Japan, Lujan opened a sales and engineering centre in 1997. As access to the market was hampered by the '*keiretsu*' structure of the industry, Lujan formed alliances with four local companies manufacturing mirrors, cables, brake systems and plastics. Lujan marketed its Japanese partners' products outside Japan, while they marketed Lujan's products in Japan.

In 1999, Lujan entered the Asia-Pacific region by acquiring an equity stake in a components manufacturer in South Korea, with the aim of supplying the big car manufacturers.

In Mercosur, most of the best-positioned car companies were already Lujan's customers and were expected to manufacture the global platforms for their latest small and medium-sized models in that area. Accordingly, in 1996, Lujan formed a JV in Brazil with a local firm and set up a plant for its three international lines of business. In 1998 the company became a fully owned subsidiary of Lujan and led the Brazilian market for rearview mirrors. In Argentina, Lujan acquired a controlling 55 per cent stake in a local component manufacturer in 1997.

In early 2000, in a major new move, Lujan acquired the mirrors division of one of its major European competitors, the biggest acquisition in the company's history. This made Lujan the third largest producer of rearview mirrors in the world and gave it new manufacturing presence in Italy (the only important European location in which it had not yet established itself), France, Spain, Poland, Brazil, Argentina, India and Turkey. The company kept its divisional structure, with highly empowered and independent divisions, however, the increase in the number and location of facilities made it impossible to carry on using its somewhat informal control system and standardization became the obvious solution. Lujan developed a highly formalized and integrated reporting system, designed to simplify corporate evaluation of the divisions. Divisions were framed as parts of a portfolio, according to their cash–growth profile and lost control over their funds. The beginning of the global strategy in 1995 brought also changes in the Board. The entry of two private equity firms as minority partners, reinforced the presence of external directors and the financial bias of the Board.

Getting tighter, 2000–2

The already tight situation of the low-growth car industry worsened as a result of the global economic slowdown that began in 2000. The components sector was expected to undergo a fresh round of consolidation, leading to an industry configuration characterized by concentration in a minority of powerful component giants. In this context, Lujan began another major strategic shift. The company level ordered the divisions to put *margin-strengthening* at the top of the agenda, leaving the global expansion plan 'on hold'. Operations located in low-cost regions were further developed. This third shift in Lujan's corporate strategy had a much greater impact on its architectural design than the previous two, as the need for cost-cutting led the corporate level to prioritize *synergy development*, even if partly at the expense of the traditional philosophy in favour of a high degree of divisional autonomy. Diversity of systems, structures and procedures had multiplied with organic growth and, particularly, with acquisitions. Significant cost-cutting opportunities resulting from cross-business collaboration became apparent. Accordingly, the corporate centre launched a series of organizational changes aimed at exploiting potential synergies, trying at the same time to preserve the 'small-company' culture that had contributed so much to Lujan's success.

A *matrix structure* was developed in all international divisions. Business units, grouped either by product or by customer decision centre, became responsible for the business strategy, revenues and return. Four global functional units: Operations, Technical, Purchasing and Quality were responsible for optimizing their areas of specialization. Business unit and functional directors had worldwide authority. Purchases and Logistics were centralized as a corporate function in an effort to obtain scale economies. The R&D functions that did not demand close interaction with customers and accounted for 60 per cent of total R&D costs were centralized in the industrial headquarters in Barcelona.

Discussion

The main features of Lujan's successful internationalization strategy show that the *corporate level* played a significant role in three ways (Caldart and Ricart 2004). First, the corporate level restated what were the relevant geographical boundaries of the firm. This new cognitive representation of the business landscape *drove* the firm's divisions to engage in an European expansion and later on in a global expansion. Second, despite divisions having authority and responsibility for business strategy, the corporate level *paced* their evolution process through a set of 'simple rules' (Eisenhardt and Sull 2001), biasing divisional initiatives, whether towards 'local search' or 'long-jumps'. Finally, the corporate level also adapted the firm's architectural design to the new realities of international competition. However these changes were not specific but just broad organizational arrangements aimed at *framing* divisions' self-organizing processes.

Drive: reinterpreting the geographic business landscape

A firm's choice of strategy is often a by-product of actors' representation of their *problem space* (Fiol and Huff 1992; Walsh 1995). *Cognition* is a forward-looking form of intelligence that is premised on an actor's belief about the linkage between the choice of actions and the subsequent impact of those actions on outcomes. Such beliefs derive from the actor's mental model of the world or 'dominant logics' (Prahalad and Bettis 1986). In contrast, *experiential wisdom* accumulates as a result of positive and negative reinforcement of prior choices (Levitt and March 1988).

Powerful analytical representations of the fitness landscape that reduce the dimensionality – and, in turn, the cognitive complexity – of the space provide a strong guide to action. The normative traditions of the management literature in particular offer low-dimensional typologies such as the BCG or GE matrixes (Hax and Majluf 1985) and 'generic strategies' (Porter 1980) that help to structure the choice of firm strategy. However, to the extent that the representation does not capture the essential structure of the real fitness landscape, it will be a mistaken guide (Levinthal and Warglien 1999).

Cognitive representations provide not only a powerful suggestion for an initial choice of organizational form, but also a useful discipline in subsequent efforts at experiential search. However, with a fixed cognition, the organization immediately identifies the highest peak with respect to its cognitive representation. Associated with this point is a subset of policy variables. Without a shift to a new cognitive representation, there is no basis for moving from the position identified initially (Gavetti and Levinthal 2000).

Changing cognitive representations can be an important form of adaptation in two different respects. First, the new representation may consist of a better *mental model* of the actor's environment, reflecting weaknesses of the prior representation or the existence of environmental shifts that render a previously adequate representation less effective. Second, shifting cognitive frameworks effectively results in a sequential allocation of attention to *different facets* of the actor's environment. The shift in policies prompted by the new representation may result in the loss of the experiential wisdom accumulated in the context of the prior representation. However, with dramatic changes in the fitness landscape, prior experiential wisdom is rendered largely obsolete. In the face of events triggering drastic environmental changes, the ability to rapidly identify attractive regions in the landscape, via a cognitive process as a result of a shift in cognitive representation, can compensate for the loss associated with foregone experiential wisdom.

As it can be seen in our story of Lujan's evolution, the corporate level of the company shifted radically its 'view of the world' twice during the period under study. First, by 1986 it had acknowledged the decreasing value of the current national position in Spain. Repositioning itself to be near the European headquarters of car manufacturers became mandatory in the context of West European economic unification and the car makers' tendency to concentrate purchasing decisions and component development in their headquarters. Second, in 1995, the globalization of the car industry and the increasing pressure on suppliers to reduce costs led Lujan's top managers to conclude that global presence would be crucial for Lujan's survival as a 'tier one' component supplier.

Pacing: evolving in the business landscape

Guided by its cognitive representation, the corporation tries to 'climb' a basin of attraction towards a peak. Hill-climbing strategies can take two extreme forms: local or incremental search, or non-incremental search or 'long-jumps'.

Local search

Search is local when the company aims at improving through experiential learning within its current cognitive representation. Local search is equivalent to the static efficiency concept developed in Ghemawat and Ricart (1993) and therefore represents one extreme in a continuous spectrum of choices. The other extreme, dynamic efficiency, corresponds to the non-incremental search presented next. This strategy permits high exploitation, as changes or organization attributes are only incremental, but limited exploration, as learning is constrained by the local topography on which the actor lies, increasing the risks of suffering the pathology labelled by Levitt and March (1988) as 'competency trap' and by Kauffman (1993) as a 'complexity catastrophe' – that is, climbing towards a local peak that is unattractive.

Non-incremental search or 'long-jumps'

In contrast to local search, 'long-jumps' involve the simultaneous alteration of many of the firm's attributes. This strategy is characterized by high exploration but limited exploitation and emphasizes sample variation. 'Long-jumps' prevent the company from falling into competency traps, and are more valuable in turbulent environments in which the value of current knowledge diminishes, making exploitation less relevant. However, the impact of alternative sampling strategies varies dramatically depending on whether the evaluation mechanism is one of on-line experimentation or off-line cognition (Gavetti and Levinthal 2000). If the evaluation of alternatives is off-line, the variation in the sample is generally an attractive property. If low outcome draws can be costlessly discarded (or at low cost), the greater variance in the sample increases the expected value of the draws that are adopted, therefore encouraging long jumps. Real options (Amram and Kulatilaka 1999), cooperation strategies for risk sharing such as strategic alliances and hedging strategies, are examples of how firms try to absorb complexity through low-cost, multiple and sometimes conflicting representations of environmental variety.

In a process of 'on-line' experimentation, however, such variation may prove fatal because the actor experiences the consequences of each experimental draw, facing the risk of falling into an 'error catastrophe' (Brown and Eisenhardt 1998). Off-line experimentation is one form of locating the search strategy between the two extremes. As elaborated in Ghemawat and Ricart (1993), there is a tendency to move towards the extremes, making the intermediate cases difficult to reach. Off-line experimentation is one alternative, recombination (as explained next) is another, as it could be possible to think of temporal arrangements that periodically move from one extreme to the other. All these solutions and others one can develop will create important *organizational tensions* (Ghemawat and Ricart 1993).

In the comfortably protected Spanish market before 1986, Lujan's strategy evolved incrementally, just adapting to the product needs of its current Spanish customers. In this context, local commercial relationships were the key success factor. However, this situation had changed rapidly by 1986. Realizing that the basin of attraction of its business model based in a national positioning was losing height, the corporate level engaged the company in an evolution strategy shaped by multiple 'off-line' 'long-jump' initiatives towards higher basins of attraction. Simple corporate rules such as 'we must have presence where the manufacturers make design and purchase decisions' inspired business units' initiatives. These bets were gradually augmented as promising results unfolded. This allowed the company to engage in intense exploration, but retaining the ability of discarding low-outcome moves at a low cost. The company engaged in multiple real options, particularly those that fitted the definition of 'corporate growth options' (Trigeorgis 1996). During the period 1986–95, building of commercial relationships with car manufacturers across Europe that could benefit every business unit in the future and the opening of new plants for single product lines with the possibility of extending the range of products in the future are examples of Lujan's intuitive application of this idea. The gradual increases in the company's position in the UK, Germany and France, thanks to successful market penetration, show how the company 'exercised' these successful growth options.

As the struggle for economies of scale in purchasing and R&D, obliged 'tier one' firms to go global, a second 'long-jump' based in 'off-line' strategic moves began around 1995. The scope of the company's geographical market shifted yet again towards the development of a global position, with new operations and engineering centers in NAFTA, Mercosur, Korea and India and commercial agreements in Japan. During this period, the strategy of engaging in multiple and varied initiatives was intensified. Entry into the USA, Mexico, Brazil and Argentina was gradual and subject to unfolding events, constituting new corporate growth options. Lujan's initial positioning in Korea and India also represented limited downside bets.

The acquisition, in early 2000, of the Mirrors Division of a major European competitor reflects the transition between this period of 'long-jumps' and the subsequent stage focused on local search or static efficiency. On the one hand, with this major acquisition the company developed new corporate growth options, such as entry into Poland, a beachhead for the fast-growing East European market, and Turkey, another fast-growing, low-cost area. At the same time, this acquisition allowed the company to obtain worldwide leadership status in the mirrors business, easing the development of economies of scale in Purchasing and R&D.

In 2000, the company moved back towards a a local search bias. However, this refocusing did not come after the company had completed its global expansion but in the middle of the process. Interviewees agreed that the company's global positioning could not be considered complete until Lujan had built up operations in the USA and China, both still unrealized objectives. However, the combination of a huge expansion effort and the global economic slowdown led the company to grind to a halt and focus on strengthening margins at the expense of fast growth. Lujan's spectacular growth during the period 1986–99 came at the expense of tolerating important organizational inefficiencies, as the corporate focus was set on aggressively gaining market share 'as the only possible path to secure survival', as one board member put it. Three interviewees remarked that, while the divisions broadly shared a common 'Lujan culture', their evolution was divergent in structure, systems and style, as these features were developed according to division leaders' own idiosyncrasy.

Drive: an architectural design for global competition

Through an analysis of the high-profile organizational initiatives that took place after 1999, we can identify several features of Lujan's corporate level architectural design initiatives concerning its international divisions: the development of *standardized processes* across divisions, the promotion of *recombination* of resources and business opportunities, the development of channels for *interdivisional collaboration* and the adoption of *performance metrics* consistent with corporate priorities. We consider these characteristics the 'building blocks' of a coherent management system, promoted by the corporate level, with the purpose of fostering a bottom-up, self-organized approach to horizontal collaboration between business units within each division and between divisions.

Recombination

Apart from 'off-line' 'long-jumps', another partial solution to the dilemma of how to get the advantages of exploration without losing the benefits of exploitation through 'on-line' experimentation, is the recombination of elements of existing partial solutions (Levinthal and Warglien 1999) through the manipulation of the interdependences (K) between different elements of N. Entrepreneurs do not randomly sample the space of alternatives, but find new, unforeseen combinations of known but previously distant elements. Galunic and Eisenhardt (2001) propose 'chartering', a competitive process between units enabling the recombination or 'patching' (Eisenhardt and Brown 1999) of product market domains between business units in response to market changes. Patching permits a company to engage in 'long-jumps' exploiting existing building blocks of knowledge without being trapped by this knowledge. In this way, the company obtains *inter-temporal economies of scope* (Helfat and Eisenhardt 2001), arising from the replacement of old businesses that used that resource by a new business that does so, in response to changing market conditions, an approach that would require a matrix type of organization.

Lujan's recently created matrix organization has been conceived in a way that facilitates the recombination of changing global business opportunities with manufacturing facilities worldwide for business units operating within each division. Operations managers have authority over plant activities worldwide and are therefore able to recombine operations' locations and business projects in such a way as to provide a competitive cost to business unit managers within each division, who also have a worldwide responsibility.

Standardization

Organizational initiatives initiated up until 1999 also included important efforts to standardize procedures. Corporate Purchases and Logistics developed companywide standardized procedures and were set with a global logic. Planning and control and information systems were unified throughout the company. Finally, Human Resources (HR) policies were unified for every unit under the company's strategic control and international career plans were developed.

Interunit collaboration

Lujan's reorganization in 2000 included the development of interdivisional functional committees designed to help divisional functional managers find a channel to explore opportunities for developing synergies through knowledge sharing (for example, interchanging best practices) and activity sharing. The creation of Corporate Purchasing and Logistics and the centralization of R&D were initiatives resulting from the interdivisional Purchases and Technology Committees' proposals, in response to the corporate 'simple rule' mandate to find new ways to lower costs in these areas. At the top management level, collaboration was also fostered by letting divisional managers join the executive committee.

Performance metrics led by corporate objectives

Performance metrics influence actors' attention to different facets of the company's environment. In this way, through architectural redesign, the cognitive representations of divisional management may be altered to make them fit with the new corporate priorities.

During the two periods of 'long-jumps' the company's metrics fostered the achievement of ambitious sales targets, paying relatively little, though gradually increasing, attention to balance sheet items and strict cost control. During the last period, in contrast, corporate concentration on static efficiency was reflected in a new set of performance metrics aimed at biasing motivation towards cost awareness. Granular metrics were developed, such as the implementation of a per-project income statement that enabled the company to fine-tune each individual project from tender to delivery. Finally, divisional directors' variable remuneration began to be linked to corporate performance in order to enhance interunit collaboration.

The important implication of these initiatives is that while Lujan 'tightened' the architectural design after becoming a global company, it promoted a 'bottom-up' approach for the creation of corporate advantage. The implication of this approach is that corporate advantage is a consequence of the firm's behavior at every level. The corporate level sets the architecture that facilitates recombination and allows collaboration opportunities to arise, but these recombination opportunities are self-generated by the different business and functional units working together.

Conclusion

Kauffman's framework helped us to approach the study of the impact of the corporate level in a car components manufacturing firm's rapid transition from a local to a global geographical scope. Our fieldwork suggests that corporate management's impact on this process was crucial.

Corporate impact on the internationalization process was substantial. It consisted in *driving*, *pacing* and *framing* the firm's evolution from a national position in Spain through a global position. Once the corporate level had reinterpreted which was the relevant geographic scope for 'tier one' car component firms, the whole firm was *driven* to engage in two subsequent and radical geographic expansion processes. Second, the corporate level enforced a set of 'simple rules', such as 'we must be present in all the central and high-growth regions of the car industry'. These rules *paced* the divisional strategic initiatives and biased them towards local search or 'off-line' 'long-jump' initiatives.

Finally, the architectural design was altered by the corporate level in such a way that self-organizing processes taking place at the divisional level were *framed* by broad organizational arrangements in order to foster interdivisional and interdivisional recombination and knowledge sharing. Particularly relevant was the development of a matrix structure within each division in order to foster recombination of resources (in this case, production facilities) and business projects.

As this study aimed at exploring new grounds, it did not suffer from the constraints derived from the highly detached division in subfields that characterizes the rich and highly interdependent field of strategic management. This work permitted us to link two subfields, international business and corporate strategy, that have tended to be studied separately, a fact that in our opinion has harmed their development. Corporate strategy literature puts the stress on the implications of diversification from an industrial standpoint, but neglects the study of geographic diversification. On the other side, international business literature can benefit from the study of how the decision making process resulting in an internationalization plan takes place at the corporate level of the firm.

Note

1. The real name of the company and its officials has been modified in order to protect confidentiality.

References

Amram, M. and N. Kulatilaka (1999) *Real Options. Managing Strategic Investment in an Uncertain World* (Boston, MA: Harvard Business School Press).

Bowman, E. and C. Helfat (2001) 'Does Corporate Strategy Matter?', *Strategic Management Journal*, 22, 1–23.

Brown, S. and K. Eisenhardt (1998) *Competing on the Edge: Strategy as Structured Chaos* (Boston, MA: Harvard Business School Press).

Brush, T. and P. Bromiley (1997) 'What Does a Small Corporate Effect Mean? A Variance Components Simulation of Corporate and Business Effects', *Strategic Management Journal*, 18, 825–35.

Caldart, A. and J. E. Ricart (2004) 'Corporate Strategy Revisited: A View From Complexity Theory', *European Management Review*, 1, forthcoming.

Chang, S. and H. Singh (2000) 'Corporate and Industry Effects on Business Unit Competitive Position', *Strategic Management Journal*, 21, 739–52.

Cyert, R. and J. March (1963) *A Behavioural Theory of the Firm* (Malden, MA: Blackwell Business).

Eisenhardt, K. and S. Brown (1999) 'Patching, Restitching business portfolio in dynamic Markets', *Harvard Business Review*, 77(3), 72–82.

Eisenhardt, K. and D. Sull (2001) 'Strategy as Simple Rules', *Harvard Business Review*, 78(1), 107–16.

Fiol, C. and A. Huff (1992) 'Maps for Managers: Where are We? Where do We Go From Here?', *Journal of Management Studies*, 29, 267–85.

Galunic and K. Eisenhardt (2001) 'Architecture Innovation and Modular Corporate Forms', *Academy of Management Journal*, 44(6), 1229–50.

Gavetti, G. and D. Levinthal (2000) 'Looking Forward and Looking Backward: Cognitive and Experiential Search', *Administrative Science Quarterly*, 45, 113–37.

Ghemawat, P. and J. E. Ricart (1993) 'The Organizational Tension Between Static and Dynamic Efficiency', *Strategic Management Journal*, 14, 59–73.

Hannan, M. and J. Freeman (1977) 'The Population Ecology of Organizations', *American Journal of Sociology*, 82, 929–64.

Hax, A. and N. Majluf (1985) *The Strategy Concept and Process: A Pragmatic Approach*, (Englewood Cliffs, NJ: Prentice-Hall).

Helfat, C. and K. Eisenhardt (2001) 'Inter-Temporal Economies of Scope, Organizational Modularity and the Dynamics of Diversification', Paper presented at the annual meeting of the Strategic Management Society.

Kauffman, S. (1993) *The Origins of Order*, (New York: Oxford University Press).

Levinthal, D. (1991) 'Organizational Adaptation and Environmental Selection: Interrelated Processes of Change', *Organization Science*, 2, 140–5.

———(1997) 'Adaptation in Rugged Fitness Landscapes', *Management Science*, 43, 934–50.

Levinthal, D. and M. Warglien (1999) 'Landscape Design: Designing for Local Action in Complex Worlds', *Organization Science*, 10, 342–57.

Levitt, B. and J. March (1988) 'Organizational Learning', *Annual Review of Sociology*, 14, 319–40.

March, J. and H. Simon (1958) Organizations (New York: John Wiley).

McGahan, A. and M. Porter (1997) 'How Much does Industry Matter, Really?', *Strategic Management Journal*, 18, 15–30.

McKelvey, B. (1997) 'Quasi-Natural Organization Science', *Organization Science*, 8, 352–80.

———(1999) 'Avoiding Complexity Catastrophe in Coevolutionary Pockets: Strategies for Rugged Landscapes', *Organization Science*, 10, 294–321.

Mintzberg, H., B. Ahlstrand and J. Lampel (1998) *Strategy Safari: A Guided Tour through the Wilds of Strategic Management* (London: Prentice-Hall).

Nelson, R. and S. Winter (1982) *An Evolutionary Theory of Economic Change*. (Cambridge, MA: Bellknap Press).

Porter, M. E. (1980) *Competitive Strategy. Techniques for Analyzing Industries and Competitors*, (New York: Free Press).

Prahalad, C. and R. Bettis (1986) 'The Dominant Logic: A New Linkage between Diversity and Performance', *Strategic Management Journal*, 7, 485–501.

Rumelt, R. (1991) 'How Much does Industry Matter?', *Strategic Management Journal*, 12, 167–85.

Schmalensee, R. (1985) 'Econometric Diagnosis of Competitive Localization', *International Journal of Industrial Organization*, 3, 57–70.

Sewell, Wright (1931) 'Evolution in Mendelian Populations', *Genetics*, 16: 97.

Trigeorgis, L. (1996) *Real Options: Managerial Flexibility and Strategy in Resource Allocation*, (Boston, MA: MIT Press).

Walsh, J. (1995) 'Managerial and Organizational Cognition: Notes from a Trip Down Memory Lane', *Organization Science*, 6, 280–321.

19

'Wireless Apostles' and 'Global Emperors': Strategies for Domination in a Global Arena

Mitchell P. Koza, Silviya Svejenova and Luis Vives

> Globalization is key to survival in the 21st century. In this day and age, no country or company can survive without becoming globalized. (Lee Kun-Hee, Chairman of Samsung)

Introduction

When competing in industries that are global, or are in the process of globalization, some scholars and practitioners have argued that firms either become global – developing more or less isomorphic strategies – or perish (Marquardt 1999; Duysters and Hagedoorn 2001). Others, however, have acknowledged that becoming a global player is not a universal solution and that there is more than one type of international strategy viable in a global context (Yip 1989). The main argument of this chapter is that *not all companies can or should forge a global strategy* (Hout, Porter and Rudden 1982). Certain environmental and internal firm characteristics may drive the firm to pursue different strategic pathways to gain influence and enhance performance in such industries.

Empirical research has shown that the existence of global companies is largely overstated and international business is primarily regional business (Rugman and Hodgetts 2001; Rugman and Bain 2003). In some global industries local or regional players not only survive but also outperform global competitors (Roth and Morrison 1990). Furthermore, contrary to the traditional notion of first-mover advantages (Porter 1985), empirical evidence shows that late movers to the global arena are not necessarily at a disadvantage (Lieberman and Montgomery 1998; Bartlett and Ghoshal 2000). These results have reinvigorated the discussion on when, under what circumstances and to what extent a firm is better off internationalizing.

While research on international strategy and globalization has focused on different strategies for competing in a global arena, little has been said on how these strategies are shaped, sustained and modified over time. There is a need for a more rigorous and systematic account of intraindustry heterogeneity and its sources (Noda and Collis 2001). This chapter contributes to the international business field by proposing a typology of strategies for achieving dominance in a global arena and suggesting how heterogeneity of firms' strategic behaviour co-evolves with their context. Hence, by contrasting the embedded characteristics of strategic behaviours in an industry context and looking at how firms' interactions with the context produce equifinal strategies for adaptation, we push forward a co-evolutionary perspective in global industries.

For the purpose we trace the evolution of the global wireless telecoms sector and account for the strategies of leading players. We focus the analysis on players who have succeeded in gaining and sustaining a leadership position in the wireless arena by using different strategic approaches. In particular, this chapter examines four strategic behaviours, which we have labelled a 'Global Emperor', a 'Technological Apostle', a 'Culture-Based Regionalist' and a 'Mighty Local'. We examine how these profiles came into being to secure a dominant position on a local, regional or global scale in the wireless sector.

'Dominance' refers to the ability of a firm 'to develop and maintain a strong and clear lead in the market share over all competitors for a prolonged period of time' (Shamsie 2003, p. 199). In a global arena we understand dominance as the firm's ability to sustain a leading position in the majority of markets in which the firm competes. Positions are not transient in nature, at least in the mid-term, and their sustainability and stability is related to a range of strategic commitments (Ghemawat 1991). Competition in multiple geographic markets (Haveman and Nonnemaker 2000) – where a firm co-evolves with a sector in several different locations and under deregulation regimes with different scope and speed – poses further difficulties for a company's adaptation and sustainable domination.

Theoretical background

To examine heterogeneity in a global industry we combine a co-evolutionary perspective with insights from resource-based view (RBV) and institutional theory. For longer-run competitive advantage 'firms need both resource capital and institutional capital' (Oliver 1997, p. 709).

RBV acknowledges heterogeneity, arguing that a dominant position in a market is an outcome of unique resource bundles and dynamic capabilities (Barney 1991; Teece, Pisano and Shuen 1997). As Barney, Wright and Ketchen (2001, p. 631) put it, 'the value of a particular set of capabilities must be evaluated in the market context within which a firm is operating'. RBV has been used in understanding global competition (Barney 1991; Collis 1991; Tallman and Fladmoe-Lindquist 2002). Considering a global market, Tallman and Fladmoe-Lindquist (2002) proposed a *competence-based* approach to global competition as an alternative to the more traditional approaches grounded in economics industry-based theories. Their 'capability-driven framework of the multinational firm considers the firm's attempts to build, protect, and exploit a set of unique capabilities and resources as ... the key forces that drive firms into international and global strategies' (Tallman and Fladmoe-Lindquist 2002, p. 118). The two key processes of this approach are capability leverage, or exploitation of current capabilities, and capability-building, or development of new competitive resources.

The development and leverage of capabilities is affected by the properties the firms have inherited at birth due to the influences of institutions and rules of competition in their local or regional markets (Duysters and Hagedoorn 2001). The idea of such imprinting goes back to Stinchcombe's (1965) claim that strategy and structure are influenced by the social, cultural, technological and competitive conditions at the time of the company's establishment and has been empirically supported in the work of Boeker (1989). It is further developed in the notion of 'administrative heritage', understood as 'the company's existing configuration of assets, its traditional distribution of responsibility, and its historical norms, values, and management style' (Bartlett and Ghoshal 1988, p. 56). As Yip (1989) acknowledges, one reason why globalization drivers are not deterministic has to do precisely with the business and parent company position and resources.

By developing and leveraging capabilities, a firm seeks a *fit with the environment* (Lawrence and Lorsch 1967). Applications of the idea of 'fit' to multinational corporations (MNCs) have placed an emphasis on differentiation of responses to diverse environments and integration of action across environments, leaving the issues of change and adaptation to new environments unanswered (Doz and Prahalad 1991). According to this view, changes in the environment are exogenous to the organization. Yet environmental change is not always exogenous. Firms could influence the direction of the environment's evolution through internal technological developments (Tushman and Romanelli 1985; Henderson and

Clark 1990) or acquisition of new resources and competencies (Collis 1991; Mahoney 1995). In such cases environmental upheavals, at least partially, become endogenous to a firm's action. Different approaches have attempted to illuminate the link between micro and macro behaviour (Granovetter 1973; Giddens 1984; McKelvey 1997). Few of them, however, analyse the simultaneous, mutual influence of organizations and their environment, adopting a co-evolutionary perspective (Baum and Singh 1994; Koza and Lewin 1998; Lewin and Volberda 1999). Two or more evolving units co-evolve when they interact in a repeated way, continuously affecting one another's evolutionary paths. Co-evolutionary analysis has 'the potential for integrating micro and macro evolution within a unifying framework, incorporating multiple levels of analyses and contingent effects, and leading to new insights, new theories, new empirical methods and new understanding' (Lewin and Volberda 1999, p. 520).

Strategic behaviour profiles

The purpose of a typology is to convey parsimoniously fundamental differences in strategic approaches (Hambrick 1980, in Boeker 1989). Rather than a fully-fledged typology, in this chapter we provide a concise depiction of four distinctive profiles of wireless service operators along the lines of the conceptual ideas advanced in the theoretical section: imprints, capability-building and leverage, and co-evolutionary processes that have shaped these heterogeneous strategic behaviours. The wireless telecoms sector was chosen for several reasons. Firstly, created in the mid-1970s, it witnessed an impressive growth in the 1990s and a significant opening to competition. Its relatively young age facilitates tracing the emergence of dominant players. Secondly, though highly reliant on technological advances, it has been strongly regulated, with government interventions determining the opening of windows of strategic opportunities. Thirdly, while the telecoms industry is still dominated by the incumbent telephone companies, the mobile market segment has witnessed the emergence of new players, exempt from the assets and liabilities of the national monopolies – the 'born wireless' firms that have entered the mobile arena, attracted by its market potential and high growth.

To understand and conceptualize heterogeneity in a globalizing arena, we collected and analysed a wealth of information from publicly available sources such as journal articles and analysts' reports. From a close reading of strategic behaviours in the wireless sector we identified four distinct positions for leadership in a global arena. The following wireless operators represent these positions: Vodafone, China Mobile,

Telefónica Moviles and NTT DoCoMo. These players are market leaders in their local markets (UK, China, Spain and Japan, respectively) and as Mitchell, Shaver and Yeung (1992, p. 430) argue, '[t]o gain from increased international presence in technically sophisticated industries, a firm must have a strong base in a key market'. Hence, the basis of sustainable competitive advantage was developed initially in the home country (Yip 1989). Faced with deregulated local arenas with increasing competition and eroding local leadership, the wireless firms undertook different pathways for further expansion.

The positions and the strategic behaviour profiles are depicted comparatively in Table 19.1, and then discussed individually. The labels – Global Emperor, Technological Apostle, Culture-Based Regionalist and Mighty Local – represent the scope of dominance and, to an extent, the way it was achieved.

Global Emperor

The label 'Global Emperor' makes reference to a company that has a dominant position in countries that provide for global reach. 'Born wireless' in the UK, Vodafone has become a dominant player in a wide geographical terrain. It has developed capabilities in acquiring and fast integration of businesses in chosen markets, managing to harmonize them while preserving some local responsiveness. Furthermore, it has developed a strong relationship with the client, and consequently such a reputable brand over time that it is now able to leverage in its relation with other (traditionally powerful) value-chain players, such as handset providers. Its capabilities are leveraged on a wide geographical scale – it has moved from being a leading UK operator to one having European stronghold and now also an increased outreach to the USA, Africa and Australia. In global strategy countries are selected for their potential contribution to globalization benefits such as efficiency in procurement, distribution, marketing, etc. on a global scale (Yip 1989). Vodafone's strategy is in a way bifurcated. In addition to using the *efficiency criterion* in choosing the countries to enter, it also enters markets with strategic importance for the *future state of competition*. Its entry into Japan as a leading market for wireless innovations with a controlling stake in J-Phone, for example, provides Vodafone with access to know-how for developing a technological edge (a capability-building with the potential to be leveraged on its wide network). The strategy of Vodafone has co-evolved with the overall globalization of the sector as well as with the context of the local markets it has entered with the opening up of opportunities.

Table 19.1 Strategic behaviour profiles

Profile	'Global Emperor'	'Technological Apostle'	'Culture-Based Regionalist'	'Mighty Local'
Company Imprints	Vodafone Group 'Born-wireless', early entrant Local market (UK)	NTT DoCoMo Offspring of a monopolist Local market (Japan): low PC–Internet penetration, high innovation	Telefónica Moviles Offspring of a monopolist Local market (Spain)	China Mobile Offspring of a monopolist Local market (China): strongly regulated, big in size
Capability-building	Acquisition and subsequent integration of new companies/markets	**Corporate parent strong** position in Asia Pacific area R&D excellence and partnering (corporate contacts) for co-development and risk-sharing	**Corporate parent strong** position in Latin America Knowledge transfer and partnering for technology improvement	**Corporate parent strong** position in China Growth of subscribers' base and improvement of infrastructure and services
Capability leverage	Fast pace Broad (geography) (from local to regional dominance, and then to global reach)	Slow pace Selective (technology)	Fast pace Selective (culture) (corporate positioning)	Fast pace Narrow (single country)
Co-evolutionary processes	Strategy of **global leadership** co-evolves with globalization of the wireless sector Shift from market development to branding and technological edge	Strategy of **technology leadership** co-evolves with handset manufacturers and content providers, and further with the strategies of local and regional wireless players in need of technological edge	Strategy of **regional leadership** co-evolves with corporate parent's positioning and with the strategies of other wireless players in search of technological edge	Strategy of **local leadership** co-evolves with the regulator's intervention

Technological Apostle

As Yip (1989, pp. 39–40) affirms, '[a] competitor with sufficiently superior technology can use it to offset globalization disadvantages'. Therefore, a technology-edge position could be a sustainable way to yield greater returns in a global industry without pursuing a global expansion strategy. In business terms an 'apostle' is a firm that strongly believes in a policy or idea and tries to make other firms adopt it. A 'Technological Apostle' is a company that innovates and puts a bet on a given techno- logy, undertaking a quest for its establishment as a standard *beyond its local domain*. DoCoMo is labelled a 'Technological Apostle' for its efforts to innovate and subsequently diffuse its technology-based know-how. Building a capability of R&D excellence and partnering for co-development using the relationships of its corporate parent (the former monopolist company of Japan, NTT), NTT DoCoMo has embarked on establishing a world wireless standard. Unlike Vodafone's fast-paced expansion through acquisitions, DoCoMo has a 'slow and careful' approach to overseas investment for the spread of its proprietary technology. The leverage of NTT DoCoMo's technological capability (for the propagation of the i-mode, for example) takes place through a slow-paced expansion and carefully selected partnerships with European and US companies that are well positioned in the respective local markets and able to do the necessary content development and customization of the technologi- cal platform. Nevertheless, technological bets increase the company's commitment (Ghemawat 1991) and may hamper its flexibility and future expansion if another technology finally becomes the winning standard.

Culture-Based Regionalist

A 'regionalist' is a company that has selected deliberate restriction of the geographical scope of its expansion to markets where relatively little adaptation of the domestic value proposition is required to be successful (Ghemawat 2003). Scholars have looked at the 'Triad blocs' of North America, Europe and Japan as bases for regional strategies, further distinguishing among home-triad, host-triad, and bi-regional strategies (Rugman and Hodgetts 2001; Rugman and Bain 2003). In this chapter, we advance a particular type of a regional strategy based on *cultural proximity* whereby a common language and behavioural patterns facilitate the transfer of expertise to local operations and at the same time diminish the need for localization.

In its expansion across Latin America Telefónica Moviles, as a 'Culture- Based Regionalist', has relied on cultural proximity and the already established positions of the corporate parent Telefónica Group in fixed telephony and related services. It builds a capability of *knowledge transfer*. It leverages its know-how and corporate parents' relations pursuing leadership in markets – with language and culture proximity to its local market – that are opening up to competition. The cultural proximity facilitates the leverage of know-how through common language and similarity in the patterns of customer behaviour. The strategy of a region-alist co-evolves with the strategies of the regulators in the respective countries it enters. A culture-based regionalist would be likely to fail in its strategic positioning if the cultural specifics of the selected regions are not significant enough to provide a distinctive advantage and competitors without the cultural advantage could have equally, or more, attractive value propositions.

Mighty Local

A 'Mighty Local' strategy is focused on achieving domination by development and exploitation of a *particular prominent market* (a country or a region) that provides a sufficient client base for the company's growth. An exceptional knowledge of the local environment and/or boundaries protecting the entry of other companies is necessary to sustain this position. China Mobile represents a 'Mighty Local' with leadership pos-ition in a single country – the Chinese wireless market with its growing size and a potential for further growth of the number of subscribers and the Average Revenue per User (ARPU). China Mobile has developed a capability of infrastructure development and an increase in the customer base. The leverage of these competencies has been across different areas of the vast country. The strategy of this firm co-evolves with that of the regulator. A Mighty Local may fall into complacency due to the sheer volume of its local market and narrow down its search for strategic growth internally, losing site of growth opportunities elsewhere.

The strategic profiles of these four companies have unique contextual characteristics imprinted on their behaviour. Vodafone is 'born wireless' without the administrative heritage of a telecoms monopoly, unlike NTT DoCoMo, Telefónica Moviles and China Mobiles, all offsprings of local monopolists. The advantages of 'born-wireless' players are greater flexibility and speed in expansion, as no bureaucratic structure of a parent is necessary for resources and approval. This could be a liability for an offspring of a monopolist company, which may require time and effort to instill a fast-paced and agile entrepreneurial culture. A case in point is NTT DoCoMo, which was transformed into more flexible and creative business with the intervention of its first president Koji Oboshi. Oboshi 'defied traditional Japanese business practice by reaching outside of NTT for marketing specialists' (Ratliff 2002, p. 58).

These four companies were not only 'born' under different institutional circumstances but also developed and leveraged different capability bundles. Vodafone has core competence in acquisition-based growth, identifying, taking majority stakes and later, integrating the acquired businesses and harmonizing the service across the network. The global reach provides for economies of scale and improved cost structure. NTT DoCoMo's competitive edge, as first in its local market and then in the expansion of its i-mode across Europe and some parts of the USA, has to do with its R&D capability, inherited from the parent company and further emphasized with dedicated investment in the area and about a thousand people working on it (Ratliff 2002). Partnering is another core capability for NTT DoCoMo, which secures fruitful co-development, know-how sharing and licensing. It manifests itself in the ability to gain power and obtain loyalty from its partners, the handset manufacturers and content providers. Telefónica's competitive resource is the ability to transfer know-how across the countries in the Latin American markets with common cultural and historical heritage. Carefully chosen local partnerships have further contributed to success in the bidding for licences in the area. Finally, China Mobile's edge – within a regulator-protected local perimeter of China – has to do with its ability to expand its network rapidly while at the same time working on the improvement of the infrastructure and services. In all four cases the developed capabilities are leveraged on global, regional or local scale, respectively. Capability-building and leverage are part of the co-evolutionary processes now discussed.

Co-evolutionary dynamics in the wireless arena

The four mobile operators' strategic behaviours co-evolve with the users, technology, (de)regulation and the strategies of handset manufacturers, content providers and the other wireless companies. Here we focus on two specific manifestations of co-evolutionary dynamics, which contribute to the shaping of the four strategic profiles over time: (1) regulator–technology–wireless operators, and (2) wireless operators–handset manufacturers.

Regulator–mobile technology–wireless operators

Historically, the telecoms industry has been subject to strong interests of the State, resulting in governmental regulation and control (Wallsten 2000; Gual and Ricart 2001). Regulation has 'protected' national players from foreign competition. At the same time IT has created constraints to their competitive initiatives. Firms operating in a regulated environment are usually constrained in attaining optimal efficiency (Pettus 2001). Public policies influence corporate behaviour by framing competitive context, rather than by promoting specific practices (Dobbin and Dowd 1997). New policies create constraints and incentives rather than dictating particular behaviours. In regulating the wireless sector the regulator has a say and an impact on technology, permitting or banning the application of available technological innovations. Initially, it selected one (or more then one, in the case of USA) standard for the local market. However, mobile technology advances opened up the possibilities for unified standards and interconnectivity and led the regulator to allow regional standards in the local marketplace. In line with these 'national settings' the first generation of mobile technology (analogue technology) was local. Interconnectivity was difficult between countries, a situation that radically changed with 2G, which allowed interconnectivity between countries as the same standards were set. The development of 2G technology coincided with the sector's deregulation and provided a unique opportunity for change in firms' strategies (Kole and Lehn 1997).

Technological developments that permitted standards' convergence reinforced the opportunities for firms to go international, as they were able to realize the economies of scale from this expansion (much more difficult and costly under different local technological standards). As mobile players started internationalizing, they kept working on technological developments that enhanced the possibilities for inter-connection. These improvements materialized in the third generation of universal mobile technology system (UMTS). Deregulation acts as a shock that requires firms to adapt or invent new rules of the game (Mahon and Murray 1981; Koza 1988; Kole and Lehn 1997) as well as to innovate and influence the regulator for further changes in policies. Regulators' policies and mobile operators' strategies thus co-evolve.

Wireless operators–mobile technology–handset providers

As an article in the *Financial Times* affirms, 'the move towards data services will change the balance of power between the mobile operators and the handset manufacturers', converting co-development to be 'The quickest way of coming into the market for smaller handset makers' (Budden 2003, pp. 8–9). In Western Europe handset manufacturers have traditionally taken the lead in technology development. Nokia is known for having increased its power over time by not tailoring its handsets to the needs and requirements of the wireless operators. Handset manufacturers have also purposefully slowed down the adoption of a more advanced technology to permit the payback of their previous investments and avoid the cannibalization of an earlier range of handsets.

With the globalization of the wireless sector, *brands* have increased in importance. Certain mobile operators have managed to develop strong brands based on strong links with the consumers. This leads to a shift in power whereby handset manufacturers are pushed to customize the handsets. For example, Vodafone chose Sharp, until recently an insignificant player, to provide tailored handsets for its new Vodafone Live service. This in turn will impact on Nokia and other dominant handset providers that have been resisting customization. In an attempt to preserve their power, handset providers are also trying to strengthen their relationship with the consumer, providing a range of complementary services aimed at achieving loyalty. This triggers further response of the wireless operators through branding.

Instead of competing, handset providers and wireless operators could *collaborate*. This leads to a different co-evolutionary dynamics, as in the case of NTT DoCoMo, for which co-development and know-how transfer and sharing with dedicated handset manufacturers (NEC and Matsushita) has led to the development and continuous incremental improvements of the i-mode platform.

Some concluding remarks

This chapter presents work in progress on the role of co-evolutionary dynamics in shaping a heterogeneous strategic response to a globalizing sector. It seeks to advance and enrich theories on global competition by combining institutional and resource-based view (RBV) insights with a co-evolutionary perspective, providing a more eclectic and better-informed view on the *dynamics of competitive behaviours* in a global market. The typology of positions and strategic behaviours – while not exhaustive – provides a useful way for depicting strategic heterogeneity. As different industries are exposed to drivers for globalization with different strength and intensity (Conn and Yip 1997), some of these positions may not be manifested in particular industries or their specifics may vary with the context. Three concluding remarks can be drawn from the study.

There is a range of alternative behaviours for leadership in a global market, some of which may not necessarily take advantage of the drivers for globalization

The environment conditions and institutions at the time of the firms' founding get imprinted on these alternative behaviours. While being 'born wireless' yields flexibility and speed of expansion, as we can see in the case of Vodafone, a background as a monopolist's offspring (for example Telefónica Moviles) permits exploitation of markets that have been already explored by the corporate parent and a reliance on parents' resources and relationships. Profiles are further differentiated over time. Unlike Vodafone, which enjoys the benefits of global reach through *economies* of scale, development of a global brand and marketing, NTT DoCoMo's strategic bet is technological and underplays these globalization drivers, forming selective licensing agreements with local partners that tailor the content and services provided locally. Region-specific bets, leveraging a common historical and cultural heritage as well as positions already taken by the corporate parent, also go against the grain of the globalization forces. Finally, dominant size could be also achieved locally if the market under consideration is of significant size and growth potential, as in China. Sustaining the dominant position in such markets, however, in conditions of market opening, may require bi-focal attention to operational details, on the one hand, and on technological advancement and improved offer, on the other hand.

Along with heterogeneity of strategic behaviours for achieving a leading position in a global arena, certain isomorphic forces are also in play

In the wireless sector further expansion and sustained leadership position require both *market reach* and *technological edge*. This further increases the importance of co-development alliances, with both competitors and with other players from the wireless value chain, such as handset manufacturers and content providers. An illustration is Vodafone's participation in China Mobile, which for Vodafone is an option for increased presence in a market with falling barriers under WTO regulations. Another example is the licensing agreement between NTT DoCoMo and Telefónica Moviles, which is complemented by a higher degree of commitment to the relationship through a specific knowledge sharing agreement. It allows DoCoMo to further spread its technological platform on the way to providing a technological standard. For Telefónica it gives access to a technological edge that could improve its customer service and allow it to sustain dominance in its core markets. While DoCoMo's contribution is the platform, Telefónica Moviles provides the platform's local adaptation of content and services' execution.

Further research is needed on the mechanisms for stability and sustainability of the different strategic profiles and their role in facilitating or blocking firms' adaptation

Inertia forces transform core capabilities into *core rigidities*, thus hampering continuous adaptation. As Oliver remarks, 'resources and capabilities that are developed and sustained over time are vulnerable to cognitive sunk costs because individuals find it difficult for reasons of loyalty, fear, or habit, to replace or abandon long-standing traditions and routines' (Oliver 1997, p. 703). Perhaps the most difficult and costly transition to be made is from a Mighty Local to an expanding Culture-Based Regionalist, even in cases of companies achieving a spectacular size and growth such as China Mobile. After all, being a 'Mighty Local' may decrease strategic vision and visibility to immediate landscapes at the expense of more distant ones. Hence, while initially permitting adaptation to a globalizing sector, some strategic profiles may more than others hamper further adaptation.

By emphasizing the importance of imprints, capabilities and co-evolutionary processes we argue for caution in adopting a global strategy for a global market. As Mitchell, Shaver and Yeung (1992, p. 430) claim, '[when] firms that are not ready try to operate outside their core capabilities, or miss opportunities to strengthen their capabilities [they] are likely to suffer more than they gain from international expansion'. Nevertheless, our understanding of how imprints and path dependence influence the evolution of the firm and co-evolution with the environment is limited, and more research from a co-evolutionary perspective is needed.

Understanding and conceptualizing the heterogeneity of strategic behaviours or pathways for dominance in global, fast-growing arenas through a co-evolutionary perspective could contribute to pushing forward the academic debate on the ways for adaptation in market sectors that are undergoing globalization. It could also help practitioners in choosing a strategic course of action in a globalizing arena, providing them with a more balanced and complete view that takes into account their administrative heritage, capabilities and important interrelations.

References

Barnett, W. P. and G. R. Carroll (1995) 'Modeling Internal Organizational Change', *Annual Review of Sociology*, 21, 217–36.

Barney, J. B. (1991) 'Firm Resources and Sustained Competitive Advantage', *Journal of Management*, 17, 99–120.

Barney, J., M. Wright, and D. J. Ketchen (2001) 'The Resource-Based View of the Firm: Ten Years after 1991', *Journal of Management*, 27(6), 625–41.

Bartlett, C. A. and S. Ghoshal (1988) 'Organizing for Worldwide Effectiveness: The Transnational Solution', *California Management Review*, Fall, 54–74.

————(2000) 'Going Global: Lessons from Late Movers', *Harvard Business Review*, March-April, 132–42.

Baum, J. A. C. and J. V. Singh (eds) (1994) *The Evolutionary Dynamics of Organizations* (New York: Oxford University Press).

Boeker, W., (1989) 'Strategic Change: The Effects of Founding and History', *Academy of Management Journal*, 32(3), 489–515.

Budden, R. (2003) 'Could I have one of those Beckham Phones, Please?', *Financial Times*, Creative Business Supplement, 8–9.

Collis, D. (1991) 'A Resource-Based Analysis of Global Competition: The Case of the Bearings Industry', *Strategic Management Journal*, 12 (Special Issue), 49–68.

Conn, H. and G. Yip (1997) 'Global Transfer of Critical Capabilities', *Business Horizons*, Vol 40(1), 22–31.

Dobbin, F. and T. J. Dowd (1997) 'How Policy Shapes Competition: Early Railroad Foundings in Massachusetts', *Administrative Science Quarterly*, 42, 501–29.

Doz, Y. L. and C. K. Prahalad (1991) 'Managing DMNCs: A Search for a New Paradigm', *Strategic Management Journal*, 12, 145–64.

Duysters, G. and J. Hagedoorn (2001) 'Do Company Strategies and Structures Converge in Global Markets? Evidence from the Computer Industry', *Journal of International Business Studies*, 32(2), 347–56.

Ghemawat, P. (1991) *Commitment* (Boston, MA: Harvard Business School Press).

————(2003) 'The Forgotten Strategy', *Harvard Business Review*, 81(11), 88–95.

Giddens, A. (1984) *The Constitution of Society* (Cambridge: Polity Press).

Granovetter, M. (1973) 'The Strength of Weak Ties', *American Journal of Sociology*, 78, 1360–80.

Gual, J. and J. E. Ricart (2001) *Estrategias Empresariales en Telecomunicaciones e Internet*, (Madrid: Fundación Retevisión).

Haveman, H. A. and L. Nonnemaker (2000) 'Competition in Multiple Geographic Markets: The Impact on Growth and Market Entry', *Administrative Science Quarterly*, 45, 232–67.

Henderson, R. M. and K. B. Clark (1990) 'Architectural Innovation: The Reconfiguration of Existing Product Technologies and the Failure of Firms', *Administrative Science Quarterly*, 35, 9–30.

Hout, T., M. Porter and E. Rudden (1982) 'How Global Companies Win Out', *Harvard Business Review*, September–October, 98–108.

Kole, S. and K. Lehn (1997) 'The Emerging New Economics of the Firm: Deregulation, the Evolution of Corporate Governance Structure, and Survival', *AEA Papers and Proceedings*, May.

Koza, M. P. (1988) *Regulation and Organization Environmental Niche Structure and Administrative Organization*, (Stamford, CT: JAI Press).

————(1999) 'The Coevolution of Network Alliances: A Longitudinal Analysis of an International Professional Service Network', *Organization Science*, 10(5), 638–53.

Lawrence, P. R. and J. W. Lorsch (1967) *Organization and Environment: Managing Differentiation and Integration*, Division of Research, Graduate School of Business Administration (Boston, MA: Harvard University Press).

Lewin, A. Y. and H. W. Volberda (1999) 'Prolegomena on Coevolution: A Framework for Research on Strategy and New Organizational Forms', *Organization Science*, 10(5), 519–34.

Lieberman, M. B. and D. B. Montgomery (1998) 'First-Mover (Dis)advantages: Retrospective and Link with the Resource-Based View', *Strategic Management Journal*, 19, 1111–25.

Mahon, J. F. and E. A. Murray (1981) 'Strategic Planning for Regulated Companies', *Strategic Management Journal*, 2, 251–62.

Mahoney, J. T. (1995) 'The Management of Resources and the Resource of Management', *Journal of Business Research*, 33, 91–101.

Marquardt, M. J. (1999) *The Global Advantage* (Houston: Gulf).

McKelvey, B. (1997) 'Quasi-Natural Organization Science', *Organization Science*, 8(4), 352–80.

Miles, M. B. and A. M. Huberman (1987) *Qualitative Data Analysis: A Sourcebook of New Methods*, (Newbury Park, CA: Sage).

Mitchell, W., J. M. Shaver and B. Yeung (1992) 'Getting There in Global Industry: Impacts on Performance of Changing International Presence', *Strategic Management Journal*, 13, 419-32.

Noda, T. and D. J. Collis (2001) 'The Evolution of Intraindustry Firm Heterogeneity: Insights from a Process Theory', *Academy of Management Journal*, 44(4), 897–25.

Oliver, C. (1997) 'Sustainable Competitive Advantage: Combining Institutional and Resource-Based Views', *Strategic Management Journal*, 18, 697–713.

Pettus, M. L. (2001) 'The Resource-Based View as a Developmental Growth Process: Evidence from the Deregulated Trucking Industry', *Academy of Management Journal*, 44(4), 878–96.

Porter, M. E. (1985) *Competitive Advantage* (New York: Free Press).

Ratliff, J. (2002) 'NTT DoCoMo and its I-mode Success: Origins and Implications', *California Management Review*, 44(3), p. 55, 77pp.

Roth, K. and A. Morrison (1990) 'An Empirical Analysis of the Integration–Responsiveness Framework in Global Industries', *Journal of International Business Studies*, 21, 541–64.

Rugman, A. and C. Bain (2003) 'Multinational Enterprises are Regional, not Global', *Multinational Business Review*, 11(1), 3–12.

Rugman, A. and R. Hodgetts (2001) 'The End of Global Strategy', *European Management Journal* 19(4), 333–43.

Shamsie, J. (2003) 'The Context of Dominance: An Industry-Driven Framework for Exploiting Reputation', *Strategic Management Journal*, 24, 199–215.

Stinchcombe, A. L. (1965) *Organizations and Social Structure. Handbook of Organizations* (Chicago, IL: Rand-McNally), 142–93.

Tallman, S. and K. Fladmoe-Lindquist (2002) 'Internationalization, Globalization, and Capability-Based Strategy', *California Management Review*, 45(1), 116–35.

Teece, D., Pisano, G., and A. Shuen (1997) 'Dynamic Capabilities and Strategic Management', *Strategic Management Journal*, 18(7), 509–33.

Tushman, M. and E. Romanelli (1985) 'Organizational Evolution: A Metamorphosis Model of Convergence and Reorientation', in L. L. Cummings and B. M. Staw (eds), *Research in Organizational Behavior*, 7 (Greenwich, CT: JAI Press), 171–222.

Wallsten, S. (2000) 'An Econometric Analysis of Telecom Competition, Privatization and Regulation in Africa and Latin America', Working Paper, Stanford University.

Yip, G. S. (1989) 'Global Strategy . . . In a World of Nations?', *Sloan Management Review*, 31(1), 29–41.

Index

3M   34

Absorptive capacity   35, 154
  spillovers and absorptive
    capacity   146
Adaptation   5, 219
  internationalization as a
    key-dimension for adaptation
    239, 244, 249, 250
advantage   4, 9, 10, 15, 16, 56, 78–93,
    113, 114, 119, 125, 134, 135, 136,
    239, 242, 245, 248
advantage of foreignness   89, 90
  firm-specific sources of
    advantage   4, 9, 73, 74, 78,
    79, 81, 84, 85, 87, 89, 91
  home advantage   84, 87, 88
  host advantage   84, 88, 89, 91
  location of the advantage   73, 76, 81
  multinational advantage   81, 84,
    86, 87, 91
  non-firm-specific sources of
    advantage   4, 9, 73, 78, 79,
    81, 85, 87, 89, 91
  parent advantage   81, 84, 85, 86
  sources of firm's advantage   78
  subsidiary advantage   81, 85, 86, 91
airlines   183, 188, 249
alliances   96, 98, 201–4, 206, 208–12
  alliances between firms from
    developed countries with firms
    from emerging countries   95,
    181, 182, 183, 227
  alliances motivation   99
  strategic alliances   95, 181, 182, 184,
    202, 204, 206, 210, 212, 231
  high-technology alliances   182,
    202, 206
Argentina   23, 45, 49, 52, 96, 97, 98,
    105, 227, 232
assets   4, 5, 89, 97, 126
  complementary assets   8, 79
associations   80, 192, 193, 194
autonomy   50, 51, 117, 128, 131–4,
    137, 139, 140, 141, 194, 197
  role of subsidiary autonomy in MNE
    innovation   183

banks   60, 186, 188
BMW   29
boards of directors   6, 7, 62
  composition of the boards   62
  French board   62, 63
  German board   62, 63
  Japanese board   62, 63
  supervisory board   62
  UK board   62
  US board   62
Brazil   15, 23, 45, 49, 97, 99, 105,
    110–15, 117, 227, 232
business group   74, 100

capabilities   23, 28, 32, 39, 65, 73, 84,
    85, 86, 125, 173, 181, 189, 240,
    242, 246, 250
  capability-building/creation of
    new capabilities   219, 240,
    242, 243, 246
  capability-leverage/exploitation of
    capabilities   219, 240, 243
  liberalization handling
    capabilities   103
  unobserved capabilities (that lead
    the firm to go global)   58, 166,
    168, 172
capacity   35
  excess capacity   84
  transfer of capacity   79, 80–5
Carrefour   110, 115
case studies   15, 37, 46, 110, 202, 207
centralization   48, 50, 51, 52,
    134, 153
  R&D centralization   153, 155
Chile   74, 95, 96, 97, 98, 100, 102, 103
Chilean firms   74, 75, 95–103
China   29, 227, 233, 242, 243, 249
China Mobile   241, 243, 245, 246,
    249, 250
clans   192, 193
clusters   12, 89, 122
Coca-Cola   11
co-evolution   219, 220, 247, 248, 250
coevolutionary processes   241, 242,
    246, 247, 250
cognition   229

cognitive representation 218, 229, 230, 235
collaboration 134, 135, 188, 197, 228, 233, 234, 235
  interunit collaboration 234, 235
competition 50, 52, 109, 111, 115, 129, 217, 219, 239, 240, 248
  competition in a host country 75
  domestic and international competition 97
  international competition 16, 73, 78, 79, 81, 82, 90, 91
  market competition and R&D 146
competitive advantage 15, 71, 73, 74, 76, 78, 79, 80, 101, 102, 103, 118, 135, 177, 195, 196, 239, 242
  competitive advantage of third world multinationals 102
  sources of advantage in international competition 78, 79, 82
Complexity Theory 220, 223
conduct 58, 132–8, 140, 141, 142
conglomerates 100
constellations 192, 194
contextual factors 206, 211
  international context 172, 173
corporate level 11, 126, 217, 220, 222, 223, 224, 228, 229, 230, 232, 233, 235, 236
  internationalization and corporate level 224, 236
corporate governance 24, 55–9, 61, 63–6
  corporate governance of the multinational firm 57
  corporate governance as a source of variance in globalization 57
  employees' influence in corporate governance 9, 56, 58, 59, 61, 63
  shareholders' influence in corporate governance 60
corporate strategy 218, 219, 220, 225, 228, 236
  a dynamic view of corporate strategy 220
costs 10, 29, 30, 32, 35, 116, 118, 119, 125, 126, 155, 156, 157, 159, 160, 166, 167, 168, 170, 171, 173, 174, 176
  coordination costs 4, 166, 167, 169, 172, 173
country-specific advantages 74, 113

cultural distance 117, 126, 171, 172, 173
  cultural distance indicators 117
  global culture 58, 61
culture 34, 65, 117, 118, 126
culture-based regionalist 239, 242, 243, 244, 250

decentralization 157, 159
  R&D decentralization 146, 149, 152, 155–8, 160, 161
decision making 131, 132, 134, 135
  decision making in established firms 33, 38
  decision making in MNCs compared with multilatinas 48, 49
  decision making in start-ups 34–9
  network approach to decision making 12
deregulation 247
developed countries 74, 81, 102, 103, 128, 148
  firms from developed countries 75, 95, 96, 102
developing countries 74, 81
  see also emerging countries
directors 56, 57, 62
  outsider 63
distance 13, 14, 28, 116, 125, 128
  costs of 116
  cultural 99, 171, 172, 173
  geographic 7, 127
  institutional 127
  psychic 6, 117
  technological 127
domestic firms 167, 172
  domestic competitors 87, 89, 91
dominance 239, 242, 243, 249, 250
driving 218, 235

eBay 34, 35
efficiency 52, 59, 71, 72, 89, 135, 230, 242
  tension between static and dynamic efficiency 219
electronics 23, 37, 119
emerging countries 95, 96
emerging MNCs 48
  emerging multinationals 43, 45, 47, 49, 51, 53
  multinational enterprise as a source of knowledge creation 145
  MNE innovation 132
  processes in MNE 31

employees 33, 50, 58, 59, 61, 63, 110, 138
Endesa 99, 101
Endesa de Chile 98, 101
entrepreneurial companies 8, 32, 206
entry mode 12, 117, 147, 168
technology transfer and entry mode 147
environmental change 24, 220
drivers of the environmental change 219
environmental pressures 131, 132, 133, 136, 139, 140, 142
responses to environmental pressures 14, 133
EU 28, 105, 117, 118, 150
EU firms and R&D 150
Europe (European MNE) 109, 111–15
Western European companies 55
evolving theory of the multinational corporation 48
expansion 4, 8, 9, 21, 22, 23, 24, 30, 31, 32, 33, 36, 39, 43, 52
cross-border expansion 27, 37
expansion decisions 23, 24, 31, 33, 37
see also internationalization
expatriates 122
exports 64, 147

federations 192, 194
firm 13, 15, 21–39, 44, 45, 46, 47, 49, 52–65, 71–5, 78–91, 110, 111, 112, 114, 120, 125, 126, 127, 130–8, 140, 142, 156, 158, 159, 165–74, 181, 183, 185–90, 194, 196, 197, 223, 229, 231, 238–42, 246, 247, 250
conduct 132
outcome 132
firm-specific advantages 74, 81, 111, 114, 134, 136
parent company creation of firm-specific advantages 136
subsidiaries as a source of firm-specific advantages 136
fitness landscape 223, 224, 229, 230
foreign direct investment (FDI) 23, 44, 57, 75, 76, 95, 97, 98, 109, 126, 165, 167, 168, 169, 171, 172, 174
Chilean FDI 95, 96, 100, 102, 103

evolution of FDIs in the 1990s 44
FDI from one emerging country to another 95
FDI made with developed country partners 102
real options perspective on FDI 165
R&D and FDI 146
home-base exploiting FDI 148
uncertainty of FDI investment 35, 36, 37, 38, 39
foreign expansion 26, 31, 44, 45, 111
as a route to profitable growth 111
foreignness 75
advantage of 84
liability of 114
food services 188
framework 13, 14, 43, 47, 56, 57, 91, 111, 114, 128, 132, 140
of MNE competition in a given host market 111
framing 219, 229, 235

game theory 146
geography 75, 76, 81, 110, 116, 118, 120
Germany 60, 62, 111, 117, 118, 174, 196, 226, 232
German firms 149
Gillette 12, 114
global 46, 47, 48, 50, 52, 53, 58, 59, 61, 65, 71, 130, 133, 140, 141, 170, 181, 182, 183, 197, 227, 228, 229, 232, 233, 234, 235, 238, 239, 240, 242, 243, 248
going global 226
global economy 185, 186, 187
global emperor 239, 242, 243
global integration 56, 58, 59
pressures of 131, 133
global strategy 24, 56, 57, 58, 59, 64, 65, 71, 78, 85, 173, 181, 183, 201, 202, 206, 210, 212, 220, 242, 250
companies creating value through global strategy 201
globalization 22, 23, 24, 44, 56–66, 131, 181, 182, 183, 187, 197, 220, 230, 239, 240, 242, 243, 248, 249
globalization drivers 220, 242, 249
globalization of the car component manufacturing industry 219

globalization – *continued*
  industries and firms
    globalization   185
  influence of the institutional
    environment on
    globalization   55
  patterns of globalization   58
  process of globalization   130
  sources of globalization   186
government   57, 60 ,61, 63, 64,
    65, 80, 83, 118, 119
  host country government   90
  interventionist governments
    64, 65
  local government influence   133, 141
  relations of the MNE with the local
    government   112

heterogeneity   91, 172, 239, 241, 249
  firm   111, 239
history   56, 76, 110, 115–18, 120

IBM   111, 114
Ikea   114, 120
industrial organization   146
industry   12, 22, 25, 50, 57, 58, 105,
    112, 132, 138, 158, 181,182, 185,
    187, 195, 196, 201, 205, 206, 211
  global industry   239
  local industries   71
innovation   50, 127, 131, 134, 136,
    137, 138, 139, 140, 141, 145, 146 ,
    149, 151, 152, 153, 242, 243
  centre for global innovations   148
  effects of conduct on   137
  effects of structure on   137
  innovative strategies   148
  MNE innovation   132
  technological innovation   153
institutions   56, 57, 59, 240, 248
  influence of institutions in the social
    and political processes   56
  institutional actor centred
    analysis   56
  institutional context/institutional
    environment   55, 56, 58, 65
  institutional influence   127
institutional Theory   56, 57, 239
integration–responsiveness framework
    43, 47
Intel   114, 120
interaction   12, 13, 56, 157
  interaction between environment
    and managerial structures   132

interaction between conduct and
    outcomes   134
internationalization   44, 46, 47, 53,
    54, 57, 80, 84, 120, 126, 218, 219,
    220, 223, 224, 229, 235, 236
  barriers to internationalizing   27
  internal perspective of the
    internationalization
    process   46, 47
  internationalization of large
    multinational firms   32,
    34, 38
  internationalization of fast-growing
    enterpreneurial firms   27
  internationalization of small (and
    medium) firms   44, 45, 46
  internationalization of an emerging
    multinational   44, 47
  internationalization process   2, 22,
    23, 44, 46, 47, 53, 222, 224,
    225, 235
  international expansion in
    knowledge-intensive
    settings   26
  learning from
    internationalization   34
  motives/rationale for
    internationalization/
    international expansion   26, 29
  uncertainty of the international
    expansion   30, 36, 37
interviews   207
investment   23, 24, 35, 36, 37, 38,
    39, 44, 48, 61, 113, 118, 157,
    158, 161, 166, 171
  home-base augmenting investment
    28, 29, 30, 35, 36, 37, 39
    (*see also* FDI)
  home-base exploiting investment
    28, 29, 30, 36, 37, 39 (*see also* FDI)
  multinational investment   29, 165,
    166
isomorphic forces   249
Israel   202, 204, 205, 206, 207,
    210, 212

Japan   27, 34, 35, 59, 60, 62, 63, 99,
    100, 109, 111, 114, 117, 118, 197,
    222, 232, 242, 243, 244
  Japanese firms and R&D   149,
    150, 151
  Japanese MNEs   99
joint ventures   74, 96, 99, 181
  cross-border joint ventures   32

Kauffman, S. 223, 224, 231, 235
knowledge 3, 5, 11, 12, 14, 22, 24, 28,
    29, 30, 32, 44, 57, 127, 135, 137,
    185, 188, 189, 190, 195, 196
  external knowledge
      management 146, 161
  knowledge base 161, 190, 191, 196
  knowledge creation and
      sharing 145, 191
  knowledge flows 28, 32, 131, 146,
      147, 152
  knowledge flows and ownership 32
  knowledge intense settings 26,
      37, 39
knowledge (or know-how)
      transfers 152, 185
  internal knowledge transfer/
      intra-firm knowledge
      transfer 153
  external knowledge transfer/
      inter-firm knowledge
      transfer 154
  multinational enterprise as a source
      of knowledge creation 145
know-how 146, 147, 148, 151, 152,
    153, 154, 245, 246, 248
  see also knowledge

labour cost 29
Latin America 22, 23, 42, 43–9,
    51, 53, 75, 102, 103, 243,
    244, 246
learning 34, 35, 46, 47, 128, 183
  effects of conduct on learning 137
  effects of structure on learning 137
  global learning 72
  learning as a source of sustainable
      competitive advantage 34, 135
  learning influence on the resource
      allocation processes 34
  learning on start-up firms because of
      internationalization 34
leadership position 239, 245, 249
  local 242, 243
  regional 243
level 11, 12, 13, 30, 37, 38, 47,
    48, 52, 58, 65, 111, 115, 119,
    122, 127, 132, 160, 161, 185,
    189, 195
  industry and firm level 185
liberalization 75, 96, 97, 101, 102, 130
  economic liberalization 95, 96
  liberalization handling
      capabilities 95, 96

responses to liberalization 103
links 111, 112, 113, 118, 120, 136
  geography and history links
      75, 76
local 11, 15, 28, 29, 34, 47, 49, 50, 58,
    128, 133, 140, 141, 155, 159, 181,
    184, 224, 225, 227, 231, 235, 238,
    239, 242, 243, 244
  competitors 81, 90, 147, 153, 154,
      156, 160
  know-how 151, 152, 154, 158,
      159, 161
  partners 99, 101, 249
  search 229, 230, 235
local responsiveness 131, 133, 242
  pressures for 131, 133
long jumps 231, 234

managers 31, 32, 34, 36, 38, 60,
    63, 64, 65, 86, 91, 118, 134, 135,
    142, 201, 207, 209, 210
  professional managers 63
manufacturing firm 185, 187,
    223, 235
  car component manufacturing
      firm 223, 235
metanational 204
Mexico 23, 45, 49, 110, 111, 227, 232
mighty local 243, 245
mobility of resources 88
  see also transfer of resources
multilevel approach 202
multinational enterprise (MNE)/MNC
    79, 145
  consolidated multinationals 47,
      48, 52
  see also emerging MNCs
multinational expansion 145,
    148, 181
multilatinas 43, 48, 49, 52
  characteristics of multilatinas 48,
      49, 52
  comparison between multinational
      corporations and multilatinas
      50, 52
  management processes at
      multilatinas 50, 52
multinationality 166–9, 172, 173
  contingencies that can affect the net
      benefits that firms derive from
      multinationality 167
  relation between risk and
      multinationality 169, 173
  transnational companies 148

natural resources 14, 196
  access to natural resources 89
Netherlands, The 45
networks 10, 14, 121, 181, 182, 185,
  186, 191, 196
  main reasons why actors join
    a network 188
  networked firm 72
  network formation 195
  networked organizations in
    professional services 196
  types of networked
    organization 192
networking 134, 135, 137, 138,
  140, 141
NK Model 224
Novartis 115
NTT DoCoMo 242–6, 248, 249

organizational design 127, 128
  in multinational enterprises 125
organizational risk 165, 171
organizations 31, 53, 56, 190,
  202, 204, 224
  networked organizations 185–93,
    195
  organizational risk 165, 171,
    172
outcomes 24, 37, 52, 56, 58, 109,
  112, 115, 118, 120, 131,
  133–7, 139
  interaction between conduct and
    outcomes 134
outperforming 110, 238
  rivals across the globe 110
ownership 38, 60, 61, 167, 170,
  171, 174
  knowledge flows and ownership 32
  ownership structure 170
  subsidiary ownership 167, 174

pacing 218, 219, 230, 235
parent company 136, 240, 246
  creation of firm-specific advantages
    by the parent company 136
partners 57, 58, 181, 182, 184,
  201, 203, 205
  partner roles 99
patching 233, 234
patent citation 151
patterns 112, 118, 244, 245
  globalization patterns 24, 56
  internationalization patterns 57
  outcome patterns 111, 114

performance 73, 75, 201, 202, 204,
  205, 208
  effects of environmental pressures
    on firm performance 131
  geography as predictor of MNE
    foreign market relative
    performance 110
  history as predictor of MNE foreign
    market relative
    performance 110
  host market relative
    performance 118
  firm performance 130, 131, 133,
    135, 137, 141, 142, 166
  paths to performance 141, 142
  possitive effects of networking on
    performance 138, 140
  relationship between geography and
    history links and MNE foreign
    performance 115
  relative performance of MNEs in
    foreign markets 120
  subsidiary performance 130, 142
Peru 23, 49, 97, 99, 105
Pfizer 111, 115
pharmaceutical industry 23, 37
Philips 111, 119
power 116, 118, 246, 247, 248
  bargaining 143
  political power 117, 195
  political power across
    professions 195
  politically influenced markets 119
privatization 119
processes 22, 23, 24, 46, 48, 52, 56,
  58, 61, 63, 65, 130, 183
  management and organizational
    processes 22, 48, 50, 51, 52
  management and organizational
    processes at MNCs 44, 48
  resource-allocation processes 26,
    27, 30, 31, 33
  product life-cycle 27
  profesional services 185, 186, 187,
    195, 196, 197
  boundary lines of professional
    services 187
  globalizing professional
    services 185
  networked organizations in
    professional services 196
  professional service providers
    (PSPs) 185
Procter & Gamble 110, 111, 115

professions 185, 186, 187, 189, 190, 191, 193, 195, 196, 197
  globalization of a profession 197
  strategy and structure in professions 197
profile 239, 241, 242, 243, 245, 249, 250
Puerto Rico 29

R&D 22, 28, 29, 37, 48, 49, 50, 113, 145–60, 161, 171, 203
  decentralization of R&D 148, 153; motives (drivers) for R&D decentralization 146; benefits and costs of R&D decentralization 146; R&D decentralization and MNE's total profits 157
  size of R&D resources decentralized 146
  R&D internationalization 146, 149, 150, 161; empirical evidence on R&D internationalization 145, 146; drivers of R&D internationalization 152
  R&D organization 146
real options 126
  theory 165, 166, 168, 173, 174, 175, 232
reforms 97, 202, 203
  influencing economic 102
regulator 243, 246, 247
regulations 249
relationship 7, 115, 116
  relations of the MNE with the local government 110, 112
  relations of the MNE with suppliers 110
  relations of the MNE with customers 110
research agenda 6, 115
resource-allocation processes 22, 28, 31, 32, 33, 34, 35, 38
  challenges of the resource-allocation processes 31
  international expansion and resource-allocation processes 27, 34, 39
  resource allocation in established firms 27
  resource allocation in start-up firms 36
resource-based view 239, 248
resources (and capabilities) 24, 73, 96, 188, 189, 195, 196, 219

advantageous resources 79, 85
cross-country transferability of resources 80, 82
disadvantageous resources 79
external resources 78, 79, 88
firm-specific resources 78, 81, 84
intangible resources 80
lack of resources and capabilities 96
location resources 79, 80, 83, 87, 88, 89
neutral resources 80, 85, 86, 88
resources and start-up firms 35
strategic resources 78, 79
tangible resources 80
transfer of resources 81, 89
risk 46, 52, 63, 126, 131, 166, 167, 168, 171, 172
  implications of FDI on organizational risk 171

shareholders 24, 59, 60, 61, 62, 63
  family 60, 61
  first generation of 60
  governmental 60
  institutional 6, 59
  large institutional 62
  neutral 59, 60, 61
  partial 60, 61
  shareholder value 59, 60, 63, 66
  shareholders' influence 60
  state 60
small firms' internationalization 45, 46
  evolutionary theory and 46
Spain 225, 227, 230, 235, 242, 243
start-up 22, 23, 33, 35
  global 32, 46, 53
  organizational routines in 30, 33
state-owned firms 62
social capital 187, 189
spillovers 29, 30, 127, 146, 147, 150, 151, 154, 156, 157, 159, 160
  internal 147
  external 147, 154, 157, 158, 159, 160, 161
  international 150
  types of external 147
  universities and 29, 30
stages, theory 43
stakeholders 24

standards 188, 247
strategic alliances 95, 202, 204, 206, 207, 210, 212
  characteristics and performance, 201, 204, 210
strategic behaviour profiles 241, 243
  sustainability 250
strategic management 132, 135
strategy 3, 10, 11, 12, 16, 23, 120, 125, 127, 128, 130, 190, 191, 197, 223, 236
  effects of environmental pressures on strategy 131
  field of strategy classification 218
  global strategy 71, 85, 173, 181, 183, 202, 206, 238, 242
  local strategy 24
  regional strategy 95
  strategy of subsidiaries 130
  typology of strategies 239
structural theories 43
structure 10, 14, 15, 32, 46, 49, 62, 87, 130, 131, 132, 134, 135, 137, 140, 186, 197, 204, 206, 240
  effects of environmental pressures on structure 131
  governance structures 187, 191
  major dimension of organizational structure 134
  ownership structure 170
  structure of subsidiaries 130
structure–conduct–performance paradigm 132
subsidiaries 29, 32, 43, 48, 57, 71, 72, 73, 74, 85, 86, 87, 126, 128, 136, 138, 142, 145, 147, 148, 149, 151, 152, 167, 174
  innovation of subsidiaries 151
  interunit learning in subsidiaries 132, 137
  market innovation in subsidiaries 132
  market pressures faced by subsidiaries 130
  production subsidiaries 148
  subsidiaries' role 160
  subsidiary performance 72, 73, 74, 128, 130, 131, 133, 135, 137, 141, 143
  subsidiary profitability and R&D decentralization 155

Taiwan 202, 204, 205, 206, 207, 208, 210, 212
Technological Apostle 239, 242, 243, 244
technology 28, 30, 50, 130, 201, 243, 244, 246, 247
technology transfer 127
  intra-company technology transfers 161
  mobile technology advances 247
technology sourcing 155, 158, 160, 161
telecom industry 241, 246
Thailand 29
ties 202, 203, 206
  alliances formed from personal ties 203
  country differences on the use of personal and organizational network ties 208
  multilevel ties 202, 204
  organizational ties 182, 183, 201, 202, 203, 204, 205, 208, 209, 210, 211
  personal ties 182, 183, 184, 202, 203, 205, 206, 208, 211
top management team 9, 24, 56, 63
Toyota 115
trade 5, 7, 28
  costs of international trade 28
  trade blocks 28
transaction costs 17, 118
transfer of capacity 79, 80, 81, 82, 83, 84, 85
transnational companies 148
trust 189, 191, 192, 193, 194, 195, 208, 211
  personal trust 205, 209, 210, 211

Unilever 45, 59, 61, 62, 110, 115
United Kingdom 55, 59, 61, 62, 242, 243
United States 89, 111, 112, 113, 114, 118, 119, 136, 181, 205, 208

value 1, 5, 14, 15, 35, 48, 88, 96, 99, 100, 101, 103, 117, 125, 173, 201, 203, 209, 211, 212, 240, 245
  value-addition by partners 96, 99, 103

venture capital funding   34
Vodafone   110
  Vodafone Live service
    248
Volkswagen   111, 115

Wal-Mart   110 ,111, 113, 115
wireless   238, 239, 241–9
  sector   239, 241, 243, 248, 249

Yahoo!   34

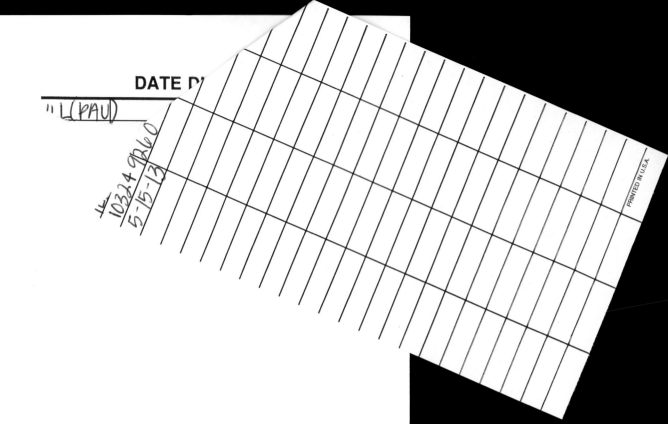

DATE D

" L (PAU)

102249260

5-15-13